Homosexuality and the European Court of Human Rights

Homosexu … -length
study of … rovides
a socio-le … ıents of
the Stras … ay men
and lesbi … iding a
systemat … lecades
of decisi … ers the
evolutior … his has
fashionec … ınalysis
by emplo … ırispru-
dence, Pa … ılity is
both soc … gh the
Conventi … ıe light
of presen … ;ed and
advanced … argues
that the … ause it
provides … mobi-
lized by l … mative
social rel … rs how
the Cour … future
to better protect lesbian and gay rights and lives.

Paul Johnson is Anniversary Reader in Sociology at the University of York.

Homosexuality and the European Court of Human Rights

Paul Johnson

Routledge
Taylor & Francis Group
a GlassHouse Book

irst published 2013
This version published 2014
by Routledge
2 Park Square, Milton Park, Abingdon, Oxon OX14 4RN

and by Routledge
711 Third Avenue, New York, NY 10017
a GlassHouse Book

Routledge is an imprint of the Taylor & Francis Group, an informa business

British Library Cataloguing in Publication Data
A catalogue record for this book is available from the British Library

Library of Congress Cataloging in Publication Data

Johnson, Paul J.
Homosexuality and the European Court of Human Rights / Paul Johnson.
p. cm.
"Simultaneously published in the USA and Canada."
Includes bibliographical references and index.
1. Homosexuality—Law and legislation—Europe—History.
2. Gays—Legal status, laws, etc.—Europe—History.
3. Homophobia—Law and legislation—Europe—History.
4. Convention for the Protection of Human Rights and Fundamental Freedoms (1950) 5. European Court of Human Rights. 6. Human rights—Europe. 7. Homosexuality—Law and legislation—Europe—Cases. I. Title.
KJC5144.G39J64 2012
342.408'7—dc23
2012009980

ISBN 978-0-415-69657-9 (hbk)
ISBN 978-1-136-21897-2 (ebk)
ISBN 978-0-415-63263-8 (pbk)

Typeset in Garamond by
RefineCatch Ltd, Bungay, Suffolk, Great Britain

For Robert Vanderbeck

Contents

Preface to the paperback edition

The publication of this book in paperback has provided the opportunity to do three things: first, in this preface, to give an overview of Strasbourg jurisprudence in respect of sexual orientation during the time since the book went to press at the beginning of 2012; second, to revise and update the chronological list of decisions and judgments found in Appendix 2; and third, to make a small number of corrections to the original text. Over the last two years the European Court of Human Rights has given decisions and judgments on a wide range of issues relating to homosexuality. I summarize these below and, at the end of this preface, consider whether this most recent jurisprudence alters my original conclusion that the 'realization of universal Convention rights for gay men and lesbians is far from complete and achieving it will require a considerable change in the Court's jurisprudence'.

In one of its most recent judgments, the Court further evolved its jurisprudence in respect of discrimination created by criminal laws regulating male homosexual acts. In *E.B. and Others v Austria*, the Court upheld a complaint by a group of applicants about the refusal of domestic authorities to delete convictions from their criminal records following convictions under Article 209 of the Austrian Criminal Code.[1] Article 209, prior to its repeal in 2002, criminalized male homosexual acts between adults and consenting males aged between 14 and 18 and, as I discuss in Chapter 5, applied a higher minimum age to sexual acts between men than that set for opposite-sex or female same-sex acts. The Court stated that because 'keeping an Article 209 conviction on someone's criminal record may have particularly serious consequences for the person concerned' that 'the legislator, when amending the relevant legal provision in order to bring it into conformity with modern standards of equality between men and women, should have provided for appropriate measures'.[2] In light of the Austrian authorities having taken no

1 *E.B. and Others v Austria*, 31913/07, 38357/07, 48098/07, 48777/07 and 48779/07, 7 November 2013.

2 Ibid., § 81.

such measures, or provided any explanation regarding the purpose of maintaining these specific convictions on the criminal record, the Court concluded that there had been a violation of Article 14 taken in conjunction with Article 8.

In respect of discrimination affecting 'family life', the Court has issued several significant decisions and judgments. In *Gas and Dubois v France*, the Court gave its first judgment addressing the differential treatment of same-sex and opposite-sex couples in respect of the adoption of a child.[3] The complaint concerned the refusal of a simple adoption order to the same-sex partner of a biological mother on the grounds that, according to French law, joint second (step) parent adoption was only available to married persons. The Court dismissed the applicants' complaint that, because they were unable to enter into marriage (a situation which has since changed in France), refusing a simple adoption order amounted to discrimination based on sexual orientation contrary to Article 14 taken in conjunction with Article 8.[4] However, in *X. and Others v Austria*, the Court subsequently upheld a complaint by three applicants, a female same-sex couple and the biological child of one of the partners, about the legal exclusion of same-sex partners from second parent adoption.[5] The chief difference between *X. and Others v Austria* and *Gas and Dubois v France* is that Austrian law permitted second parent adoption for both unmarried and married opposite-sex partners whilst prohibiting it for same-sex partners.[6] Because the Court was prepared to consider same-sex couples and unmarried opposite-sex couples as comparable for the purposes of Article 14, it felt able to conclude that there were no 'particularly weighty and convincing reasons to show that excluding second-parent adoption in a same-sex couple, while allowing that possibility in an unmarried different-sex couple, was necessary for the protection of the family in the traditional sense or for the protection of the interests of the child'.[7] Although this is significant, it demonstrates that complaints about discrimination on the ground of sexual orientation under Articles 8 and 14 will often be unsuccessful when they concern rights linked to marriage. The Court's unwillingness to disturb the privileged status often afforded to married couples was confirmed in *Boeckel and Gessner-Boeckel v Germany* in which, declaring inadmissible a complaint by a same-sex couple about their inability to record their joint names on the birth certificate of a child in the same way as opposite-sex couples, the Court stated that 'it cannot be said that the applicants found themselves in a

3 *Gas and Dubois v France*, no. 25951/07, 15 March 2012.

4 For a discussion see: P. Johnson, 'Adoption, homosexuality and the European Convention on Human Rights: *Gas and Dubois v France*', *Modern Law Review* 75(6), 2012, 1123–1149.

5 *X. and Others v Austria*, [GC], no. 19010/07, 19 February 2013.

6 For a discussion see: P. Johnson, 'X and Others v Austria – Judgment', ECHR Blog, 21 February 2013, http://echrblog.blogspot.co.uk/2013/02/x-v-austria-judgment.html.

7 *X. and Others v Austria*, [GC], no. 19010/07, 19 February 2013, § 151.

relevantly similar situation as a married husband and wife in respect of the entries made into the birth certificate at the time of birth'.[8]

In respect of the question of same-sex marriage, in *H. v Finland* the Court reaffirmed its view that Article 12 of the Convention 'enshrines the traditional concept of marriage as being between a man and a woman' and that, although 'some Contracting States have extended marriage to same-sex partners, this reflects their own vision of the role of marriage in their societies and does not flow from an interpretation of the fundamental right as laid down by the Contracting States in the Convention'.[9] In doing so, the Court dismissed the complaint of a male-to-female transsexual about the requirement that she transform her existing marriage into a civil partnership in order to gain full legal recognition of her acquired gender. The Court held that requiring the applicant to change her marriage to a civil partnership – a form of partnership recognition 'which provides legal protection for same-sex couples which is *almost* identical to that of marriage'[10] – did not amount to a violation of Article 8 or Article 14 taken in conjunction with Article 8 and, furthermore, that no separate examination under Article 12 was necessary.[11] This judgment reiterates the Court's trenchantly heteronormative interpretation of marriage which I discuss in Chapter 5. It remains to be seen if and when, in light of pending complaints relating to the exclusion of same-sex couples from marriage,[12] the Court will evolve its interpretation of Article 12 and give same-sex couples access to this important Convention right.

In *Vallianatos and Others v Greece*, the Grand Chamber held that the blanket exclusion of same-sex couples living in Greece from registering a civil union – a legal form of partnership available only to opposite-sex couples – violated Article 14 taken in conjunction with Article 8.[13] Although the Court upheld the applicants' complaint, it was careful to clarify that the scope of the case did not relate 'in the abstract to a general obligation on the Greek State to provide for a form of legal recognition in domestic law for same-sex relationships' but, rather, concerned the question of 'whether the Greek State was entitled [. . .] to enact a law introducing alongside the institution of marriage a new registered partnership scheme for unmarried couples that was limited

8 *Boeckel and Gessner-Boeckel v Germany* (dec), no. 8017/11, 7 May 2013.
9 *H. v Finland*, no. 37359/09, 13 November 2012, § 38.
10 Ibid., § 50. My emphasis.
11 At the request of the applicant, *H. v Finland*, now *Hämäläinen v Finland*, was referred to the Grand Chamber on 29 April 2013 and a hearing was held in Strasbourg on 16 October 2013.
12 For example: *Oliari and Others v Italy*, nos. 18766/11 and 36030/11, Statement of facts, 3 December 2013; *Orlandi and Others v Italy*, no. 26431/12, Statement of facts, 3 December 2013.
13 *Vallianatos and Others v Greece* [GC], nos. 29381/09 and 32684/09, 7 November 2013.

to different-sex couples and thus excluded same-sex couples'.[14] In concluding that the Greek state was not entitled to do this, the Court established the principle that if a contracting state makes available a system of registered partnerships as an 'alternative to marriage' it cannot exclude same-sex couples from its scope. Whilst this is important, it currently has direct relevance to only two of the 47 contracting states (Greece and Lithuania) that have enacted such legislation and does not impose any positive obligation on the majority of Council of Europe member states that do not offer same-sex couples any legal system for registering a partnership.[15] Of particular relevance in *Vallianatos and Others*, in relation to the broader discussion found in Chapter 3, is the Court's use of 'consensus analysis' in reaching its judgment.[16]

Expanding its Article 11 jurisprudence that I discuss in Chapter 7, the Court upheld a complaint in *Genderdoc-M v Moldova* about a refusal to allow an LGBT-focused organization to hold a peaceful public demonstration aimed at encouraging the adoption of laws protecting sexual minorities from discrimination.[17] The Court found that the refusal violated a range of the applicant's Convention rights and, specifically in respect of Article 14 taken in conjunction with Article 11, held that an interference with freedom of assembly based on the domestic 'authorities' disapproval of demonstrations which they considered to promote homosexuality' amounted to discrimination contrary to the Convention.[18] This is welcome in light of the enactment of a federal law in the Russian Federation prohibiting the promotion of 'non-traditional sexual relationships' to minors.[19] The Russian federal law, as well as similar regional laws that are discussed in Chapter 7, has been subject to scrutiny by the Committee of Ministers of the Council of Europe in its supervision of the execution of the judgment in *Alekseyev v Russia*[20] but the Court has recently communicated a complaint about regional laws that regulate 'homosexual propaganda'.[21] It is to be hoped that in response to

14 Ibid., § 75

15 For a discussion of the judgment see: P. Johnson, 'Vallianatos Judgment on Sexual Orientation Discrimination in Civil Partnerships', ECHR Blog, 8 November 2013, http://echrblog.blogspot.co.uk/2013/11/vallianatos-judgment-on-sexual.html.

16 For a discussion of the use of consensus analysis see: P. Johnson, 'Consensus analysis in Vallianatos and Others v Greece', ECHR Sexual Orientation Blog, 11 November 2013, http://echrso.blogspot.co.uk/2013/11/consensus-analysis-in-vallianatos-and.html.

17 *Genderdoc-M v Moldova*, no. 9106/06, 12 June 2012.

18 Ibid., § 54.

19 For a discussion see: Article 19, 'Russia: Federal laws introducing ban of propaganda of non-traditional sexual relationships', June 2013; P. Johnson, '"Homosexual Propaganda" Laws in the Russian Federation: Are They in Violation of the European Convention on Human Rights?', Working Paper, 8 July 2013, http://papers.ssrn.com/sol3/papers.cfm?abstract_id=2251005.

20 *Alekseyev v Russia*, nos. 4916/07, 25924/08 and 14599/09, 21 October 2010.

21 *Bayev v Russia*, no. 67667/09, Statement of facts, 16 October 2013.

complaints about laws of this type that the Court evolves its Article 10 jurisprudence to better protect the freedom of expression of sexual minorities. Relatedly, the conclusion by the Court in *Molnar v Romania*, that public speech intended to incite hatred against a 'homosexual minority' is incompatible with Article 10, is welcome in further reiterating the principle that sexual minorities require protection from particular forms of hostile public expression.[22]

One of the most important recent evolutions in the Court's sexual orientation jurisprudence has been in respect of Article 3. In *X. v Turkey*, the Court found that holding a male homosexual prisoner in total isolation from other prisoners for more than eight months on the grounds of sexual orientation amounted to inhuman and degrading treatment contrary to Article 3 and discrimination contrary to Article 14 taken in conjunction with Article 3.[23] This judgment is extremely significant, given that it represents the first successful use of Article 3 to complain about legally mandated discrimination based on sexual orientation. Furthermore, it represents the first successful use of Article 3 to complain about conditions imposed on an individual whilst in detention because they are homosexual. Also of note in this respect is *Zontul v Greece*, in which the Court upheld a complaint by a homosexual man under Article 3 about his rape by a public official whilst he was detained as an illegal immigrant.[24] The Court held that the rape of the applicant amounted to a form of torture that was a substantive violation of Article 3 and that the subsequent inadequate redress afforded by the Greek state also amounted to a procedural violation of Article 3. Whilst *Zontul* is not explicitly concerned with sexual orientation (and the Court would have certainly reached the same conclusion regardless of the sexual orientation of the applicant) it is to be hoped that, taken together, these judgments signal the development of greater protection from discrimination based on sexual orientation under Article 3. However, such protection was not extended to the applicant in *M.K.N. v Sweden*, a (heterosexual) married man seeking asylum, who feared deportation to Iraq because of the risk of ill-treatment he would be subjected to as a result of knowledge about a previous homosexual relationship.[25] In declaring that the deportation of the applicant would not amount to a violation of Article 3, the Court stated that 'the applicant's claim concerning the homosexual relationship is not credible',[26] thereby raising the legal and sociological question of how it is possible, especially for those who do not claim a homosexual identity, to 'prove' a previous or existing homosexual relationship.

22 *Molnar v Romania* (dec), no. 16637/06, 23 October 2012.
23 *X. v Turkey*, no. 24626/09, 9 October 2012.
24 *Zontul v Greece*, no. 12294/07, 17 January 2012.
25 *M.K.N. v Sweden*, no. 72413/10, 27 June 2013.
26 Ibid.

Assessing the Court's sexual orientation jurisprudence over the last two years does not lead me to any conclusions that fundamentally differ from those expressed in this book. Although the Court has issued some significant judgments that enhance the protection of sexual minorities under the Convention – and, in this respect, I regard its recent Article 3 jurisprudence as especially important – it has largely continued its established practice of piecemeal and limited evolution. At the same time, the Court has reaffirmed, in a number of judgments, that gay men and lesbians do not have access to some of the human rights and fundamental freedoms available to heterosexuals under the Convention. For example, the Court has reiterated on a number of occasions that no right to marriage is available to same-sex couples under Article 12 of the Convention and, furthermore, that there is no positive obligation for contracting states to offer same-sex couples access to rights and benefits equivalent to marriage. In this and other respects, the Court continues a long-term reluctance to fully recognize that legal distinctions based on sexual orientation amount to violations of the Convention. A revealing insight into what may be a hostility among some of the Court's judges to the further expansion of human rights in respect of sexual orientation can be found in the distinction drawn between 'gay rights' and 'fundamental human rights' by Judges Vučinić and De Gaetano in *Eweida and Others v the United Kingdom*.[27] In an otherwise welcome judgment, in which the Court dismissed two complaints about national legislation that required the applicants to treat homosexuals equally during the provision of services to the public,[28] these dissenting judges ostensibly argued that the protection of a 'conscientious objection' to homosexuality was of greater importance than ensuring equal treatment on the grounds of sexual orientation. The opinion of Vučinić and De Gaetano, and the wider body of Strasbourg jurisprudence relating to homosexuality that is examined in this book, demonstrates that there is still a gap between the just demands of gay men and lesbians for full and equal protection under the Convention and the Court's willingness to recognize these.

Paul Johnson
York, January 2014.

27 *Eweida and Others v the United Kingdom*, nos. 48420/10, 59842/10, 51671/10 and 36516/10, 15 January 2013, Joint partly dissenting opinion of Judges Vučinić and De Gaetano, § 5.

28 For an extensive discussion see: R. Wintemute, 'Accommodating religious beliefs: Harm, clothing or symbols, and refusals to serve others', *Modern Law Review* 77, 2014, 223–253.

Acknowledgements

I am very grateful to the Department of Sociology at the University of Surrey for the period of sabbatical research leave in which I wrote this book. In particular, I would like to thank Karen Bullock, Kate Burningham, Geoff Cooper, Christine Hine, Jo Moran-Ellis and Katharine Tyler for being such supportive colleagues and friends.

The staff at the European Court of Human Rights have been extremely helpful in supplying documents from their archives and, in particular, I must thank Geneviève Woods for patiently and efficiently dealing with my many requests. My thanks also go to Janet Bendell for assistance with translation.

I am, as always, greatly indebted to my family and friends who provide me with continuous encouragement and support. My thanks to Marilyn Bedford, Terence Bedford, Mary Castiglione, Anthony Johnson, James Johnson, Stephen Johnson, Steph Lawler, Andy Nercessian, Audrey Palmer, Sue Parker, David Pringle, Ian Roberts, Brian Statham and Sue Williams. I am particularly grateful to my partner Rob for the many conversations we have had and the insightful ideas that he has so generously shared with me.

Table of cases cited in the book

European Commission of Human Rights and European Court of Human Rights

Other courts

Introduction

We are living through a profound transformation in the social regulation of homosexuality. At the heart of this transformation are fundamental changes in law. In many jurisdictions around the world, where the role of law was once long established as a mechanism for discouraging homosexual acts through their total or partial criminalization, a range of new statutory legislation (which, for example, prohibits discrimination in the provision of goods and services, criminalizes 'hate speech' and enables the registration of same-sex partnerships) now protects and enhances the 'sexual citizenship'[1] of homosexuals. In other jurisdictions, however, law continues to criminalize homosexual sex (for example, in 41 of the 53 states comprising the Commonwealth of Nations[2]) and is increasingly being amended in an attempt to suppress and eradicate homosexuality. We are therefore witnessing a striking variegation in the global landscape of the legal regulation of homosexuality. For example, whilst in 2010 Argentina became the latest state to permit same-sex civil marriage,[3] in 2011 the Senate of Nigeria approved legislation prohibiting and criminalizing marriage between same-sex partners.[4] Similarly, whilst in 2009 Uganda considered making 'aggravated homosexuality' a capital offence,[5] in 2011 the Supreme Court of Gibraltar invalidated existing laws criminalizing buggery and gross indecency.[6]

One of the most important recent changes in global debates about the relationship between law and homosexuality has been the ascendency of

1 D.T. Evans, *Sexual Citizenship: The Material Construction of Sexualities*, London: Routledge, 1993.

2 M. Kirby, 'Human Rights Insights: Homosexuality and Love', *The National Legal Eagle* 17(1), 2011, 3–7.

3 'Matrimonio Civil', Decreto 1054/2010, Boletín Oficial de la República Argentina No. 31, 22 July 2010.

4 'A Bill for An Act to Prohibit Marriage Between Persons of Same Gender, Solemnization of Same and for Other Matters Related Therewith', Parliament of Nigeria, SB.05/C895, 2011.

5 'The Anti Homosexuality Bill' (Bill no. 18), Bills Supplement No. 13, *Uganda Gazette* No. 47 Volume CII, 25 September 2009.

6 *The Chief Minister of Gibraltar and Her Majesty's Attorney General for Gibraltar v Equality Group GGR and The Secretary of State for Foreign and Commonwealth Affairs*, Supreme Court of Gibraltar, 2009 C No. 272, Judgment of 8 April 2011.

'human rights'. Human rights discourse has become one of the most effective vehicles for mobilizing a range of moral and political claims that contest the widespread social and legal discrimination experienced by sexual minorities. Over the past two decades, gay and lesbian human rights have moved from a marginal position once associated with the 'loony left'[7] to gain mainstream acceptance in national and international politics. For instance, when in 2011 the United States Secretary of State, Hillary Clinton, made the unprecedented policy commitment to challenge all forms of legal discrimination experienced worldwide by homosexuals, it was through the framework of human rights: 'gay rights are human rights, and human rights are gay rights'.[8]

There has been a recent and sudden expansion at the transnational level in the commitment to guaranteeing the effective legal protection of human rights in respect of sexual orientation. For example, in July 2011, 17 years after the judgment in *Toonen v Australia*,[9] the United Nations adopted its first resolution on human rights and sexual orientation in which it expressed '*grave concern* at acts of violence and discrimination, in all regions of the world, committed against individuals because of their sexual orientation and gender identity'.[10] This resolution commissioned a study of 'discriminatory laws and practices and acts of violence against individuals based on their sexual orientation and gender identity, in all regions of the world, and how international human rights law can be used to end violence and related human rights violations'.[11] The study was subsequently published in November 2011 and confirmed 'a pattern of human rights violations' around the world that 'demands a response'.[12] Similarly, in March 2010, the Committee of Ministers of the Council of Europe

7 In a speech to the Labour Party Conference on 28 September 2004, the then Prime Minister of the United Kingdom, Tony Blair, reflected on how in the past 'to be in favour of gay rights was to be a loony leftie' but '[n]ow the parties compete for the gay vote'. Available HTTP: <http://news.bbc.co.uk/1/hi/uk_politics/3697434.stm> (accessed 17 February 2012).

8 H.R. Clinton, 'Remarks in Recognition of International Human Rights Day', Geneva: Palais des Nations, 6 December 2011, available HTTP: <http://www.state.gov/secretary/rm/2011/12/178368.htm> (accessed 17 February 2012).

9 In *Toonen v Australia*, the United Nations Human Rights Committee held that the criminalization of consensual male homosexual acts in private violated Article 17 of the International Covenant on Civil and Political Rights. Whilst it did not consider the merits of whether such criminalization violated Article 26 of the Covenant – which states that 'law shall prohibit any discrimination and guarantee to all persons equal and effective protection against discrimination' – the Human Rights Committee declared that sexual orientation fell within its scope. *Toonen v Australia*, Communication No. 488/1992, U.N. Doc CCPR/C/50/D/488/1992 (1994).

10 United Nations Human Rights Council, 'Human Rights, Sexual Orientation and Gender Identity', A/HRC/RES/17/19, 34th Meeting, 17 June 2011.

11 Ibid.

12 United Nations Human Rights Council, *Discriminatory Laws and Practices and Acts of Violence Against Individuals Based on their Sexual Orientation and Gender Identity: Report of the United Nations High Commissioner for Human Rights*, A/HRC/19/41, 17 November 2011.

made its first commitment to combatting discrimination on the grounds of sexual orientation and gender identity through a set of recommendations designed to 'ensure respect for the human rights of lesbian, gay, bisexual and transgender persons and to promote tolerance towards them'.[13]

These commitments to guaranteeing the human rights of sexual minorities have been given by political organizations that play a central role in the construction and enforcement of human rights around the world. They are, in part, a response to the globalization of human rights demands that have been advanced through local demonstrations, national campaigns and international agreements such as the Yogyakarta Principles.[14] However, despite this recent and high-profile recognition, gay and lesbian human rights remain marginal to the political and social policy of many states. As Thomas Hammarberg, Commissioner for Human Rights at the Council of Europe, argued in a 2011 report on discrimination on the grounds of sexual orientation in Europe:

> There is considerable resistance among many people to discuss the full enjoyment of universal human rights by LGBT persons. Even if this may not be a popular human rights topic, the time has now come to take the discussion forward and make it concrete.[15]

The voting record on sexual orientation issues in the United Nations evidences Hammarberg's candid acknowledgement that lesbian and gay rights are not a 'popular' topic in many countries that maintain an intense hostility towards homosexuality.[16]

13 Council of Europe, 'Recommendation CM/Rec(2010)5 of the Committee of Ministers to Member States on Measures to Combat Discrimination on Grounds of Sexual Orientation or Gender Identity', adopted 31 March 2010 at the 1081st meeting of the Ministers' Deputies.

14 'The Yogyakarta Principles on the Application of International Human Rights Law in relation to Sexual Orientation and Gender Identity', available HTTP: < http://www.yogyakartaprinciples.org/> (accessed 17 February 2012).

15 Council of Europe, *Discrimination on Grounds of Sexual Orientation and Gender Identity in Europe*, Strasbourg: Council of Europe Publishing, 2011.

16 For example, the United Nations Human Rights Council resolution 'Human Rights, Sexual Orientation and Gender Identity' (A/HRC/RES/17/19, 34th Meeting, 17 June 2011) was only marginally adopted by a vote of 23 to 19, with 3 abstentions. Those voting in favour were: Argentina, Belgium, Brazil, Chile, Cuba, Ecuador, France, Guatemala, Hungary, Japan, Mauritius, Mexico, Norway, Poland, Republic of Korea, Slovakia, Spain, Switzerland, Thailand, Ukraine, United Kingdom of Great Britain and Northern Ireland, United States of America and Uruguay; those voting against were: Angola, Bahrain, Bangladesh, Cameroon, Djibouti, Gabon, Ghana, Jordan, Malaysia, Maldives, Mauritania, Nigeria, Pakistan, Qatar, Republic of Moldova, Russian Federation, Saudi Arabia, Senegal and Uganda; and those abstaining were: Burkina Faso, China and Zambia. For a general discussion of the development of human rights in respect of sexual orientation at the United Nations see: I. Saiz, 'Bracketing Sexuality: Human Rights and Sexual Orientation: a Decade of Development and Denial at the UN', *Health and Human Rights* 7(2), 2004, 48–80.

The European Convention on Human Rights and the Strasbourg organs

This book is a study of one organization, the European Court of Human Rights (hereafter 'the Court'), which has played a prominent role in developing gay and lesbian human rights and could, in the future, make the full enjoyment of universal human rights by sexual minorities a concrete reality. The principal role of the Court is to adjudicate complaints brought under the Convention for the Protection of Human Rights and Fundamental Freedoms (more commonly referred to as the European Convention on Human Rights and hereafter 'the Convention').[17] The Convention is an international human rights treaty that was drafted by the Council of Europe in 1949, signed by 12 of the member states that comprised it in 1950,[18] and entered into force in 1953. The Convention has since been amended by a number of protocols and has been ratified by all 47 member states of the Council of Europe. The Convention is a regional human rights instrument that guarantees rights first set out in the Universal Declaration of Human Rights, which was adopted by the United Nations General Assembly in 1948.[19] Unlike the more expansive Universal Declaration, which protects civil, political, economic, social and cultural rights, the Convention focuses predominantly on civil and political rights. The rights of the Convention that are most commonly invoked in complaints relating to homosexuality can be found in Appendix 1.

'To ensure the observance of the engagements undertaken by the High Contracting Parties', the Convention created two part-time institutions, commonly referred to as the Strasbourg organs, to be its 'control machinery': the European Commission of Human Rights (hereafter 'the Commission') and the Court.[20] On its entry into force in 1998, Protocol 11 of the Convention abolished the Commission and established a full-time Court to which all European citizens have the right to directly petition. Prior to its abolition, the purpose of the Commission was to determine the admissibility of applications brought by both states and individuals and, where these were accepted, provide a mediating function with a view to reaching a friendly settlement between parties. In cases where no settlement could be reached, the Commission produced a report on the facts of the case and expressed its opinion on whether a complaint amounted to a violation of the Convention. The Commission's report and advisory opinion were then transmitted to the Committee of Ministers and, where appropriate, to the Court for consideration. The Commission's

17 Council of Europe, *Convention for the Protection of Human Rights and Fundamental Freedoms*, 4 November 1950, ETS No. 005.

18 Belgium, Denmark, France, Germany, Iceland, Ireland, Italy, Luxembourg, Netherlands, Norway, Turkey and the United Kingdom signed on 4 November 1950.

19 United Nations General Assembly, G.A. res. 217A (III), U.N. Doc A/810 at 71 (1948).

20 Ex Article 19 of the European Convention on Human Rights.

interpretation of the Convention over 40 years remains an integral aspect of Strasbourg case law and, throughout this book, I examine its decisions and reports as well as judgments issued by the Court.

The work of the Strasbourg organs has changed dramatically since they were created in the aftermath of the Second World War. As a response to the effects of fascism before and during the war, and to guard against the future growth of Communism, the Convention was conceived as 'the rules of the Club' that 'laid down the minimum standards of human dignity and freedom compatible with membership' of the Council of Europe.[21] The Strasbourg organs were not originally designed to deal, as they do today, primarily with applications from individuals (who sometimes incorrectly regard the Court as a court of fourth instance) but rather from states seeking to address violations of human rights in other contracting states. Over time, however, the Convention has assumed the function of a European bill of rights and, because of this, the Court's casework has reached significant levels. At the end of 2011, the Court had 151,600 applications pending before a judicial formation and 22,600 applications at a pre-judicial phase.[22] In 2011, it delivered 1,511 judgments and gave decisions (by deeming applications inadmissible or striking them out) on 50,677 other complaints.

Applications to the Court ostensibly involve an individual or group of individuals complaining that the actions of a nation state violate rights guaranteed by the Convention. Complaints also often involve a range of other actors, such as non-governmental organizations and pressure groups, who organize complaints or make written submission to the Court in support of them. The involvement of these organizations and groups shows that whilst the Court is often imagined to be a mechanism of adjudication within the traditions of liberal individualism – a machinery designed to resolve discrete disputes between an individual and the state – there is frequently a broader social dimension to many of the complaints it receives. As Hodson argues, the contemporary importance of the Court lies less in its role as an adjudicator in the 'epic battle' between the individual and the nation state, and more in the stage that it provides for political movements seeking to effect legal change.[23] Because human rights is an 'arena of transformative political practice that disorients, destabilizes, and at times even helps destroy deeply unjust concentrations of political, social, economic and technological power',[24] the

21 From a speech given at the signing of the Convention by Sir David Maxwell Fyfe who was instrumental in drafting it. Human Rights Information Bulletin, *The European Convention on Human Rights at 50*, Strasbourg: Council of Europe, 2000, p. 47.

22 European Court of Human Rights, *Analysis of Statistics 2011*, Strasbourg: European Court of Human Rights, 2011.

23 L. Hodson, *NGOs and the Struggle for Human Rights in Europe*, Oxford: Hart Publishing, 2011.

24 U. Baxi, *The Future of Human Rights*, Oxford: Oxford University Press, 2002, p. 10.

Court has become one of the key sites at which this political practice is manifest and played out. This is an aspect of its judicial work that the Court increasingly acknowledges. In *Ireland v the United Kingdom*, the Court stated that its

> judgments in fact serve not only to decide those cases brought before the Court but, more generally, to elucidate, safeguard and develop the rules instituted by the Convention, thereby contributing to the observance by the States of the engagements undertaken by them as Contracting Parties.[25]

And in *Karner v Austria*, the Court went on to state that:

> Although the primary purpose of the Convention system is to provide individual relief, its mission is also to determine issues on public-policy grounds in the common interest, thereby raising the general standards of protection of human rights and extending human rights jurisprudence throughout the community of Convention States.[26]

The Court's 'policy' in respect of a wide range of political issues is significantly influenced by its partners within the Council of Europe and by its close relationship with the Committee of Ministers. The Committee of Ministers provides not only the supervisory mechanism through which the Court's judgments are executed but also produces the human rights policy of the Council of Europe that underpins the work of the Court. This policy is produced by a range of actors within the Council of Europe who 'feed' into the Committee of Ministers: under the Directorate General of Human Rights and Legal Affairs, the Directorate of Standard-Setting houses the Human Rights Intergovernmental Co-operation Division, which encompasses the Steering Committee for Human Rights. The policy produced by these organizational actors is mandated by the Committee of Ministers and provides a significant steer to the Court's interpretation of the Convention. For this reason, the first official policy recommendations by the Committee of Ministers on sexual orientation and human rights in 2010 were of considerable importance.[27] These recommendations were given immediate effect by the Court in *Alekseyev v Russia*[28] and, as I discuss in Chapter 7, underpinned a significant development in the Court's judicial policy.

25 *Ireland v the United Kingdom*, no. 5310/71, 18 January 1978, Series A no. 25, § 154.

26 *Karner v Austria*, no. 40016/98, 24 July 2003, ECHR 2003-IX, § 26.

27 Council of Europe, 'Recommendation CM/Rec(2010)5 of the Committee of Ministers to Member States on Measures to Combat Discrimination on Grounds of Sexual Orientation or Gender Identity'.

28 *Alekseyev v Russia*, nos. 4916/07, 25924/08 and 14599/09, 21 October 2010.

The Parliamentary Assembly of the Council of Europe has also played an important role in shaping and developing human rights policy in respect of sexual orientation and, since 1981, has passed a number of recommendations and a resolution supporting gay and lesbian rights.[29] In addition, the Commissioner for Human Rights, established by the Committee of Ministers in 1999,[30] reports annually on the state of human rights in member states and makes recommendations about current issues. The jurisprudence of the Court must therefore be seen within the landscape of a dense network of human rights policies and mechanisms designed to enforce them.[31]

The aims of this book

In writing this book, I set out to achieve three principal aims:

My first aim is to provide a comprehensive overview of Strasbourg jurisprudence in respect of homosexuality. Whilst some of the Court's judgments in this area are well known, many of the Commission's decisions remain obscure. I hope that the book will be a useful 'map' of all decisions and judgments issued on matters relating to homosexuality and aid interested parties to better navigate this now dense case law.

My second aim is to offer a sociological (rather than simply doctrinal) analysis of the Court's jurisprudence. To achieve this, I consider a number of sociological issues, including: the social construction of homosexuality by the Court; the influence of the Court's moral reasoning about homosexuality on its use of legal method; and the relationship between the Court's interpretation of the Convention and heteronormativity.

My third aim is to suggest how the Court might more effectively protect the rights and lives of gay men and lesbians. To meet this aim I have inevitably identified limitations in the Court's current jurisprudence in respect of homosexuality, and proposed ways in which it might better guarantee human rights in the future. These proposals are made in the spirit of critique welcomed by Judge Costa who, as then President of the Court, argued that

29 Parliamentary Assembly of the Council of Europe Recommendation 924 (1981) 'On Discrimination Against Homosexuals'; Recommendation 1470 (2000) 'Situation of Gays and Lesbians and Their Partners in Respect of Asylum and Immigration in the Member States of the Council of Europe'; Recommendation 1474 (2000) 'Situation of Lesbians and Gays in Council of Europe Member States'; Recommendation 1635 (2003) 'Lesbians and Gays in Sport'; Resolution 1728 (2010) 'Discrimination on the Basis of Sexual Orientation and Gender Identity'; Recommendation 1915 (2010) 'Discrimination on the Basis of Sexual Orientation and Gender Identity'.

30 Council of Europe, Committee of Ministers Resolution (99) 50, 7 May 1999.

31 For an overview of the organization of human rights within the Council of Europe, see: G. de Beco (ed.), *Human Rights Monitoring Mechanisms of the Council of Europe*, Abingdon: Routledge, 2011.

the Court 'can accept a fair degree of criticism' and that '[f]rank and even blunt commentary can serve as a stimulus to further improve'.[32]

A sociological approach to the Court's jurisprudence

Although the term 'human rights' evades definition and is deployed across multiple sites in different ways, its essential utility to gay men and lesbians is its capacity to discursively construct sexuality as an innate and inalienable characteristic of human beings and claim recognition for this as a 'right'. The potential for human rights discourse to (re)fashion conceptions of 'humanness' is, as Douzinas argues, what makes it attractive to those who wish to challenge the social and political relations that underpin discrimination:

> The prime function of rights is to construct the individual person as a subject (of law). Rights are tools and strategies for defining the meaning and powers of humanity. The human and its derivatives, humanism and humanitarianism, are all intimately linked with the work of rights. We acquire our identity in an endless struggle for recognition, in which rights are our bargaining chips in our desire of others. The law and rights make a central contribution to the project of becoming subject through the reciprocal acknowledgement of self and the (mis)recognition of others.[33]

Human rights discourse has become, as I argue throughout this book, a framework through which 'the homosexual' has been (re)imagined as a specific kind of human being in possession of a certain 'nature' that both requires and is worthy of protection. A key focus of the book, therefore, is on how the Court constructs homosexuality and the implications of this construction for the development of lesbian and gay rights in Europe and the rest of the world.

Approaching homosexuality as a social construction, rather than as an innate biological or psychological condition of individuals, has been an ongoing concern of the human sciences since the late 1960s.[34] Throughout this book I draw upon the work of Michel Foucault and, specifically, his idea that sexuality, far from being a congenital or immutable aspect of an individual, is socially produced in and through discourse. Discourse, for Foucault, both produces and constrains sexuality: it is the mode by which sexuality is

32 J-P. Costa, 'On the Legitimacy of the European Court of Human Rights' Judgments', *European Constitutional Law Review* 7, 2011, 173–182 at 182.

33 C. Douzinas, *Human Rights and Empire: The Political Philosophy of Cosmopolitanism*, London: Routledge, 2007, p. 7.

34 See, for example: M. McIntosh, 'The Homosexual Role', *Social Problems* 16, 1968, 182–192.

conceived and proliferated by a range of experts across a number of sites and it is the mechanism that delimits sexuality (as both identity and practice) into its contemporary coherent forms. Through a historical analysis of key professional discourses, most notably medicine and psychology, Foucault sought to determine the constitutive elements through which both the object and subject of sexuality have been 'incited' into existence:

> Sexuality must not be thought of as a kind of natural given which power tries to hold in check, or as an obscure domain which knowledge tries gradually to uncover. It is the name that can be given to a historical construct: not a furtive reality that is difficult to grasp, but a great surface network in which the stimulation of bodies, the intensification of pleasures, the incitement to discourse, the formation of special knowledges, the strengthening of controls and resistances, are linked to one another, in accordance with a few major strategies of knowledge and power.[35]

Law is an integral aspect of the 'great surface network' through which sexuality is socially constructed. It is both an important site at which the 'formation of special knowledges' about sexuality are interpreted and reproduced, and a vital nexus at which 'controls and resistances' around sexuality are negotiated. Law is therefore significant because it is one of the most authoritative mechanisms through which the normative 'truths' of sexuality are established.[36] Whilst the value of Foucault's work for understanding law has been the subject of academic commentary and critique,[37] it is useful for illuminating the ways in which law is an arena in which discourses of sexuality are cited, mobilized, deployed and normalized.

In this book, I use Foucault's 'method' to consider the discursive construction of homosexuality in the Court.[38] I examine how the development of the Court's case law, based on the incremental process of legal citation, has had a 'sedimenting' effect in relation to discourses of sexuality that has entrenched and normalized particular ideas about what homosexuality 'is' and who homosexuals 'are'. From the time of its earliest judgments, the Court has shown a specific interest in the aetiological aspects of homosexuality and has discursively constructed the homosexual as a subject in possession of a

35 M. Foucault, *The History of Sexuality: Volume 1*, London: Penguin, 1979, pp. 105–6.

36 Patterson discusses this more generally in relation to the realist properties of law: see D. Patterson, *Law and Truth*, New York: Oxford University Press, 1996.

37 For example, see: A. Hunt and G. Wickham, *Foucault and Law: Towards a Sociology of Law as Governance*, London: Pluto Press, 1994. See also: B. Golder and P. Fitzpatrick, *Foucault's Law*, Abingdon: Routledge-Cavendish, 2009.

38 M. Foucault, 'Politics and the Study of Discourse', in G. Burchell, C. Gordon and P. Miller (eds.), *The Foucault Effect: Studies in Governmentality with Two Lectures by and an Interview with Michel Foucault*, Chicago: Chicago University Press, 1991.

congenital sexual orientation.[39] Because of this, the Court has contributed to what Foucault termed the 'specification of individuals' by imagining homosexuals as a 'species'[40] in possession of a common ontology.[41] Whilst Grigolo argues that the 'homosexual as a legal subject was introduced into the Convention using traditional essentialist narratives',[42] it is important to recognize that sexual essentialism is itself a recently invented discourse and that the Court has played an important role in stabilizing and perpetuating it. Although the contemporary preoccupation with the essential nature of 'the homosexual', as opposed to the pre-twentieth-century concern with the aberrant perversions of 'the sodomite',[43] reflects broader developments in the social construction of sexuality, I argue that the Court's contribution to this discursive construction is significant.

Strasbourg case law has produced a settled conception of the 'European homosexual subject' around which the Court's interpretation of the Convention continues to evolve. In Part I, I outline the Court's progressive ontological construction of homosexuality and, throughout Part III, show how this underpins its interpretation of the Convention. I argue that because the Court has produced and sustained a distinctive discursive construction of homosexuality that has endured across three decades, it must be seen as having a significant role in fashioning the discursive landscape of sexuality in contemporary Europe and beyond. Furthermore, the Court's construction of homosexuality has provided applicants with an important means through which to contest, disrupt and change not only the legal regulation of same-sex practices but wider social conceptions of homosexuality. As Foucault argued, since the time that homosexuality first appeared in nineteenth-century jurisprudence, law has provided a 'reverse discourse'[44] that enables resistance to dominant discourses about sexuality. Because of this, and with the caveat that the power of the law does not make it 'all-powerful',[45] I argue that the Court must be regarded as one of the most important performative sites at which discourses on sexuality are given ontological effect.[46] I argue that the Court should be

39 L.J. Moran, *The Homosexual(ity) of Law*, London: Routledge, 1996, p. 176.

40 M. Foucault, *The History of Sexuality: Volume 1*, pp. 42–43.

41 B. Turner, *Regulating Bodies: Essays in Medical Sociology*, London: Routledge, 1992.

42 M. Grigolo, 'Sexualities and the ECHR: Introducing the Universal Sexual Legal Subject', *European Journal of International Law* 14, 2003, 1023–1044 at 1027.

43 For a consideration of pre-twentieth-century legal discourses on sexuality, see: I. McCormick, *Secret Sexualities: A Sourcebook of 17th and 18th Century Writing*, London: Routledge, 1997.

44 Foucault argues that from the nineteenth century 'homosexuality began to speak in its own behalf, to demand that its legitimacy or "naturality" be acknowledged, often in the same vocabulary, using the same categories by which it [had been] disqualified'. M. Foucault, *The History of Sexuality: Volume 1*, p. 101.

45 C. Smart, *Feminism and the Power of Law*, London: Routledge, 1989.

46 For a discussion of the relationship between discourse, performativity and effect, see: J. Butler, *Bodies that Matter: On the Discursive Limits of Sex*, London: Routledge, 1993.

seen as one of the most important discoursing machines in the world and pre-eminent in shaping the global discourse on homosexuality. As such, the Court can be seen to have made a significant contribution to nothing short of the ongoing making of the 'modern homosexual'.[47]

The Court and heteronormativity

A key focus of my analysis of Strasbourg jurisprudence is a consideration of how it sustains or contests heteronormativity. By 'heteronormativity', I mean what Berlant and Warner call, 'the institutions, structures of understanding, and practical orientations that make heterosexuality seem not only coherent [. . .] but also privileged'.[48] Throughout the book, I explore the ways in which the Strasbourg organs have responded to the privilege of heterosexuality and the 'effortless superiority' that it commonly achieves in social life.[49] I draw upon a range of critical and 'queer' theory to examine how Strasbourg jurisprudence is implicated in what Ingraham calls the 'heterosexual imaginary': that 'way of thinking which conceals the operation of heterosexuality [. . .] and closes off any critical analysis of heterosexuality as an organizing institution'.[50] I argue that the Court's role in adjudicating sexual orientation complaints gives it significant scope to challenge and interrupt the heteronormative social relations of contemporary societies. I therefore examine the extent to which the Court's jurisprudence reproduces heteronormative social relations or subjects them to critical scrutiny.

In considering the Court's jurisprudence in respect of heteronormativity, my aim is to address a wider set of questions about the impact and effectiveness of the Court's case law in addressing and challenging both direct and indirect discrimination based on sexual orientation. Academic commentators based in law and politics tend to address questions of impact and effectiveness through an examination of the execution of the Court's judgments by the Council of Europe and/or their implementation at a national level. This analytic approach produces a range of divergent opinions. For instance, Stone Sweet argues that in 'hundreds of important cases' the Court has 'steadily raised standards of protection with regard to every Convention right, thereby requiring ongoing adjustment on the part of

47 K. Plummer, *The Making of the Modern Homosexual*, London: Hutchinson, 1981.

48 L. Berlant and M. Warner, 'Sex in Public', *Critical Inquiry* 24(2), 1998, 547–566 at 548.

49 C. Smart, 'Collusion, Collaboration and Confession: On Moving Beyond the Heterosexuality Debate', in D. Richardson (ed.), *Theorising Heterosexuality*, Buckingham: Open University Press, 1996, p. 173.

50 C. Ingraham, 'The Heterosexual Imaginary: Feminist Sociology and Theories of Gender', in S. Seidman (ed.), *Queer Theory/Sociology*, Oxford: Blackwell, 1996, p. 169.

laggard States'.[51] He argues that, in consistently expanding rights across contracting states, the Court has created a 'cosmopolitan legal order' in Europe.[52] In contrast, Helfer and Voeten argue that judgments from the Court have a limited effect on nullifying discriminatory laws in contracting states,[53] and Nash argues that 'cosmopolitan law' may encourage conditions that exacerbate violations of human rights.[54] There are those, such as Anagnostu, who argue that the Court's effectiveness is variable because of differences in the national legal and political systems of member states and the policy agendas that they pursue.[55] However, such debates are, in many ways, speculative since there is no agreed methodology through which to measure the impact of the Court's judgments, save for the immediate relief they give to individual applicants.

My approach to considering the impact of the Court is not to attempt to identify direct causal relationships between its jurisprudence and the domestic legal arrangements of nation states. Rather, my aim is to examine the ways in which its jurisprudence reproduces or challenges 'compulsory heterosexuality'.[56] I am interested in the extent to which the Court functions as one of 'the numerous ways in which heterosexual privilege is woven into the fabric of social life, pervasively and insidiously ordering everyday existence'.[57] To assess this, I analyze various aspects of the Court's case law on homosexuality to consider how it contributes to sustaining or contesting the social and legal relations that privilege heterosexuality and, as a consequence, discriminate against non-heterosexuals. I do this in acknowledgement of the widespread effects of the Court's jurisprudence on the social organization of sexuality. Whilst there are those, such as Spackman, who regard the Court as 'restrictive and conservative' and see it as largely ineffective because of its 'unwillingness to protect gays and lesbians in areas other than private consensual sex',[58]

51 A. Stone Sweet, 'A Cosmopolitan Legal Order: Constitutional Pluralism and Rights Adjudication in Europe', *Journal of Global Constitutionalism* (forthcoming), 2012, available HTTP: <http://works.bepress.com/cgi/viewcontent.cgi?article=1043&context=alec_stone_sweet> (accessed 17 February 2012).

52 Ibid.

53 L.R. Helfer and E. Voeten, 'Do European Court of Human Rights Judgments Promote Legal and Policy Change?', unpublished paper, available HTTP: <http://scholarship.law.duke.edu/cgi/viewcontent.cgi?article=3025&context=faculty_scholarship> (accessed 17 February 2012).

54 K. Nash, 'Between Citizenship and Human Rights', *Sociology* 43(6), 2009, 1067–1083.

55 D. Anagnostou, 'Does European Human Rights Law Matter? Implementation and Domestic Impact of Strasbourg Court Judgments on Minority-Related Policies', *The International Journal of Human Rights* 14(5), 2010, 721–743.

56 A. Rich, *Blood, Bread and Poetry: Selected Prose 1979–1985*, London: Virago Press, 1986.

57 S. Jackson, 'Gender, Sexuality and Heterosexuality: the Complexity (and Limits) of Heteronormativity', *Feminist Theory* 7(1), 2006, 105–121 at 108.

58 P.L. Spackman, 'Grant v. South-West Trains: Equality for Same-Sex Partners in the European Community', *American University Journal of International Law and Policy* 12, 1997, 1063–1120 at 1078.

I argue that the Court's jurisprudence can be understood in much more positive terms. The effects of the Court's judgments can, for example, be considered in terms of the 'evolution of consciousness'[59] they have created through the assertion of 'the reality of lesbian and gay lives as a reality' and an insistence that 'these are lives worthy of protection in their specificity and commonality'.[60] The Court's role in the development of a global consciousness about gay and lesbian human rights is evidenced by the reproduction of its jurisprudence in national and international Courts around the world.[61] In comparison to other regional human rights courts (for instance, the Inter-American Court of Human Rights, which heard its first case relating to homosexuality in 2011,[62] or the African Court on Human and Peoples' Rights, which has never considered a complaint in respect of sexual orientation discrimination), the Court remains the most important site at which human rights discourse and policy relating to sexual orientation is formulated.

The social impact of Strasbourg jurisprudence is both wide and deep. The Court's self-styled image as the 'Conscience of Europe' acknowledges its significant influence on shaping the 'collective conscience' of its member states and fashioning what Jacques Delors once called the 'soul of Europe'.[63] As Durkheim argued, law and its associated mechanisms for enforcement are the embodiment of the primary moral relations of organic societies[64] and the Court can be seen as one of the principal modes by which a distinctive 'European morality' is expressed. However, whilst the Court often suggests that it merely amplifies the collective morality of member states – interpreting the Convention 'in the light of present-day conditions'[65] – its jurisdiction over the radically different social and cultural communities that together comprise in excess of 800 million people means that its jurisprudence is inevitably a highly selective representation of social morality.[66] In acting as the moral nervous system of a body of highly differentiated European societies, the Court is inexorably required to conceive and execute a particular moral vision through its judgments. In producing, sustaining and imposing a moral view, the Court must therefore be regarded as one of the most important

59 E. Heinze, *Sexual Orientation: A Human Right, An Essay on International Human Rights Law*, Dordrecht: Martinus Nijhoff Publishers, 1995.

60 J. Butler, *Undoing Gender*, New York: Routledge, 2004, pp. 29–30.

61 International Commission of Jurists, *Sexual Orientation, Gender Identity and Justice: A Comparative Law Casebook*, Geneva: ICJ, 2011.

62 *Karen Atala and Daughters v Chile*, IACHR, Report No. 139/09 (merits), Case 12.502, 18 December 2009.

63 J. Coleman, *The Conscience of Europe*, Strasbourg: Council of Europe, 1999.

64 E. Durkheim, *The Division of Labour in Society*, London: Macmillan, 1893/1998.

65 *Tyrer v the United Kingdom*, no. 5856/72, 25 April 1978, Series A no. 26, § 31.

66 C.F. Stychin, 'Same-Sex Sexualities and the Globalization of Human Rights Discourse', *McGill Law Journal* 49, 2004, 951–968.

mechanisms through which normative ideas about the 'present-day conditions' of Europe are fashioned. Because of this, some commentators see a direct causal relationship between the Court's judgments and the moral evolution of European societies.[67] It is certainly the case that the Court possesses a unique capacity to challenge the established moral relations of European states and, using the symbolic authority of law, 'socialize' contracting states within the terms of its own moral vision.[68] It is this capacity that has made the Court a popular site to which gay men and lesbians have brought their complaints. As I explore throughout the book, the Court (and the Convention that it interprets) has become a vital instrument for contesting the heteronormative morality of European societies.

Sample of cases

The book contains an analysis of a body of case law relating to homosexuality that comprises decisions, reports and judgments issued by the Commission and the Court between 1955 and 2012. This body of documents relates to approximately 95 individual complaints, a full list of which can be found in Appendix 2. To produce this 'data set' I sampled cases from the now vast case law of the Strasbourg organs in which homosexuality was a central issue in the facts of the original complaint. I have therefore excluded the body of case law relating to transsexual rights. However, along with other aspects of the Court's case law, I discuss the Court's jurisprudence in respect of transsexual rights where it is of significance to complaints relating to homosexuality. It is important to note that although the data set comprises all of the published decisions and judgments of the Strasbourg organs in respect of homosexuality, these reflect a fraction of the complaints made by gay men and lesbians. The Court continues to deem 90 per cent of the complaints that it receives inadmissible and therefore publishes judgments in only a small number of cases.[69]

A note on terminology

Throughout this book, I use the terms 'homosexual' and 'homosexuality' rather than the now more ubiquitous range of nomenclature such as 'LGBTI' or 'queer'. I do this for three primary reasons. First, the Strasbourg organs

67 A. Mowbray, 'The Creativity of the European Court of Human Rights', *Human Rights Law Review* 5(1), 2005, 57–79 at 57.

68 For a discussion of the socialization thesis of human rights, see: J.T. Checkel, 'International Institutions and Socialization in Europe: Introduction and Framework', *International Organization* 59, 2005, 801–826. See also: R. Goodman and D. Junks, 'How to Influence States: Socialization and International Human Rights Law', *Duke Law Journal*, 2004, 621–703.

69 European Court of Human Rights, *Annual Report 2011*, Strasbourg: Registry of the European Court of Human Rights, 2012.

have consistently and exclusively used the terms 'homosexual' and 'homosexuality' since 1955 and this remains unchanged to the present day. Second, the focus of this book is on homosexual sexuality and not the separate (albeit related) matters of bisexuality, transsexuality or intersexuality. Third, many of the complaints considered by the Court relate to specific practices ('homosexual acts') or relationships that are not equivalent or reducible to matters of orientation or identity captured by other nomenclature. The terms homosexual and homosexuality can therefore be used descriptively to more precisely discuss the substance of complaints to the Court. Whilst I acknowledge that the terms carry with them the baggage of their historical usage and their association with ideas of pathology – something that I explore in Chapter 2 – I retain them for analytic expediency. I use other terminology – such as 'gay men and lesbians', 'sexual orientation' and the more inclusive 'sexual minorities' – where appropriate.

Outline of the book

The book is divided into three parts.

In Part I, I explore the ways in which the Strasbourg organs have conceived of homosexuals and homosexuality from 1955 until the present day. Part I is divided between two chapters, which explore the period before and after the Court's 1981 judgment in *Dudgeon v the United Kingdom*.[70] *Dudgeon* was the first successful complaint relating to homosexuality in the Court and, because of this, it and subsequent judgments have become well known. However, prior to 1981 the Commission had received a substantial number of complaints from homosexual men and, with only one exception, had deemed them inadmissible. An understanding of this pre-*Dudgeon* period is of vital importance in explaining the Court's subsequent evolution of homosexual rights. As I demonstrate, a key reason for the success of *Dudgeon* was the Court's decisive break with the Commission's earlier and long-standing conceptualization of homosexuality. In *Dudgeon*, the Court adopted a new ontological understanding of homosexuality and this has remained foundational to its jurisprudence. The Court's construction of homosexuality, which hinges upon essentialist ideas about sexual 'personality', can be seen as a response to the long-standing struggle between complainants and contracting states. The constant debate and contestation about the ontological substance of 'the homosexual' over nearly seven decades, and whether this subject possesses characteristics protectable by the Convention, has required the Strasbourg organs to 'make up' a homosexual subject of human rights. The Court's construction of the homosexual after *Dudgeon*, as I show, has underpinned an

70 *Dudgeon v the United Kingdom*, no. 7525/76, 22 October 1981, Series A no. 45.

interpretation of the Convention that continues to both enable and constrain the development of gay and lesbian human rights.

In Part II, I consider the methods used by the Strasbourg organs in their adjudication of complaints relating to homosexuality. The Court regularly attracts the criticism that it has failed to deliver the full human rights available to homosexuals under the Convention or, conversely, that it consistently over-extends its authority. As a defence to such accusations, the Court, in common with all legal institutions, has developed and applied a distinct suite of methods in an attempt to encourage judicial objectivity and maintain legal consistency. In examining three of the Court's primary methods – the margin of appreciation doctrine, consensus analysis and the 'living instrument' principle – I show that the use of these has consistently been subservient to the Court's 'moral policy' towards homosexuality. The Court can be seen to deploy its methods in particular ways and at particular times to mandate its moral reasoning. The variations in the use of these methods across the Court's case law can be explained by a number of factors, including changes in Council of Europe policy and differences in moral views among the Court's individual judges. An important issue for homosexuals seeking access to Convention rights is that the Court's methods give it considerable scope to legitimize a conservative interpretation of the Convention and prevent the success of complaints. An understanding of the moral foundations of the Court's use of method is therefore important for those seeking to bring future complaints that attempt to evolve the landscape of gay and lesbian human rights.

In Part III, I examine the Court's jurisprudence on homosexuality in respect of the substantive rights of the Convention. Part III is divided into chapters that each provide a critical reflection on the Court's interpretation of individual Convention articles. This approach is not intended as a purely doctrinal form of analysis but as a sociological consideration of how the Court has framed matters relating to homosexuality within the scope of the Convention. Beginning with an analysis of the Court's Article 8 jurisprudence, I argue that the Court's understanding of homosexuality as 'a private manifestation of the human personality' has provided an important foundation on which to guarantee salient rights for homosexuals. The Court's interpretation of Article 8 has also been vital in evolving Article 14 to deem various forms of differential treatment based on sexual orientation to be discriminatory. However, as I show in later chapters, the Court's conception of homosexuality as a matter of 'private life' has limited its interpretation of other aspects of the Convention. In considering Articles 3, 10, 11 and 12 in detail, I show that the Court's jurisprudence in these areas is significantly under-evolved and currently offers limited protection to various forms of discrimination suffered by gay men and lesbians in contemporary European societies.

Part I

Making the homosexual of human rights

Chapter 1

Emerging voices

Homosexuality and the Commission 1955–1980

In 1981 the European Court of Human Rights issued its landmark judgment in *Dudgeon v the United Kingdom*,[1] holding that the criminalization of consensual sexual acts between adult males committed in private violated the right to respect for private life guaranteed by Article 8 of the European Convention on Human Rights. Whilst the Court's jurisprudence relating to homosexuality subsequent to *Dudgeon* is well known and has become the subject of extensive debate, it is pre-dated by a substantial number of decisions issued by the European Commission of Human Rights that have received little systematic attention and remain obscure.[2] In this chapter, I examine the decisions of the Strasbourg organs issued in respect of complaints relating to homosexuality that were lodged by applicants between 1955 and 1980. All of the complaints in this period were brought by men seeking redress for their treatment under national laws that criminalized consensual and private homosexual sexual activities. The Commission, which until its abolition by Protocol 11 of the Convention in 1998 provided the quasi-judicial function of assessing the admissibility of all individual applications, declared all but one of the applications relating to homosexuality inadmissible and, in the main, deemed them to be 'manifestly ill-founded'.[3] No applications during this period reached the Court and therefore none were successful.

Whilst the period between 1955 and 1980 is characterized by a startling lack of success on the part of applicants in persuading the Strasbourg organs that male homosexual sexual activities were protectable under the Convention, the decisions made by the Commission remain important for a number of reasons. First, the decisions issued during this time provided the foundation on which subsequent evolutions in the interpretation of the Convention in

1 *Dudgeon v the United Kingdom*, no. 7525/76, 22 October 1981, Series A no. 45.

2 For an exception, see: D.J. Kane, 'Homosexuality and the European Convention on Human Rights: What Rights?', *Hastings International and Comparative Law Review* 11, 1998, 447–486.

3 Under ex Article 27(2) of the Convention.

respect of homosexuality were based. An understanding of these decisions is therefore essential because of their important contribution in establishing the framework through which the Court continues to approach homosexuality today. Second, it was in these early complaints that applicants developed particular 'strategies' of complaint that have since become axiomatic in petitions to the Court. In contrast to the 'scattergun' use of articles of the Convention in the earliest petitions, applications progressively demonstrate the emergence of the tactical use of particular articles (most notably Article 8) that continues to the present day. Third, decisions in this period show the formulation of distinctive ontological understandings of homosexuality by the Commission and the considerable influence of these on its reasoning. Ontological debates about sexual orientation, as I discuss in Chapter 2, remain ongoing and vital to the Court's current jurisprudence. And fourth, the reasoning of the Commission during this period has strong resonances with contemporary political and legal arguments that favour restricting the human rights of homosexuals. Understanding the Commission's decisions to systematically deny homosexuals protection under the Convention provides crucial insights into legally mandated processes of homophobia today.

The legal context of the applications lodged between 1955 and 1980

All of the applications relating to homosexuality between 1955 and 1980 originated in three states contracted to the Convention: Austria, the Federal Republic of Germany and the United Kingdom. A German applicant lodged the first complaint with the Commission on 10 October 1955, three months after it was recognized as competent to receive individual applications under the terms of ex Article 25(4) of the Convention, and the majority of complaints during this period were made against Germany. Although criminal laws enforced a total prohibition on male homosexual sex during some of the period between 1955 and 1980 in 10 of the 20 states that had ratified the Convention, not every contracting state afforded individuals the right of petition to Strasbourg. The United Kingdom, for instance, granted the right of individual petition in 1966, just prior to the partial decriminalization of male homosexual acts in 1967,[4] and this explains the absence of complaints against it before the first application relating to homosexuality in 1975.[5] However, it is notable that the Commission received no applications from two other states during this period, which both criminalized male homosexual sex and granted the right of individual petition: Norway, for instance, granted the right of individual petition from 1955 and operated

4 Sexual Offences Act 1967 in respect of England and Wales.
5 *X. v the United Kingdom*, no. 7215/75, Committee of Ministers, 12 June 1979.

total prohibition on male homosexual sex until 1972; similarly, Ireland granted the right of individual petition in 1953 but there was no complaint against its prohibition on male homosexual sex until *Norris v Ireland* was lodged in 1983.[6]

The decisions taken by the Commission during this period in respect of applications relating to homosexuality must be seen within the context of the Strasbourg machinery of the time. The role of the Court in European law, from its establishment as a part-time institution in 1959 until the mid-1970s, was peripheral and its profile was low.[7] As the Commission recognized in 1959: 'It appears that the Convention is little known to jurists in general and to practising lawyers in particular, even those in countries where it has been incorporated in the domestic legislation.'[8] During these 'sleeping beauty years',[9] the Commission's authority was limited by the reluctance of the more powerful contracting states to recognize its role (France, for instance, did not ratify the Convention until 1974). As a result of this, from the point that the Commission began to receive individual applications in 1955, it developed and forcefully implemented mechanisms for dismissing complaints. Myers describes these as 'procedures to dispose of absurd or frivolous applications and to avoid transmission to governments of applications of no interest or of malicious intent'.[10] The Commission did this within the remit of ex Article 27 of the Convention that allowed it to deem inadmissible any application it considered 'incompatible with the provisions of the present Convention, manifestly ill-founded, or the abuse of the right of individual petition'. Whilst the Commission found all but one of the complaints relating to homosexuality prior to *Dudgeon* inadmissible, this was not uncharacteristic in terms of its general approach. In its earliest days, between 5 July 1955 and 1 March 1960, the Commission received a total of 713 applications and, of these, declared 710 inadmissible.[11] Nevertheless, as I describe below, the reasoning that underpinned the decisions to declare inadmissible the applications relating to homosexuality demonstrates a fundamental unwillingness by the Commission to regard homosexual sex as in any way protectable under the Convention.

6 *Norris v Ireland*, no.10581/83, 26 October 1988, Series A no. 142.

7 E. Bates, *The Evolution of the European Convention on Human Rights. From its Inception to the Creation of a Permanent Court of Human Rights*, Oxford: Oxford University Press, 2010.

8 European Commission of Human Rights, *Documents and Decisions*, The Hague: Martinus Nijhoff, 1959, p. VIII.

9 J. Frowein, 'European Integration Through Fundamental Rights', *Michigan Journal of Law Reform* 18, 1984, 5–28 at 8.

10 D.P. Myers, 'The European Commission on Human Rights', *The American Journal of International Law* 50(4), 1956, 949–951 at 950.

11 G.L. Weil, 'Decisions on Inadmissible Applications by the European Commission of Human Rights', *The American Journal of International Law* 54(4), 1960: 874–881.

Germany and the 'paragraph 175' applications

The first applications lodged with the Commission relating to homosexuality were from men who complained about convictions for homosexual offences under paragraph 175 of the Criminal Code of the Federal Republic of Germany. Paragraph 175 had existed in the Criminal Code since 1871 and criminalized 'unnatural fornication' between men. However, as a consequence of an amendment in 1935, paragraph 175 was expanded to prohibit any 'lewd act' between males. The 1935 amendment also introduced a further statutory provision, paragraph 175a, that allowed for an increased term of imprisonment for lewd acts between men that involved: violence or the threat of violence as a form of compulsion; the abuse of a relationship of dependence based upon service, employment or subordination; a male over 21 years and a person under 21 years; any activity in a public place. These changes to the law broadened the scope of regulation from a limited range of 'intercourse-like acts', such as 'anal, oral and thigh intercourse',[12] and criminalized any sexual act between males that included 'as little as a mere kiss or embrace'.[13] The 1935 amendment of paragraph 175 – very similar in scope to the Criminal Law Amendment Act 1885 in the United Kingdom that criminalized gross indecency between males[14] – was a response by the National Socialist Party to their frustration at the difficulties posed in securing convictions under the existing law:

> Bad experiences in the recent period have made it seem advisable to bring into force [. . .] harsher provisions against homosexual offences between men [. . .] the essential defect of the previous [paragraph] 175 of the Penal Code lay in the fact that – at least in former case law – it applied only to intercourse-like acts, so that public prosecutors and the police could not proceed against evidently homosexual practices unless they were able to prove such acts. This gap has now been filled, so that any sex offence between males renders them liable to imprisonment.[15]

Paragraph 175 was an essential tool used by the Nazis to increase arrest rates and secure approximately 50,000 convictions for homosexual offences between

12 G. Grau, *Hidden Holocaust? Gay and Lesbian Persecution in Germany 1933–45*, London: Cassell, 1995, p. 64.

13 H. Heger, *The Men with the Pink Triangle*, London: GMP, 1972, p. 11.

14 Section 11 of the Criminal Law Amendment Act 1885 stated that: 'Any male person who, in public or private, commits, or is a party to the commission of, or procures, or attempts to procure the commission by any male person of, any act of gross indecency shall be guilty of a misdemeanour, and being convicted shall be liable at the discretion of the Court to be imprisoned for any term not exceeding two years, with or without hard labour'.

15 Commentary by Dr Leopold Schäfer, Assistant Head of the Department at the Reich Ministry of Justice, on the 1935 amendment to the Criminal Code, quoted in G. Grau, *Hidden Holocaust? Gay and Lesbian Persecution in Germany 1933–45*, p. 66.

1933 and 1945.[16] During the Nazi era, such convictions resulted in mass imprisonment and, as a series of biographical accounts now testify, frequent deportation to concentration camps.[17] At the point that the first complaint against a paragraph 175 conviction was lodged with the Commission in 1955, the 1935 amendment to the Criminal Code was still in force. Whilst no complaints for convictions during the Nazi period could be brought before the Commission – since the Convention has no retrospective scope – German men complained that convictions under paragraph 175 subsequent to the entry into force of the Convention in 1953 violated their human rights.

In *W.B. v Federal Republic of Germany*, the first application of this kind, the complainant had been convicted of 'two cases of homosexuality' (contrary to paragraph 175) and 'attempted serious homosexuality' (contrary to paragraph 175a) and, as a consequence, was serving a 15-month term of imprisonment.[18] Whilst convicted of crimes under both paragraph 175 and 175a, no details are given in the Commission's decision regarding the nature of the offences. The applicant claimed his conviction violated a wide range of rights guaranteed by Articles 2, 8, 14, 17 and 18 of the Convention. The use of Article 2 in the complaint, which guarantees the right to life, is unusual and has since been used in only four other applications relating to homosexuality. The use of Article 2 is made even more remarkable by the Commission's failure to engage with it. When reviewing the complaint, the Commission focused solely on the applicant's claim that his conviction under paragraph 175 infringed his right to respect for private life guaranteed by Article 8 and that, because the law applied only to men, this violated his right to non-discrimination under Article 14.

The Commission disposed of the complaint in *W.B.* with extreme brevity, stating that 'the Convention permits a High Contracting Party to legislate to make homosexuality a punishable offence'.[19] In doing so, it established the important principle that any legal measure taken by a state to regulate 'homosexuality' (and not just 'homosexual acts') would not be regarded as infringing any of the substantive rights of the Convention. The Commission went on to blandly state that paragraph 175 did not violate Article 8 rights because 'the law relating to private and family life may be the subject of interference by the laws of the said Party dealing with the protection of health or morals'.[20] Similarly, in respect of the Article 14 complaint, the Commission stated that it did 'not exclude the possibility of a High Contracting Party differentiating

16 R. Hoffman, J. Hutter and R. Lautmann, 'Germany', in D.J. West and R. Green (eds.), *Sociolegal Control of Homosexuality: A Multi-Nation Comparison*, New York: Kluwer, 1997, 255–268.

17 See, for example: P. Seel, *I, Pierre Seel, Deported Homosexual: A Memoir of Nazi Terror*, New York: Basic Books, 1995. See also: H. Heger, *The Men with the Pink Triangle*.

18 *W.B. v Federal Republic of Germany*, no. 104/55, Commission decision, 17 December 1955.

19 Ibid.

20 Ibid.

between the sexes in the measures it takes with regard to homosexuality for the protection of health or morals'.[21] As a result of this, the Commission declared the complaint manifestly ill-founded and inadmissible.

Wintemute rightly describes the decision in *W.B.* as 'tersely stated',[22] but it was certainly not unusual at the time. In the first published collection of its decisions, the Commission recognized that it 'drafted its decisions with comparative brevity' but that it had 'since become the Commission's practice to include in their decisions a much fuller statement of their reasoning'.[23] Whilst published decisions did become more expansive later in this period, decisions relating to paragraph 175 provided few details about the reasoning of the Commission. For instance, given that the Convention was conceived as an instrument to promote a common understanding and observance of human rights among 'Governments of European countries which are like-minded and have a common heritage of political traditions, ideals, freedoms and the rule of law', and that in 1955 only four contracting states out of 14 operated a total legal prohibition on homosexual acts, it is striking that the Commission gave no details of its reasoning in respect of paragraph 175, which did not reflect the 'common heritage' of contracting states.

Despite the failure of the complaint in *W.B.*, the Commission's decision established the important principle that the criminalization of homosexual sex fell within the ambit of Article 8 of the Convention. Although the criminalization of homosexual sex did not amount to a violation of Article 8, it was recognized to interfere with private life. This was significant, since it provided a foundation for future applicants to concentrate their complaints on challenging the justification for the interference with private life created by paragraph 175. However, in response to a series of subsequent complaints the Commission continued to baldly assert its reasoning in the manner established in *W.B.* In *K.H.W. v Federal Republic of Germany,*[24] for example, the applicant, who had been imprisoned for eight months following his conviction for an offence under paragraph 175, requested that the Commission consider his application admissible under the terms of ex Article 26 of the Convention (which, like the current Article 35, required that applicants exhaust all domestic remedies before making a complaint). The applicant made this request despite having an outstanding appeal lodged with the Federal Court of Constitutional Justice. The Commission stated that 'it is

21 Ibid. This reiterated the decision in *P.S. v Federal Republic of Germany* (no. 54/55, Commission decision, 17 December 1955) that differential treatment on the basis of sex did not constitute discrimination contrary to Article 14.

22 R. Wintemute, *Sexual Orientation and Human Rights: The United States Constitution, the European Convention, and the Canadian Charter*, Oxford: Clarendon Press, 1995, p. 92.

23 European Commission of Human Rights, *Documents and Decisions*, p. VI.

24 *K.H.W. v Federal Republic of Germany*, no. 167/56, Commission decision, 28 September 1956.

superfluous in the circumstances to examine whether or not the petitioner has satisfied the requirements of Article 26 of the Convention as to the exhaustion of domestic remedies' because 'investigation of the file does not appear to show a breach of a right recognized in the Convention'. In a slightly expanded statement, the Commission reiterated its decision in *W.B.*:

> the Convention permits a High Contracting Party to legislate to make homosexuality a punishable offence: in a democratic society, the right to respect for private and family life may be subject to interference in accordance with the laws of that Party if such interference is for the protection of health and morals.[25]

In *X. v Federal Republic of Germany*,[26] contestation of the necessity of criminalizing private homosexual acts 'in a democratic society' showed some tentative development. The applicant, a German national who had submitted a previous application to the Commission that was deemed inadmissible,[27] had been convicted under paragraph 175 'as a recidivist' and, following an unsuccessful appeal, received an increase in his term of imprisonment. He complained that he had been convicted 'despite procedural irregularities and, in particular, by false evidence' and that his conviction 'was essentially motivated by his Polish ethnic origins and his anti-fascist political views'.[28] To support his complaint, the applicant argued that 'the general ban on homosexuality in Germany contravenes Human Rights, given that [. . .] this sexual behaviour is not punishable in other countries'.[29] This represents the first use by an applicant of 'consensus analysis' – which, as I discuss in Chapter 3, has since become a hallmark of the Court's adjudication of complaints relating to homosexuality – as a method for interpreting the Convention in light of the legal arrangements of other contracting states. The Commission failed to engage with this argument, simply restating its view that the Convention permitted a contracting state to legislate to make homosexuality a punishable offence and declared the application inadmissible.

These decisions by the Commission bear considerable similarity with the reasoning of the German Federal Constitutional Court in a judgment issued in 1957 in respect of a case concerning the constitutionality of paragraph 175.[30] The case was brought by two men who, having been

25 Ibid.
26 *X. v Federal Republic of Germany*, no. 261/57, Commission decision, 16 December 1957.
27 *E.G. v Federal Republic of Germany*, no. 135/55, Commission decision, 31 May 1956.
28 Ibid.
29 Ibid.
30 Federal Constitutional Court (Entscheidungen des Bundesverfassungsgerichts), *The Constitutionality of Penal Regulation Against Male Homosexuality (vol. 6)*, Tübingen: J.C.B. Mohr Verlag, 1957.

convicted under paragraph 175, complained that the law embodied 'National Socialist racial teaching' and represented a 'striking violation of democratic principles'.[31] The Constitutional Court rejected this claim, stating that homosexuality violated the moral code and that, although the law had been enacted by an undemocratic government, it was not unconstitutional.[32] Linart argues that the Constitutional Court's reasoning relied upon 'allegations and plain statements rather than developing founded and convincing arguments' and in relying upon 'arguments that have no logical connection to the conclusion drawn [. . .] it violates the principle of proportionality'.[33] The failure to develop arguments that convincingly demonstrate the stringency of its methodology or the robustness of its reasoning in respect of the key principles of judicial adjudication – such as proportionality – is the defining characteristic of the Commission's earliest decisions in respect of homosexuality.

However, despite the Commission's trenchant opposition, applicants continued to lodge complaints claiming that paragraph 175 was a disproportionate measure in a democratic society. In *A.S. v Federal Republic of Germany*,[34] for example, the applicant, who was convicted of multiple paragraph 175 offences and sentenced to indefinite detention as a 'dangerous and habitual criminal', complained that paragraph 175 was 'a survival from Nazi times and is anti-democratic: all democratic States, even Poland, tolerate homosexuality [and to] make it an offence is a violation of the right to life, the corollary of which is the right to love'.[35] This invocation of 'love' represents the earliest attempt to widen complaints from a narrow focus on private sexual acts. The applicant also, atypically, relied on Article 3 of the Convention but the Commission, as I discuss in Chapter 8, failed to address this aspect of the application. In response to the argument that interference with loving, intimate relationships between men was deemed to be unnecessary in most European democratic societies (including Poland, which, although sharing a similar legal system with Germany, had never criminalized homosexual sex), the Commission stated that the 'case does not disclose any appearance of a violation of the rights or freedoms protected by the Convention' and that paragraph 175 was 'in no way in contradiction with the provisions of the Convention'.[36]

31 For an extensive discussion of this case, see: R.G. Moeller, 'The Homosexual Man Is a "Man", the Homosexual Woman Is a "Woman": Sex, Society, and the Law in Postwar West Germany', *Journal of the History of Sexuality* 4(3), 1994, 395–429.

32 R. Hoffman, J. Hutter and R. Lautmann, 'Germany'.

33 K. Linhart, 'Decriminalization of Homosexuality and Its Effects on Family Rights: A German-US-American Comparison', *German Law Journal* 6, 2005, 943–966 at 947.

34 *A.S. v Federal Republic of Germany*, no. 530/59, Commission decision, 4 January 1960.

35 Ibid.

36 Ibid.

The Commission reached the same decision in *H.S. v Federal Republic of Germany*[37] in which the applicant, having been convicted and detained in a concentration camp between 1940 and 1945 for paragraph 175 offences, stated that a subsequent conviction in 1956 was based on the 'biased' judgment of the trial judges who were 'former Nazis'. Like several applicants during this period, the applicant brought a complaint about violations of his right to a fair trial guaranteed by Article 6 of the Convention. For example, in *X. v Federal Republic of Germany* the applicant complained that, having been previously convicted for paragraph 175 offences in 1941 and 1953, and again arrested in 1958 on suspicion of having committed a similar offence, he was denied legal assistance by the police.[38] Following the applicant's 1958 conviction, the Federal Court set aside the decision and returned the case to the Regional Court, where it remained pending at the time the applicant lodged his complaint with the Commission. The applicant alleged that an order issued by the Regional Court indicated that he was guilty and stated that, although the Federal Court had quashed his conviction, it would sentence him without giving him the opportunity to contest his guilt. He complained that the Regional Court was not impartial, refused to hear evidence requested by him, and that his defence was obstructed by the late appointment of lawyers. Because the Federal Court had quashed the applicant's conviction, and his re-trial was outstanding, the Commission dismissed his complaint about the misadministration of justice. To the present day, no applicant has brought a successful complaint under Article 6 of the Convention in respect of sexual orientation discrimination.

One of the most striking examples of the Commission's approach to homosexuality during this period is found in its admissibility decision in *G.W. v Federal Republic of Germany*, which was lodged by an applicant who had brought five previous complaints between 1957 and 1961.[39] These complaints related to the applicant's arrest by the Gestapo in 1937 and 1939 for a paragraph 175 offence and, following his subsequent conviction in 1940, his expulsion as a lawyer from the Bar of Bremen. The applicant complained that at the point of his arrest by the Gestapo, he was photographed and his fingerprints were taken but, despite having his conviction set aside after the end of the war on procedural grounds, the authorities refused his request that they destroy records of his photographs and fingerprints. The applicant argued that retention of his photographs, fingerprints and other biographical details was incompatible with his rights under Articles 3, 8 and 14 of the Convention and that, since 'homosexual relations between adults are exempted from punishment in 33 countries',[40] the consensus in other democratic societies supported his claim.

37 *H.S. v Federal Republic of Germany*, no. 704/60, Commission decision, 4 August 1960.
38 *X. v Federal Republic of Germany*, no. 986/61, Commission decision, 7 May 1962.
39 *G.W. v Federal Republic of Germany*, no. 1307/61, Commission decision, 4 October 1962.
40 Ibid.

The Commission stated that, since 'the keeping of records, including documents, photographs and fingerprints, relating to criminal cases of the past is necessary in a modern democratic society for the prevention of crime', the applicant had 'failed to show that the refusals complained of were not in accordance with law and were not dictated by legitimate interests of the society and of the necessity to prevent crime and protect the health and morals of others'.[41] However, the Commission went on to state that the series of complaints lodged by the applicant were 'proof' of a 'querulous and abusive exercise of the right of petition'.[42] The use of the word 'querulous' (a term not found in the Convention) is unusually revealing and suggests that the Commission regarded complaints brought by homosexual men as not only ill-founded but also peevish, petulant and petty. The issue raised in the complaint, however, remains pertinent and the Court currently has several outstanding complaints against Austria in respect of the retention of police records for convictions under (now repealed) laws that criminalized male homosexual sex.[43]

All of the Commission's admissibility decisions in respect of the paragraph 175 complaints show a strong resistance to recognizing homosexual men as having any right to the most minimal protection under the Convention. This is made all the more striking when one considers that, although the Convention was conceived as a direct response to fascism ('a beacon to those at the moment in totalitarian darkness [that] will give them a hope of return to freedom'),[44] the Commission repeatedly upheld Nazi legislation as compatible with basic human rights. Because of this, the Convention played no part in persuading the German legislator that a total prohibition on male homosexual sex was disproportionate to any legitimate policy aims it sought to achieve. At the point that homosexual acts were partially decriminalized between men aged over 21 years in the Federal Republic of Germany by the Criminal Law Reform Act 1969 (subsequently amended in 1973 to 18 years of age), the Commission had never found a violation of the Convention in respect of a paragraph 175 complaint. The repeal of paragraph 175 was not driven by any commitment of the Council of Europe to human rights but by the government of the German Democratic Republic who, opposed to paragraph 175, negotiated a provision in the treaty of German unification that invalidated it.[45] Although paragraph 175 existed until 1994, and criminalized a broad

41 Ibid.

42 Ibid.

43 *F.J. v Austria*, no. 2362/08, Statement of facts, lodged 4 January 2008; *E.B. v Austria*, no. 26271/08, Statement of facts, lodged 29 April 2008; *H.G. v Austria*, no. 48098/07, Statement of facts, lodged 18 October 2007.

44 From a speech given at the signing of the Convention by Sir David Maxwell Fyfe, who was instrumental in drafting it. Quoted in Human Rights Information Bulletin, *The European Convention on Human Rights at 50*, Strasbourg: Council of Europe, 2000, p. 47.

45 C. Schultz, *Paragraph 175*, Hamburg: MännerschwarmSkript Verlag, 1994.

range of 'homosexual acts' between males where one partner was under the age of 18, no complaint was ever successfully brought against it in Strasbourg.

The Austrian cases

Throughout the 1960s the Commission received a series of applications from men who complained about the criminalization of homosexual sexual activity by the Austrian Criminal Code 1852. Sections 129 and 130 of the Criminal Code prohibited any form of 'lewdness against the order of nature' and, unlike German law, criminalized same-sex sexual acts between women as well as men. The Supreme Court of Austria held in several judgments that the Criminal Code prohibited all homosexual acts – not simply acts of penetration – but that 'mere touching' of the genitals fell below its threshold.[46] Prosecutions of both men and women for homosexual offences were common during this period: in 1960, for instance, 713 men and 15 women were convicted of offences under section 129,[47] an annual figure that was typical throughout that decade. Although women were subject to conviction for private and consensual same-sex sexual acts, no complaint was ever brought to the Commission by a female applicant.

In *W.R. v Austria*, the first complaint of this type, the applicant complained about his conviction and sentence (five months' 'rigorous imprisonment', including two days of fasting and two nights of 'hard bed') for homosexual acts committed with one partner in 1959.[48] At his original trial the applicant 'denied vigorously' the charges against him and, whilst he admitted to meeting his alleged sexual partner in 'a café in Vienna frequented by homosexuals and taking him home by car towards midnight', he claimed he was 'acting only to help [the other man] who was jobless at the time, by giving him a shirt'.[49] He also argued that 'the young man [had] left the building after no more than about 10 minutes' and asked that two witnesses be called to testify to this fact.[50] The court that tried the applicant refused to hear these witnesses on the grounds that 10 minutes was sufficient time for the commission of the offence. The applicant had also argued at trial that he suffered from a medical condition that rendered him incapable of committing the alleged sexual acts and requested that the court hear expert medical opinion with regard to this. This request was dismissed on the grounds that impotence did not preclude the applicant from committing a homosexual offence (of which

46 H. Graupner, 'Austria', in D.J. West and R. Green (eds.), 269–287.

47 K. Krickler, 'Homosexuals in Austria: Nazi Persecution and the Long Struggle for Rehabilitation', *Working Paper Series No. 12 of the Canadian Centre for German and European Studies*, Toronto: Canada, 2008.

48 *W.R. v Austria*, no. 1138/61, Commission decision, 18 June 1963.

49 Ibid.

50 Ibid.

he had previously been convicted). Upon conviction, the applicant appealed to the Supreme Court who, in a private session and in the absence of the applicant and his lawyer, found that the appeal was ill-founded. The applicant's complaint to the Commission was that the original court's failure to consider his evidence, and the private decision made by the Supreme Court, violated his rights under Article 6 of the Convention. The Commission dismissed this complaint as manifestly ill-founded. It also failed to make any comment on the applicant's claim that 'to all effective purposes, of Articles 5, 8 and 14: the suppression of homosexuality constitutes a "medieval" interference with the rights defined in these articles'.[51]

In a subsequent petition, *X. v Austria*, the applicant complained that his conviction and sentence (six years' 'severe imprisonment' and one day of fasting and 'hard bed' every three months) contravened his rights under Articles 1, 2, 3, 5, 7, 8 and 14 of the Convention.[52] Following his original conviction, the applicant had made a number of appeals in the domestic courts with the result that the Supreme Court ordered that he be committed to a labour institution after the expiration of his term of imprisonment. In his application to the Commission, the applicant complained about procedural irregularities at his original trial and in the Supreme Court. He also complained that prison authorities had subjected him to disciplinary measures because of his correspondence with the Commission. The Commission requested a response from the Austrian government to this element of the complaint and the Federal Ministry of Justice provided the following explanation:

> It is untrue that the prisoner X was subjected to disciplinary measures in 1962 for lodging an application with the European Commission of Human Rights. Disciplinary action was taken against him because, over a period of time and in addition to the stationery issued to him, he unlawfully appropriated (stole) and hoarded specific types of stationery for other purposes. In the interests of the maintenance of prison order and discipline, such behaviour could clearly not be tolerated, the more so since prisoners who wish to lodge an application with the European Commission of Human Rights are immediately given the necessary stationery. It is true that, in January 1962, the prisoner was deprived of privileges for a month as a disciplinary measure for the insults levelled at Austrian justice in general and prison administrations in particular, in an application addressed to the Commission in which he used such expressions as: murderers of justice, murderers of the people, court terror, robbers of freedom, double-dealing, Nazi hierarchy, etc. It is obvious that such

51 Ibid.
52 *X. v Austria*, no. 1593/62, Commission decision, 4 July 1964.

> slander cannot be tolerated by the judicial authorities and calls for disciplinary measures.[53]

Whilst hindrance of the right to individual petition is prohibited by the Convention, the Austrian government revealed that prison authorities not only read letters addressed to the Commission but, when deeming them to be 'slanderous', implemented disciplinary measures against correspondents. Yet the Commission accepted the explanation offered by the government, stating that 'it is no part of the effective exercise of the right of petition to make unnecessary or irrelevant offensive statements in an Application'.[54] The Commission went on to state that whilst it 'would be more in accord with the spirit of the Convention that letters addressed to the Secretary should not first be submitted unsealed to the prison authorities [. . .] it recognises that Governments may have reasonable grounds for making this requirement'.[55] The Commission did not give any indication as to whether maintaining 'prison discipline' constituted a reasonable ground. The Commission concluded by arguing that whilst it 'believes that [. . .] the punishment imposed might be considered as a violation of [the Convention] because of its general deterrent effects' it did 'not consider that X's Application was in fact frustrated and therefore decides in this case to take no further steps'.[56]

These complaints made against Austria, like those made against the Federal Republic of Germany, show that attempts by applicants to challenge the legal prohibition of homosexual sex were frustrated by both domestic authorities and by the Commission. As in Germany, the Convention played no part in the partial decriminalization of homosexual sex in Austria, which resulted from the Criminal Law Amendment Act 1971. Nor, as I discuss in Chapter 5, can complaints to Strasbourg be seen as decisive in removing the discriminatory minimum age of sexual activity for homosexual sex that existed in Austria until 2002.

The Commission and 'the homosexual' in the 1950s and 1960s

It is clear from the decisions in respect of complaints originating in Austria and Germany during this period that the Commission robustly rejected the claim that the criminalization of homosexual sex violated any rights protected by the Convention. Whilst this cannot be seen as the outcome of any explicit or coherent principle or policy on homosexuality, none of the Commission's decisions reveal any extensive consideration of the necessity of suppressing

53 Ibid.
54 Ibid.
55 Ibid.
56 Ibid.

homosexual practices in a democratic society. Whilst the Commission repeatedly stated that the criminalization of homosexual sex fell within the ambit of Article 8, because it interfered with private life, it never fully explained its reasoning as to why such an interference was justified. In *G.W. v Federal Republic of Germany*, the Commission implicitly and tacitly endorsed the view that the legal regulation of homosexuality was 'necessary for the protection of society' because 'this particular sort of crime [. . .] often led to recidivism'.[57] However, whilst the Commission can be seen to legitimize the view that homosexuality constituted a sufficient 'danger' or 'threat' (to either the state or to individuals) to allow an interference with Article 8 rights – primarily to enable the protection of health or morals – it provided no details about the types of threats or dangers that homosexuality posed or what specific responses to these could be regarded as necessary (and proportionate) in a democratic society. In making the blanket statement that a state could take measures to prohibit 'homosexuality' the Commission endorsed the view that national authorities possessed unlimited discretion (or, as I discuss in Chapter 3, a wide 'margin of appreciation') to criminalize any homosexual behaviour.

The decisions of the Commission during this period could be understood to express a broader social antipathy towards homosexuality and, when contextualized within the wider 'world view' of the period, may appear unsurprising. In the United States, for instance, homosexuality was, as Leznoff and Westley argue, 'defined both legally and socially as a criminal and depraved practice and the homosexual [was] threatened by powerful legal and social sanctions such as imprisonment, physical violence, social and occupational ostracism and ridicule'.[58] From 1952, the American Psychiatric Association had regarded homosexuality as a mental disorder,[59] and in Europe homosexuality was frequently discussed as the manifestation of a mental or physical pathology.[60] The legal regulation of homosexuals was often justified on the grounds that it stemmed the 'germ' of sexual deviancy from 'contaminating' wider society.[61] The male homosexual was variously understood as a menace to the health of a nation, a danger to 'the family', and a paedophilic predator capable of corrupting the innocence of boys.[62]

57 *G.W. v Federal Republic of Germany*, no. 1307/61, Commission decision, 4 October 1962.

58 M. Leznoff and W.A. Westley, 'The Homosexual Community', in P.N. Nardi and B.E. Schneider (eds.), *Social Perspectives in Lesbian and Gay Studies: A Reader*, New York: Routledge, 1998, p. 6.

59 American Psychiatric Association, *Diagnostic and Statistical Manual of Mental Disorders (DSM I)*, Arlington: American Psychiatric Association, 1952.

60 K. Waaldijk and A. Clapham, *Homosexuality: A European Community Issue*, Dordrecht: Martinus Nijhoff Publishers, 1993.

61 D. Fuss, *Identification Papers*, New York: Routledge, 1995.

62 M. Hyde, *The Other Love: An Historical and Contemporary Survey of Homosexuality in Britain*, London: Heinemann, 1970.

Against this social, political and cultural landscape, the Commission's decisions in this period might be seen as reflective of a hegemonic hostility towards homosexuality. Yet, when the Convention was conceived, the majority of contracting states did not criminalize homosexual acts between adults in private and, even in those states that continued to operate a total prohibition, strong opposition was being advanced by state-sponsored law commissions – most notably in the *Report of the Committee on Homosexual Offences and Prostitution* in the United Kingdom in 1957[63] and by the Austrian Criminal Law Reform Commission in 1956.[64] Set within the highly contested terrain of social and legal debate about homosexuality that characterized this period, and bearing in mind the precarious position occupied by the Commission and the Court as emerging supranational institutions dependent upon the voluntary agreement of nation states,[65] the Commission's decisions show that it adopted a strongly conservative interpretation of the Convention in respect of matters relating to homosexuality.

In light of this, it is all the more remarkable that applicants continued to lodge complaints with the Commission during this period. In doing so, these applicants should be seen as nothing less than the first 'voices' in European human rights law who, through tenacious and persistent petitioning, established the foundations for the subsequent development of gay and lesbian rights under the Convention. Their most important contribution, which I will explore in detail in Chapter 2, was their attempt to establish a particular ontological understanding of homosexuality in order to encourage recognition for gay and lesbian rights. For example, in *A.S. v Federal Republic of Germany*, the applicant's claim that European states should 'tolerate homosexuality' was underpinned by the argument that homosexuals 'have an innate propensity towards it, which is the case with him'.[66] Similar claims about the innateness of sexual orientation are present in many of the applications of this period and, as an early form of the 'strategic essentialism' that would later become expressed through the vocabulary of lesbian and gay 'identity',[67] represent attempts to establish homosexuality as an inherent, inborn and immutable characteristic of 'human nature'. In attempting to establish homosexuality as an innate human characteristic, applicants were making the first appeals to, what Moran describes as,

63 Home Office, *Report of the Committee on Homosexual Offences and Prostitution* (Cmnd. 247), London: Home Office, 1957.

64 H. Graupner, 'Austria', in D.J. West and R. Green (eds.), 269–287.

65 L.R. Helfer, 'Lesbian and Gay Rights as Human Rights: Strategies for a United Europe', *Virginia Journal of International Law* 32, 1991, 157–212.

66 *A.S. v Federal Republic of Germany*, no. 530/59, Commission decision, 4 January 1960.

67 M. Bernstein, 'Celebration and Suppression: The Strategic Uses of Identity by the Lesbian and Gay Community', *American Journal of Sociology* 103(3), 1997, 531–65.

> the rhetoric of legal humanism through which the judicial subject of human rights is imagined. Here the judicial subject of human rights is imagined as a subject position in law grounded in the true self, and in the idea of an authentic identity, the congenital self.[68]

This rhetoric has become, as I explore in Chapter 2, an important foundation for the expansion of lesbian and gay rights under the Convention. In early applications, it was expressed in the crudest forms as an attempt to persuade the Commission that 'homosexuals should not be blamed for their inclinations, which are the result of an inherent physical condition'.[69] These arguments quickly developed into claims that, because homosexuality was an innate 'condition', the practice of homosexual 'acts' was determined rather than voluntaristic. As one applicant stated: because he was 'constitutionally a homosexual', and since 'homosexuality is an inherent factor in the personality of certain individuals', homosexuals 'cannot be blamed or punished'.[70] The deployment of 'personality' by this applicant can be seen as an early use of a concept that, as Loukaidēs argues, has since become fundamental to the ontological basis of rights discourse.[71] More generally, these claims represent the earliest attempts by homosexuals to deploy essentialist understandings of sexual orientation in order to establish homosexuality as a form of personhood that is comprehensible within the terms of liberal humanism and protectable as a 'human right'.

Constructing the homosexual in the 1970s: the 'age of consent' applications

The arguments advanced by applicants about homosexuality throughout the 1950s and 1960s can be seen to gain significant momentum in complaints to the Commission during the 1970s. In two important decisions, the Commission produced more expansive written reports that outlined its approach to homosexuality and, for the first time, gave a full account of its reasoning in respect of its interpretation of the Convention. In *X. v Federal Republic of Germany*,[72] the Commission considered the first complaint made

68 L.J. Moran, *The Homosexual(ity) of Law*, London: Routledge, 1996, p. 179.

69 *H.K. v Federal Republic of Germany*, no. 600/59, Commission decision, 2 April 1960.

70 *H.S. v Federal Republic of Germany*, no. 704/60, Commission decision, 4 August 1960.

71 L.G. Loukaidēs, *Essays on the Developing Law of Human Rights*, Leiden: Martinus Nijhoff Publishers, 1995. The European Convention on Human Rights does not use the word 'personality', but it appears three times in the Universal Declaration of Human Rights 1948 (Res. 217A(III), A/810 91): Article 22 protects 'the free development of his personality'; Article 26 states: 'Education shall be directed to the full development of the human personality'; and Article 29 states: 'Everyone has duties to the community in which alone the free and full development of his personality is possible.'

72 *X. v Federal Republic of Germany*, no. 5935/72, Commission decision, 30 September 1975.

about national laws that maintained a higher minimum age for male homosexual sexual activities than for heterosexual or female homosexual acts. The applicant, who had previously complained to the Commission about convictions under paragraph 175,[73] complained of a further conviction for offences contrary to paragraphs 175 and 176 of the German Criminal Code. Whilst the applicant was convicted under paragraph 176 (which criminalized any adult who engaged in sexual activities with a child below the minimum age of 14 years) as well as under paragraph 175 (which criminalized sexual acts between men under 21 years of age), the Commission focused its attention on the applicant's complaint that the existence of a differential age of consent established by paragraph 175 was an unjustified interference with his private life and a form of discrimination based on sex.

I will examine the complaint made by the applicant in respect of the different minimum ages for sexual activities in Chapter 5, but here want to consider the Commission's discursive construction of homosexuality. The Commission's consideration of homosexuality in *X. v Federal Republic of Germany* is more extensive than in previous cases because, departing from its earlier practice, it took the step of requesting a written submission from the state on the difference in treatment between male homosexuals and other individuals. The German government responded by stating that the difference in treatment for male homosexuality was justified by the 'requirements of a policy of deterrence'.[74] Central to the government's justification for this policy were specific ontological claims about homosexuality. It was 'not necessary to provide special protection for girls against homosexual acts by adults', the government argued, because it is 'generally admitted that there are comparatively few female homosexuals as compared with males', that 'adult female homosexuals prefer partners of their own age', 'seldom change their partners' and, as a consequence, 'homosexual relationships between an adult woman and a girl underage are very rare'.[75] In the 'rare cases of the seduction of a girl by an adult woman', the government claimed, 'experience shows that the girl's personal development and the insertion in society are not generally affected because female homosexuality does not usually show itself in public'.[76] By contrast, the government argued, male homosexuality was 'much more frequent' and, because homosexual men had a preference for 'young partners' and often changed their partners, this placed young males at greater risk.[77] In addition, the government argued that '[o]n account of the tendency of masculine homosexual couples to show themselves in public [. . .] a young

73 Ibid.
74 Ibid., p. 53.
75 Ibid.
76 Ibid.
77 Ibid.

man or adolescent is much more exposed to social isolation and conflicts with society'.[78]

The justification offered by the German government for its policy of deterrence depended upon ontological ideas about male homosexuals as sexual predators orientated towards adolescents (a view given unfortunate credence in this case by the applicant's conviction for child sex offences under Paragraph 176 of the German Criminal Code). The conflation of male homosexuality with paedophilia – still a common trope in contemporary anti-gay discourse – was used to legitimize the regulation of all male homosexual acts by the criminal law. Such regulation was necessary, the government argued, because of the detrimental impact of homosexuality on both the sexual and social development of young people. The Commission was convinced of this argument, stating that there existed 'a specific social danger in the case of masculine homosexuality' that resulted 'from the fact that masculine homosexuals often constitute a distinct socio-cultural group with a clear tendency to proselytise adolescents'.[79] As a result, the policy of deterrence pursued by the German government was deemed to be necessary because 'a minor involved in homosexual relationships with an adult might in fact be cut off from society and seriously affected in his psychological development'.[80] Whilst the Commission clearly stated that a 'person's sexual life is undoubtedly part of his private life of which it constitutes an important aspect',[81] its decision was that the interference with private life created by the policy of deterrence was justified. In reaching this conclusion, the Commission not only established the axiomatic principle that 'sexual life' is 'undoubtedly' an 'important aspect' of the private life protectable by Article 8, but it endorsed the idea that homosexuals constitute a distinct 'socio-cultural' group. As I discuss in Chapter 2, the idea that homosexual orientation is a feature of a class of human beings who share distinctive traits has become foundational to complaints that seek to establish a 'common ontology'[82] based on sexual orientation.

Ontological ideas about homosexuality were given further expression in *X. v the United Kingdom*, the first complaint relating to homosexuality to be declared admissible by the Commission.[83] Whilst the complaint was ultimately unsuccessful and never reached the Court,[84] the Commission's

78 Ibid.
79 Ibid., p. 56.
80 Ibid., p. 54.
81 Ibid.
82 B. Turner, *Regulating Bodies: Essays in Medical Sociology*, London: Routledge, 1992, p. 254.
83 *X. v United Kingdom*, no. 7215/75, Commission decision, 7 July 1977; Commission report, 12 October 1978; Committee of Ministers, 12 June 1979.
84 The case was decided by the Committee of Ministers because, under the terms of the Convention at the time, the case had not been referred to the Court within the maximum time period allowed.

published report reveals a distinctive conception of homosexuality underpinning its interpretation of the Convention. The applicant's complaint concerned his conviction and imprisonment for buggery contrary to the Sexual Offences Act 1956, which, subject to amendment by the Sexual Offences Act 1967, criminalized sexual acts between a male over 21 years of age with another male under 21 years. The applicant complained that his conviction for 'a private and reciprocal homosexual relationship' when he was 26 years old with an '18-year-old male adult' violated his rights under Articles 8, 10 and 14 of the Convention:

> The applicant admits that, according to United Kingdom standards, in law he is guilty of an offence. He nevertheless contends that he has done no wrong socially or morally and that the unjust, archaic and old-fashioned United Kingdom law is in violation of the Convention's provisions. He complains that in England the age of consent for private acts between homosexuals is 21 years of age while a heterosexual relationship is permitted at the age of 16, a difference of 5 years. Furthermore, the age of legal majority is 18. Hence he claims that homosexuals are discriminated against [. . .] He has been victimised, hauled through the courts and imprisoned because he is a homosexual.[85]

The reasons underpinning the Commission's decision to declare the complaint admissible are obscure. Wintemute suggests that the Commission's interpretation of the Convention had been subject to increased criticism and this may have produced a change in attitude towards complaints relating to homosexuality.[86] A more likely explanation is that it was one aspect of a more general change in Strasbourg – characterized by Bates as the transition from the Court's 'formative' to 'judicial' phase[87] – in which the Commission, as well as the Court, began to exercise a greater role in a wider range of civil liberty issues. The Commission explained its break with its previous decisions – and, in particular, with *X. v Federal Republic of Germany*[88] – by stating that it would 'examine the issues presented by this application, taking into account the development of moral opinion in recent years concerning State interference with the private, consensual sexual lives of adults'.[89]

In deeming the application admissible, the Commission set in motion the first systematic examination of a complaint relating to homosexuality and, as a

85 *X. v the United Kingdom*, no. 7215/75, Commission decision, 7 July 1977.

86 R. Wintemute, *Sexual Orientation and Human Rights: The United States Constitution, the European Convention, and the Canadian Charter*.

87 E. Bates, *The Evolution of the European Convention on Human Rights. From its Inception to the Creation of a Permanent Court of Human Rights*.

88 *X. v Federal Republic of Germany*, no. 5935/72, Commission decision, 30 September 1975.

89 *X. v the United Kingdom*, no. 7215/75, Commission decision, 7 July 1977, p. 43.

result, both the applicant and the government were required to make extensive written and oral submissions. The Commission's report shows that its decision to find against the applicant was significantly influenced by its acceptance of ontological claims, advanced by the United Kingdom government, about the threat and danger of male homosexuality. The government had argued that the complaint should be deemed inadmissible because the English courts had established that the relationship between the applicant and his partner was characterized by coercion. The government relied upon a passage from the judgment given by the English Court of Appeal, which had found that the relationship

> was one which did not involve any coercion or particular unpleasantness at the beginning, but later in the history of the matter there was evidence that at some stage the applicant had virtually made a prisoner of [his partner] and had beaten and forced him to take part in homosexual acts.[90]

The Court of Appeal had also concluded that 'the fact that the applicant is orientated towards the late teenagers and the younger men of the next generation does make him a person who in our view is a danger to the public'.[91] During hearings at the Commission, the government had expanded this claim to argue that 'the applicant himself was concerned with sado-masochistic practices, and no doubt a certain amount of beating of that kind took place in the course of the homosexual incidents upon which the case was based'.[92] As a result, they argued, it was necessary to use the criminal law to protect young men from 'attentions and pressures of an undesirable kind'.[93] The applicant disputed that there was any element of force or coercion in his relationship with his partner and that, although the police had put this allegation to him during questioning, he had never been charged with or convicted of any acts of violence. He argued that the remarks about coercion in the English Court of Appeal were made by 'judges, brought up in a different era, [who] would view anyone, of whatever age, a danger to the public if they were homosexual', and stated that their view was "'absurd" and "dangerous" in the light of the fact that most other European countries have ages of consent for homosexuals at sixteen or eighteen years of age'.[94] The applicant further disputed the government's allegations that young men needed protection from the dangers of corruption by older homosexual men: 'homosexuality is a natural phenomenon and not something which is inculcated in a person after the age of puberty'.[95]

90 Ibid., p. 38.
91 Ibid.
92 *X. v the United Kingdom*, no. 7215/75, Commission report, 12 October 1978, § 131.
93 Ibid., § 143.
94 *X. v the United Kingdom*, no. 7215/75, Commission decision, 7 July 1977, p. 41.
95 *X. v the United Kingdom*, no. 7215/75, Commission report, 12 October 1978, § 43.

What is striking about the Commission's reasoning in *X. v the United Kingdom* is that, when assessing whether the interference with the applicant's private life was justifiable within the terms of Article 8, it placed significant emphasis on the issues of sexual coercion and violence raised by the government. The Commission decided that the fact that the applicant had not been charged with any offence of violence did not mean that force was not a characteristic of his sexual relationship with the younger man. In light of this, the Commission stated that the interference with the applicant's private life pursued the legitimate aim of protecting 'the rights and freedoms of others'. This gave significant weight to its view that, in attempting to meet that legitimate aim, the criminalization of the applicant was necessary in a democratic society:

> The Commission is of the opinion that it is an important function of the criminal law in a democratic society to provide safeguards in order to protect individuals from harm, particularly those who are specially vulnerable because of their age. The criminal law achieves this purpose directly by prosecuting those who have inflicted harm on others and indirectly through the deterrent effect of such prosecutions. It has been established, in the present case, that although the applicant was not charged with buggery without consent, there was an element of force involved in the relationship.[96]

The Commission concluded that, since there was a 'realistic basis' to the claim that young men 'who are involved in homosexual relationships would be subject to substantial social pressures which could be harmful to their psychological development', it was necessary to maintain a higher age of consent for male homosexual acts in a democratic society.[97] The Committee of Ministers endorsed the Commission's view and found no violation of the Convention.[98] Motivated by ideas about the danger of homosexuality and its threat to the mental, physical and social development of young men, the Strasbourg organs upheld interferences with the most basic rights (to sexual privacy) under the Convention.

Conclusion

The decisions issued in Strasbourg during 1955 and 1980 in relation to homosexuality show that the Convention provided no protection from any interference with the sex, love and citizenship rights that homosexuals now

96 Ibid., § 137.
97 Ibid., § 154.
98 *X. v the United Kingdom*, no. 7215/75, Committee of Ministers, 12 June 1979.

commonly seek. They show that the Commission robustly rejected claims that sexual orientation was an immutable human characteristic protectable in any way under the Convention. Furthermore, they demonstrate a strong tendency to accept ontological claims about the danger of homosexuality to the moral and social development of individuals and the nation state. Such claims continue to form the basis for the maintenance and development of contemporary anti-gay law around the world. In Uganda, for example, the Anti Homosexuality Bill 2009, which proposed the introduction of the death penalty for 'aggravated homosexuality' (a provision resonant with paragraph 175 of the German Criminal Code), has been argued to be necessary in order to protect the 'traditional family' and children from the threat of homosexuality.[99] Such claims about the danger of homosexuality are an entrenched and persistent aspect of contemporary global sexual politics. Furthermore, claims about the dangerousness of homosexual 'nature', the threats that it poses to individuals or to society and the need to limit rights and freedoms to deter such dangers, remain fundamental to the Court's interpretation of the Convention today. The Court's jurisprudence shows, as I will explore in the next chapter, that the development of human rights for homosexuals has essentially involved, and continues to comprise, an ontological struggle over 'who' and 'what' the homosexual subject is.

99 'The Anti Homosexuality Bill' (Bill no. 18), Bills Supplement No. 13, *Uganda Gazette* No. 47 Volume CII, 25 September 2009.

Chapter 2

An ontological struggle

The Court and the homosexual since 1981

In the previous chapter, I discussed the tentative use of ontological claims about sexual orientation in complaints to the Commission as a strategy for establishing homosexuality as an immutable human characteristic protectable under the Convention. In this chapter, I focus on the development of this conceptualization of sexual orientation, as an 'innate personal characteristic'[1] of the individual, and examine its centrality to the Court's interpretation of the Convention. I show how the Court, in response to competing claims from applicants and contracting states, has developed a stable discursive repertoire of concepts and theories relating to homosexual sex, sexuality and personhood. Through the repetitive deployment of this discourse the Court has constructed a distinctive understanding of homosexuality that remains vital to the evolution of its jurisprudence in this area. By actively conceiving of homosexuality in particular ways, I argue that the Court can be seen as proactive in what Michel Foucault termed the 'incitement to discourse', through which both the object and subject of sexuality are given ontological shape.[2]

I approach the Court, therefore, not simply as a judicial organization that determines the scope of Convention rights for those homosexual subjects who come before it, but as a site at which the homosexual subject of rights is 'made up'.[3] In other words, I consider the Court not only as an institutional gatekeeper that grants human rights to sovereign homosexual subjects, but as a performative mechanism through which the homosexual subject is given legal and social coherence. Understanding the Court in this way means that I do not begin from the premise that the development of gay and lesbian rights in the Court is a history of the progressive recognition of an immutably

1 *Smith and Grady v the United Kingdom*, nos. 33985/96 and 33986/96, 27 September 1999, ECHR 1999-VI, § 93.

2 M. Foucault, *The History of Sexuality: Volume 1*, London: Penguin, 1979.

3 I. Hacking, 'Making Up People', in T.C. Heller, M. Sosna and D.W. Wellbery (eds.), *Reconstructing Individualism: Autonomy, Individuality, and the Self in Western Thought*, Palo Alto: Stanford University Press, 1986.

homosexual subject who, previously marginalized, has been increasingly successful at making human rights claims. Rather, my starting point is that the Court is one of the most important European sites at which the immutable characteristics of the modern homosexual subject have been imagined and maintained. Like several other scholars (for example: McGhee,[4] Moran[5] and Stychin[6]) I argue that sexuality is a socially constructed phenomenon and that law plays an important role in its construction. Consequently, I seek to show how the Court is implicated in the social constitution of homosexuality.

The subject of ontology

Throughout this chapter, I examine a number of ontological debates about homosexuality that have arisen in the Court. These debates – which concern questions of what homosexuality is, how it is determined and how it becomes manifest – are the result of ongoing contestations about how law should conceive and regulate homosexual sexuality. In response to these debates, and as a way of adjudicating the competing claims of applicants and contracting states, the Court has progressively developed a distinctive conception of the homosexual subject on which to base its interpretation of the Convention. Since the early 1980s, a central feature of its understanding of homosexuality has been essentialist ideas about the innate and inherent characteristics of the homosexual subject. In producing a coherent conception of the 'European homosexual subject' through its case law, the Court can be seen to be engaged in what Foucault termed the 'specification of individuals' whereby the homosexual subject is imagined as 'a personage, a past, a case history, and a childhood, in addition to being a type of life, a life form, and a morphology, with an indiscrete anatomy and possibly a mysterious physiology'.[7]

The importance of the Court's conception of homosexuality is that it gives legal stability to particular ontological ideas. Law, as Moran argues, is an 'idiosyncratic practice that seeks systematically to appropriate, privilege and secure a specific and limited set of meanings, accents and connotations by displacing and rejecting alternative and competing meanings, connotations and accents'.[8] It is precisely this capacity of law, to privilege and exclude, which has made the Court a key arena in which conceptions of 'the homosexual' have been contested. It is because law, as Stychin argues, 'plays a role in constituting and maintaining coherent sexualities'[9] that the Court

4 D. McGhee, *Heterosexuality, Law and Resistance*, London: Routledge, 2001.
5 L.J. Moran, *The Homosexual(ity) of Law*, London: Routledge, 1996.
6 C.F. Stychin, *Law's Desire: Sexuality and the Limits of Justice*, London: Routledge, 1995.
7 M. Foucault, *The History of Sexuality: Volume 1*, p. 43.
8 L.J. Moran, *The Homosexual(ity) of Law*, p. 11.
9 C.F. Stychin, *Law's Desire: Sexuality and the Limits of Justice*, p. 1.

has become one of the most important sites at which sexual ontology is both conceived and disputed. On the one hand, there are those who continue to look to the Court as a mechanism through which to establish particular ontological understandings of homosexuality and homosexual subjects as a way of marginalizing non-heterosexual sexualities. On the other hand, there are those who ask the Court to recognize the homosexual as a type of being who, regardless of the national, social or cultural context in which s/he exists, is in possession of innate characteristics worthy of protection as human rights.[10]

The capacity of the Court to legitimize particular ontological understandings of homosexuality has always underpinned the potential it offered to applicants seeking to contest discrimination. This is why, even in the face of blanket rejections between 1955 and 1981, applicants continued to lodge complaints in Strasbourg. In seeking relief from legal discrimination, applicants looked to the Court as a mechanism through which to challenge not just domestic law, but the wider social and cultural relations that underpin legal inequalities. An essential aspect of applications to the Court in respect of homosexuality, therefore, is their attempt to use the Court as a mechanism to challenge the dominant discursive constructions of homosexuality that underpin and perpetuate legal discrimination. In this sense, whilst applications to the Court address the interests of the individual who brings the complaint, they must also be seen as vehicles through which the interests of a community[11] and a social movement[12] are both imagined and advanced.

An important aspect of complaints to the Court, as I outline below, is that they contest the 'violence of derealization'[13] that non-heterosexuals experience when they are situated within cultures that are dominated by homophobic and heterosexist discourse. Complaints to the Court can be seen as attempts to use the Convention in order to 'speak' in ways that challenge discourses promoting hostility towards homosexuality. An essential aspect of all complaints is that, relying on the possessive individualism that underwrites natural and human rights law, they attempt to 'humanize' the homosexual subject in particular ways. As I demonstrate below, complaints to the Court advance the claim that homosexuality is an essential and innate state that characterizes a particular class of human persons and that the Convention should protect this class of persons from discrimination when they give expression (through their identities, intimate relationships, family life,

10 J.A. Massad, 'Re-Orienting Desire: The Gay International and the Arab World', *Public Culture* 14(2), 2002, 361–385.

11 B. Golder, 'Foucault's Critical (Yet Ambivalent) Affirmation: Three Figures of Rights', *Social and Legal Studies* 20(3), 283–312.

12 N. Stammers, 'Social Movements and the Social Construction of Human Rights', *Human Rights Quarterly* 21(4), 980–1008.

13 J. Butler, *Precarious Life: The Powers of Mourning and Violence*, London: Verso, 2004.

political speech etc.) to this inner aspect of themselves. Whilst there is every reason to be sceptical about the use of human rights discourses in this way – not least because, in relying on essentialist ideas about a universal homosexual subject, there is an inherent tendency to reproduce the homosexual/heterosexual binary from which heteronormative privilege is derived[14] – applications to the Court can be seen to fundamentally contest the discursive relations through which non-heterosexuals are continually dehumanized. This is important because, as Butler argues:

> On the level of discourse, certain lives are not considered lives at all, they cannot be humanized; they fit no dominant frame for the human, and their dehumanization occurs first, at this level. This level then gives rise to a physical violence that in some sense delivers the message of dehumanization which is already at work in the culture.[15]

Applications to the Court are an attempt to habilitate the homosexual subject as a *human* subject in possession of a universally shared characteristic (a sexual orientation) that is worthy of protection.

It may seem ironic that, given the role of law in both criminalizing and regulating homosexuality in the twentieth century, individuals should look to human rights law as a way of challenging legal inequalities. Foucault, for example, was highly critical of human rights discourse and argued that, far from delivering freedom, it supported the relations of 'non-egalitarian and asymmetrical' disciplinary society.[16] Foucault's belief that human rights law has a tendency to reiterate and legitimate broader social relations of power has found expression in the work of a range of commentators who have remained critical about the reliance upon human rights mechanisms, like the Convention, for securing benefits for non-heterosexuals. For instance, Morgan argues:

> increasingly, legal institutions adopt mechanisms of disciplinary power to better *know* and regulate the subject. And this legal *will to know* applies doubly to sexualized subjects, who perform upon the acts of desire seen as dangerous not only to themselves and other individuals but to the polity as a whole. Indeed, the whole genus of human rights law can be read as examples in the exercise of disciplinary power. Human rights law *normalizes*. It takes abuses suffered by those who assert difference, and colonizes their experience to make them comfortable to the structures

14 D.M. Halperin, *Saint Foucault: Towards a Gay Hagiography*, New York: Oxford University Press, 1995.

15 J. Butler, *Undoing Gender*, New York: Routledge, 2004, p. 25.

16 M. Foucault, *Discipline and Punish: The Birth of the Prison*, Harmondsworth: Penguin, 1977, p. 222.

> and imperatives of the mythological nation state. And along the way, it usually exonerates governments of any wrongdoing'.[17]

It is certainly the case that the Court has sought to 'know' homosexual subjects and, as a consequence, has come to regulate these subjects in particular ways. Through the development of its case law, and the incremental process of legal citation, the Court's jurisprudence has 'sedimented' a discourse about sexuality that has entrenched and normalized ideas about what homosexuality 'is' and who homosexuals 'are'. Yet to argue that the Court's construction of homosexuality simply normalizes inequality would be to miss the very real and positive effects that have resulted from its jurisprudence. If we understand the Court's judgments as performative – that is, 'not as a singular or deliberate "act", but, rather as the reiterative and citational practice by which discourse produces the effects that it names'[18] – then its case law can be seen as an important way in which the social construction of sexuality is both maintained and challenged. It is for this reason that applicants have attempted to use the Court as a performative mechanism to amplify their voices in challenging dominant discourses on homosexuality. The Court, in turn, has interpellated homosexual subjects in particular ways and, in doing so, has offered a resource to resist the heteronormativity that underpins discriminatory legal practices. The Court's construction of homosexuality, as I argue below, continues to provide an important platform from which to contest enduring social and cultural norms through which homosexuals are conceived as less than human and, therefore, unworthy of human rights.

In the remainder of this chapter I will examine the long-standing 'ontological struggle' in the Court about sexual orientation. At the heart of this struggle is a contestation about the very 'humanness' of the homosexual. Debates about 'human nature' continue to be foundational to competing attempts to expand or delimit judicial recognition of the homosexual subject within the terms of the Convention. These ontological struggles in the Court are not fanciful 'theoretical' debates that are less important than the 'real' issue of guaranteeing human rights for 'real' homosexuals. Rather, it is through such debates that human beings become intelligible as 'real' subjects capable of claiming and accessing rights. If, as Butler argues, 'the task of international lesbian and gay politics is no less than a remaking of reality, a reconstituting of the human',[19] then the Court is an important site at which these politics are played out.

17 W. Morgan, 'Queering International Human Rights Law', in C.F. Stychin and D. Herman (eds.), *Law, Sexuality: The Global Arena*, Minneapolis: University of Minnesota Press, 2001, p. 212.

18 J. Butler, *Bodies that Matter: On the Discursive Limits of Sex*, London: Routledge, 1993, p. 2.

19 J. Butler, *Undoing Gender*, p. 30.

The declarations of applicants

As I outlined in the previous chapter, applicants to the Court have deployed essentialist claims about homosexuality since the first petitions were lodged in the 1950s. However, from *Dudgeon v the United Kingdom*[20] onwards, such claims have gained a central prominence in the discourses on sexuality that are used in the Court. Applicants have increasingly utilized the idea that homosexuality is a congenital characteristic of the individual in order to, as Moran argues, lend weight to the claim that sexual orientation is an embodied and authentic aspect of human nature.[21] Ontological claims that sexuality is 'inborn' and 'natural' have been used because they are conducive to the key epistemological tenets of human rights discourse through which human beings are conceived as individuated 'units' in possession of fundamental and universal features common to all humanity. Pettman describes how human rights discourse depends upon a conception of subjects as 'objectifying individuators' who are not only in possession of certain inalienable features but are also capable of discerning and articulating a claim for these as human rights.[22] In attempting to gain recognition for homosexuality as a human right (as opposed to a political or social privilege), applicants have attempted to demonstrate that sexual orientation is both an *embodied* and *conscious* feature of all individuals.

The first systematic attempt to articulate homosexuality in this way was in *Dudgeon v the United Kingdom*, in which the applicant made a number of claims regarding the 'status' of the 'homosexual person':

> The applicant stated that he had been consciously homosexual from the age of 14 years and that he had been aware since adolescence of severely disapproving social attitudes towards homosexual behaviour [. . .] From the onset of homosexual consciousness he had experienced fear, which was augmented by the lack of guidance available and caused him suffering and distress. His fear had increased through adulthood and was directly caused by the existence of offences against homosexual behaviour in the criminal law. As a result of the criminal law he had permanently suffered prejudice including psychological distress, and fear of harassment, blackmail, prosecution and resultant exposure. Relationships within his family had been affected by parental fears that his homosexual status might become known and lead to exposure and the destruction of normal parental arrangements has caused constant psychological upset and retarded his motivation to advance himself in life. He alleged that he had

20 *Dudgeon v the United Kingdom*, no. 7525/76, 22 October 1981, Series A no. 45.

21 L.J. Moran, *The Homosexual(ity) of Law*.

22 R. Pettman, 'A Phenomenology of Human Rights', *Human Rights Research Journal* 2, 2004, 1–10 at 3.

therefore suffered direct economic prejudice from 'the criminalizing of my status as a homosexual person'.[23]

In this account of himself, the applicant in *Dudgeon* sought to establish a particular ontological understanding of homosexual personhood. Homosexuality is depicted as a congenital feature of the individual that is experienced as an integral aspect of selfhood. The applicant's claim that he became 'consciously homosexual' from a particular age presupposes a prior state in which he was 'unconsciously homosexual' and suggests that his sexual orientation is an inherent feature of his human nature of which he became gradually aware. That such nature is not altered in the face of tremendous social hostility to it provides further evidence of its immutability.

In *Norris v Ireland*, this ontological understanding of homosexuality was given more forceful expression by the applicant's claim that 'he had realized at a young age that he was irreversibly homosexual, and had become traumatized by the fear that any overt expression of his sexuality would expose him to criminal prosecution'.[24] In this account, homosexuality is characterized as an innate and immutable characteristic that, regardless of the social or cultural context in which it exists, endures as a feature of individual personhood. As in *Dudgeon*, the applicant in *Norris* argued that homosexuality is an inherent characteristic that is 'realized' by an individual who simultaneously develops an awareness of the social hostility toward it. In describing the traumatizing effects of existing in environments hostile to homosexual sexuality, these applicants articulate the ontological claim that homosexuality is an aspect of human nature that is *a priori* to the social, cultural and legal contexts in which it is expressed.

Complaints to the Court demonstrate a variety of ways in which applicants have attempted to establish homosexual orientation as an essential feature of human personhood. In *C. and L.M. v the United Kingdom*,[25] for example, one of the applicants stated that '[s]ince the age of 17, [she] has recognized herself to be a lesbian'. For this applicant, establishing that she was 'a lesbian' was achieved by articulating her self-knowledge and awareness of herself as a particular 'type' of person. In *Lustig-Prean and Beckett v the United Kingdom*, one of the applicants 'confirmed that he was homosexual, acknowledging that he had been a practising homosexual since his teenage years'.[26] In this account, the state of *being* a homosexual is separated from any sexual practice to convey sexual orientation as an inherent aspect of personhood. And in *Fretté v France*, the applicant was described as an 'avowed' homosexual[27] who had

23 *Dudgeon v the United Kingdom*, no. 7525/76, Commission decision, 3 March 1978, p. 118.

24 *Norris v Ireland*, no. 10581/83, Commission report, 12 March 1987, § 33.

25 *C. and L.M. v the United Kingdom*, no. 14753/89, Commission decision, 9 October 1989.

26 *Lustig-Prean and Beckett v the United Kingdom*, no. 31417/96 and 32377/96, 27 September 1999, § 13.

27 *Fretté v France*, no. 36515/97, 26 February 2002, ECHR 2002-I, § 37.

'courageously revealed'[28] this aspect of himself to others. In all of these accounts of homosexuality, significant emphasis is placed on sexual orientation as an innate and naturally occurring feature of the individual's nature.

One of the key ways in which (homo)sexuality is articulated as an essential aspect of personhood is through a discourse about adolescent development. It is common across applications to find homosexuality conceived as an aspect of the individual that becomes established through a 'natural' process of child-to-adult development. In *Sutherland v the United Kingdom*, for example, sexual orientation is imagined as an inherent state that originates from and resides within the adolescent subject:

> The applicant became aware of attraction to other boys at about the age of 12. As his contemporaries became more interested in girls, he became more aware that he was sexually attracted to boys. From around that time, he felt sure that his sexual orientation was homosexual. He tried going out with a girl when he was 14. They are still friends, but there was no sexual attraction with her, and the experience confirmed for the applicant that he could only find a fulfilling relationship with another man. The applicant had his first homosexual encounter when he was 16, with another person of his own age who was also homosexual.[29]

Everything about this description is orientated towards articulating the fixity of an essential and innate sexual nature. Homosexual orientation, which is experienced and confirmed through sexual attraction, is articulated as an innate state of which the individual can be 'sure'. A very similar claim is found in *S.L. v Austria*:

> At about the age of eleven or twelve the applicant began to be aware of his sexual orientation. While other boys were attracted by women, he realized that he was emotionally and sexually attracted by men, in particular by men who are older than himself. At the age of fifteen he was sure of his homosexuality.[30]

What is being argued across all of these applications is that homosexuality constitutes an inherent feature of personhood that inevitably gives rise to a range of human experiences and actions. Central to these accounts of homosexuality is an attempt to interpellate the homosexual as a pre-social, pre-cultural and pre-legal subject who, in possession of an inalienable nature, is recognizable within the framework of natural and human rights. This does

28 Ibid., Partly concurring opinion of Judge Costa joined by Judges Jungwiert and Traja.
29 *Sutherland v the United Kingdom*, no. 25186/94, Commission report, 1 July 1997, § 17–18.
30 *S.L. v Austria*, no. 45330/99, 9 January 2003, ECHR 2003-I (extracts), § 9.

not mean that applicants 'consciously' deploy essentialism as a strategy but, as Butler argues, that they orientate their 'speech' in a discursive landscape to make claims that are intelligible.[31] In attempting to speak about homosexuality within the terms of the Convention, which presupposes the individual as a sovereign subject, applicants have utilized particular discourses to demonstrate that sexual orientation is an innate feature of their individuality. In imagining sexuality in this way, applicants have attempted 'to fix, to freeze, to delimit, to render substantial [homosexuality as] a metaphysics of substance, of discrete and singular kinds of beings'.[32]

Recognizing the essentiality of homosexuality

Some scholars have criticized the reliance upon 'traditional essentialist narratives'[33] to establish human rights for non-heterosexuals under the Convention. As I will explore later in the book, there is every reason to be critical of essentialism because of the ways in which it underpins forms of social and legal regulation. But it is important to acknowledge that essentialist understandings of homosexual 'nature' have been vital in gaining recognition for sexual orientation as an aspect of humanness that is protectable by the Convention. The evolution of the Court's interpretation of the Convention in respect of homosexuality has been symbiotic with its acceptance of essentialist understandings of homosexuality. For instance, in *Dudgeon v the United Kingdom*, the Court's decision to find in favour of the applicant – who complained that the existence of criminal laws which prohibited all male homosexual acts[34] violated his right to respect for private life under Article 8 – was largely driven by its acceptance of the applicant's claim that a 'homosexual was *ipso facto* affected by the laws in question [because by] definition the law interfered with his private life as it criminalized behaviour he might indulge in within the sphere of his private life'.[35] Because the applicant in *Dudgeon* had not been prosecuted or convicted of any offence, his complaint relied upon the claim that the very existence of law that criminalized homosexual acts made him a victim by virtue of being a 'homosexual person' who might indulge in homosexual acts. The Court was highly receptive to this claim:

> In the personal circumstances of the applicant, the very existence of this legislation continuously and directly affects his private life [. . .] either he

31 J. Butler, *Excitable Speech: A Politics of the Performative*, New York: Routledge, 1997.
32 Ibid., p. 35.
33 M. Grigolo, 'Sexualities and the ECHR: Introducing the Universal Sexual Legal Subject', *European Journal of International Law* 14, 2003, 1023–1044 at 1027.
34 Offences Against the Person Act 1861; Criminal Law Amendment Act 1885.
35 *Dudgeon v the United Kingdom*, no. 7525/76, Commission report, 13 March 1980, § 45.

> respects the law and refrains from engaging – even in private with consenting male partners – in prohibited sexual acts to which he is disposed by reason of his homosexual tendencies, or he commits such acts and thereby becomes liable to criminal prosecution.[36]

Central to the Court's recognition that the criminalization of private, homosexual acts constitutes a violation of Article 8 was the idea that the applicant's 'personal circumstances' and his 'tendencies' predisposed him towards particular sexual acts. In this sense, acknowledging the congenital nature of the applicant's sexual orientation was foundational to accepting his status as a victim of the criminal law.

In *Dudgeon*, the Court made the unprecedented statement that it considered homosexuality to be 'an essentially private manifestation of the human personality'[37] and this has remained axiomatic to its jurisprudence. The Court's construction of sexual orientation as an aspect of 'personality' is foundational to its now settled view that individuals gain entitlement to protection for their private sexual behaviours under the Convention because these behaviours are the manifestations of an immutable and essential human nature. In *Dudgeon*, the Court implicitly endorsed the Commission's view that this innate element of human nature is common to 'a particular class of persons'.[38] In doing so, the Court inaugurated the homosexual of contemporary human rights law.

There was strong resistance to the conception of homosexuality adopted by the majority in *Dudgeon* from dissenting Judge Walsh. Walsh argued that the 'fact that a person consents to take part in the commission of homosexual acts is not proof that such person is sexually orientated by nature in that direction'.[39] Whilst Walsh acknowledged that there were 'homosexuals who are such because of some kind of innate instinct or pathological constitution judged to be incurable', he stated that it was more likely that homosexual behaviours resulted from 'a lack of normal sexual development or from habit or from experience or from other similar causes but whose tendency is not incurable'.[40] Walsh went on:

> Sexual behaviour is determined more by cultural influences than by instinctive needs. Cultural trends and expectations can create drives mistakenly thought to be intrinsic instinctual urges. The legal arrangement and prescriptions set up to regulate sexual behaviour are

36 *Dudgeon v the United Kingdom*, no. 7525/76, 22 October 1981, Series A no. 45, § 41.
37 Ibid., § 60.
38 *Dudgeon v the United Kingdom*, no. 7525/76, Commission report, 13 March 1980, § 86.
39 *Dudgeon v the United Kingdom*, no. 7525/76, 22 October 1981, Series A no. 45, Partially dissenting opinion of Judge Walsh, § 13.
40 Ibid.

> very important formative factors in the shaping of cultural and social institutions.[41]

Walsh's argument is strongly anti-essentialist. It depicts sexual orientation as the result of 'culture' that creates the conditions through which individuals come to experience their sexual desires as 'intrinsic instinctual urges'. Adopting a constructivist understanding, Walsh argued for the necessity of the criminal law to prevent the development of cultural and social relations that encourage the 'mistaken' belief that homosexual urges are intrinsically innate.

A consequence of the judgment in *Dudgeon* was that contracting states wishing to defend laws criminalizing homosexual sex now had to contend with the Court's view that this interfered with an aspect of human personality. In *Norris v Ireland*, this presented a problem for the Irish government because, wishing to continue its total prohibition on male homosexual acts, it was now forced to negotiate the claim that law that criminalized behaviours adversely affected the very nature of the individual. In attempting to defend the law, the Irish government argued:

> whilst the applicant as a person with a homosexual nature can validly claim to be prohibited by the laws complained of from performing homosexual acts in private, and in that sense his claim is neither abstract nor academic, nevertheless, his application represents as extreme a case in this respect as can be envisaged, in view of the freedom he has enjoyed in his public avowals and his uninhibited campaign for reform.[42]

The government's argument that the applicant could not be regarded as a victim, because he was free to make public avowals of his 'homosexual nature' during his campaign for reforms, was weakened by its concession that his homosexual nature predisposed him to commit acts prohibited by law. The Court upheld the applicant's claim that as a 'declared homosexual' he had 'suffered great stress as a result of his sexual proclivities and the fear of prosecution because of them'.[43]

Recognition of the essential nature of homosexuality has remained a key feature of the Court's approach to complaints relating to sexual orientation discrimination. In *Smith and Grady v the United Kingdom*, for example, which concerned the discharge of individuals from the armed forces as a 'consequence of the fact of their homosexuality',[44] even Judge Loucaides (who during his

41 Ibid., § 15.
42 *Norris v Ireland*, no. 10581/83, Commission report, 12 March 1987, § 43.
43 Ibid., § 55.
44 *Smith and Grady v the United Kingdom*, nos. 33985/96 and 33986/96, 27 September 1999, ECHR 1999-VI, § 125.

term at the Court was consistently hostile to all claims brought on grounds relating to homosexuality) legitimized the view that sexual orientation was an immutable aspect of human nature. In dissenting from the majority view of the Court, that to be discharged from the armed services on the grounds of sexual orientation constituted a violation of the applicants' rights under Article 8, Loucaides argued that a total prohibition on homosexuality was necessary to deal with the problems that it gave rise to:

> It is the compulsory living together of groups of people of different sexual orientation which creates the problem. I should add here that if homosexuals had a right to be members of the armed forces their sexual orientation could become known either through them disclosing it or manifesting it in some way.[45]

Loucaides endorsed the notion that homosexuality is a feature of personhood that 'could' become manifest in some undesirable way and, because it was not possible to introduce new 'conduct codes and disciplinary rules' to 'change the sexual orientation of people',[46] a form of social segregation was necessary.

The use of essentialist discourses about homosexual nature has proved successful in expanding Convention rights for non-heterosexuals. In *Sutherland v the United Kingdom*, the Commission's recognition of the essentiality of sexual orientation was a key aspect of its decision to find that differential legal ages for male homosexual and other sexual activities contravened the applicant's Convention rights. In response to the government's claim that 'certain young men between the ages of 16 and 18 do not have a settled sexual orientation and that the aim of the law is to protect such vulnerable young men from activities which will result in considerable social pressures and isolation', the Commission adopted the view that 'sexual orientation is fixed in both sexes by the age of 16 and that men aged 16–21 are not in need of special protection because of the risk of their being "recruited" into homosexuality'.[47] Acceptance of the fixity of sexual orientation was foundational to recognizing homosexuality as an inalienable aspect of human nature that is protectable as a human right.

Contesting an ontology of 'danger'

One of the key reasons that applicants have deployed essentialist discourses in the Court is the need to establish an understanding of homosexual nature that contests constructions of homosexuals as dangerous, abnormal and monstrous

45 *Smith and Grady v the United Kingdom*, nos. 33985/96 and 33986/96, 27 September 1999, ECHR 1999-VI, Partly concurring, partly dissenting opinion of Judge Loucaides.

46 Ibid.

47 *Sutherland v the United Kingdom*, no. 25186/94, Commission report, 1 July 1997, § 64.

deviants who embody and propagate disease and perversion. Such constructions have a long history and, as I argued in the previous chapter, were accepted by the Commission until the 1980s as a justification for interfering with the right to respect for private life under Article 8. Such ideas have not disappeared from the Court and in 2008, Judge Loucaides referred to homosexuals as 'persons with some peculiarity',[48] arguing that such 'peculiarity' was a legitimate basis on which to treat homosexuals differently from heterosexuals. Whilst such a view was at its most prominent in applications prior to the 1980s, it has remained a constant part of the discourse on homosexuality in the Court.

For example, in *Dudgeon*, dissenting Judge Zekia referred to homosexuality as 'unnatural immoral practices' that arose from 'physiological, psychological or other reasons',[49] and dissenting Judge Matscher referred to the 'tendencies' of homosexual men to desire sexual relations with minors. Matscher argued that because 'it is well known that this is a widespread tendency in homosexual circles', and because the 'difference of character between homosexual conduct and heterosexual conduct' is 'obvious', laws prohibiting homosexual sex were justifiable.[50] Dissenting Judge Walsh argued that, even if homosexuality was recognized as an aspect of 'human personality', 'the human personality in question may in private life manifest dangerous or evil tendencies calculated to produce ill-effects upon himself or upon others'.[51] Judge Walsh, who elsewhere in his dissenting opinion advanced a strongly constructivist approach to homosexuality, lapsed into essentialism to convey the dangers created by abnormal and incurable sexual deviants:

> So far as the incurable category [of homosexuals] is concerned, the activities must be regarded as abnormalities or even as handicaps and treated with the compassion and tolerance which is required to prevent those persons from being victimized in respect of tendencies over which they have no control and for which they are not personally responsible. However, other considerations are raised when these tendencies are translated into activities [. . .] Even assuming one of the two persons involved has the incurable tendency, the other may not. It is known that many male persons who are heterosexual or pansexual indulge in these activities not because of any incurable tendency but for sexual excitement.[52]

Since *Dudgeon*, contracting states have consistently advanced ontological claims, similar to Judge Walsh's, about the dangers of homosexual sexuality.

48 *E.B. v France* [GC], no. 43546/02, 22 January 2008, Dissenting opinion of Judge Loucaides.
49 *Dudgeon v the United Kingdom*, no. 7525/76, 22 October 1981, Series A no 45, Dissenting opinion of Judge Zekia, § 3-4.
50 Ibid., Dissenting opinion of Judge Matcher.
51 Ibid., Partially dissenting opinion of Judge Walsh, § 8.
52 Ibid., § 13.

For instance, in *Norris v Ireland*, the government unsuccessfully relied on a judgment of the Supreme Court of Ireland to argue that homosexuality was recognized as 'an offence against nature', that 'whether the condition be congenital or acquired [it resulted] in great distress and unhappiness', and that the 'homosexually oriented can be importuned into a homosexual life-style which can become habitual'.[53] In *B. v the United Kingdom*, the government found temporary success for their argument that the policy of prohibition on homosexuality in the armed forces was necessary to prohibit the recruitment of men into homosexual practices.[54] A key aspect of their defence was that 'the potentially disruptive influence of homosexual practices should be excluded' from the armed forces so that 'those in authority over younger or junior men do not use their position to coerce or persuade those in their charge to perform acts in which they would not otherwise engage'.[55] However, in a subsequent complaint, this argument was successfully contested and the Court accepted that the policy of prohibition violated the applicants' Convention rights.[56] In *Johnson v the United Kingdom*, the government again found temporary support for their argument that the criminalization of private sexual relations involving more than two adults was justified by the prevalence of disease: 'A new consideration has emerged recently with the spread of the disease AIDS, which makes it clear that on the grounds of protection of health, the procuring of promiscuous homosexual acts should remain discouraged by the criminal law.'[57] In a subsequent judgment, the Court upheld the complaint of a 'practising homosexual' against laws that criminalized sex involving more than two men.[58]

One of the most striking challenges to ideas about the dangers of homosexuality can be found in *Salgueiro da Silva Mouta v Portugal*, in which the applicant complained that the Lisbon Court of Appeal had based its decision to award parental responsibility for his daughter to his ex-wife, rather than to himself, exclusively on the ground of his sexual orientation.[59] The Lisbon Court of Appeal had argued that:

> The fact that the child's father, who has come to terms with his homosexuality, wishes to live with another man is a reality which has to be accepted. It is well known that society is becoming more and more tolerant of such situations. However, it cannot be argued that an

53 *Norris v Ireland*, no. 10581/83, 26 October 1988, Series A no. 142, § 24.
54 *B. v the United Kingdom*, no. 9237/81, Commission decision, 12 October 1983.
55 Ibid., p. 70.
56 *Smith and Grady v the United Kingdom*, nos. 33985/96 and 33986/96, 27 September 1999, ECHR 1999-VI.
57 *Johnson v the United Kingdom*, no. 10389/83, Commission decision, 17 July 1986.
58 *A.D.T. v the United Kingdom*, no. 35765/97, 31 July 2000, ECHR 2000-IX.
59 *Salgueiro da Silva Mouta v Portugal*, no. 33290/96, 21 December 1999, ECHR 1999-IX.

> environment of this kind is the healthiest and best suited to a child's psychological, social and mental development, especially given the dominant model in our society, as the appellant rightly points out. The child should live in a family environment, a traditional Portuguese family, which is certainly not the set-up her father has decided to enter into, since he is living with another man as if they were man and wife. It is not our task here to determine whether homosexuality is or is not an illness or whether it is a sexual orientation towards persons of the same sex. In both cases it is an abnormality and children should not grow up in the shadow of abnormal situations; such are the dictates of human nature and let us remember that it is [the applicant] himself who acknowledged this when [. . .] he stated that he had definitively left the marital home to go and live with a boyfriend, a decision which is not normal according to common criteria.[60]

The applicant argued that this 'decision had been prompted by atavistic misconceptions which bore no relation to the realities of life or common sense'.[61] The Court found in favour of the applicant and, upholding his complaint that the domestic authorities had discriminated against him by invoking distinctions based on sexual orientation, implicitly rejected the claim that homosexuality is 'abnormal' or against the 'dictates of human nature'.

A key aspect of the complaints examined above is that they rely upon essentialist discourses to claim that a homosexual personality (and the sexual practices that result from it) is an innate and fixed 'core' of an individual's human nature and not the result of 'corruption' or 'seduction' by dangerous and perverse deviants. One example where this argument was noticeably unsuccessful was in *Laskey, Jaggard and Brown v the United Kingdom*, in which the applicants complained about the criminalization of sadomasochistic sexual practices.[62] The applicants, who had been convicted of a variety of assault charges under the Offences Against the Person Act 1861, argued that 'their case should be viewed as one involving matters of sexual expression, rather than violence'.[63] They also submitted that their convictions were the result of them having been 'singled out partly because of the authorities' bias against homosexuals'.[64] The Court did not accept this argument, stating that it found 'no evidence in support of the applicants' allegations' that their conviction

60 Ibid., § 14.
61 Ibid., § 24.
62 *Laskey, Jaggard and Brown v the United Kingdom*, nos. 21627/93, 21628/93 and 21974/93, 19 February 1997, Reports of Judgments and Decisions 1997-I.
63 Ibid., § 39.
64 Ibid., § 47.

were motivated by bias, and held that their conviction was based on 'the extreme nature of the practices involved and not the sexual proclivities of the applicants'.[65] Stychin has argued that the prosecutions and convictions of those involved was motivated by understandings of homosexual men as pathological and homosexual sex as an expression of addiction, seduction and contagion.[66] The concurring opinion of Judge Pettiti supports Stychin's argument and indicates that particular ontological understandings of homosexuality underpinned the Court's judgment:

> The dangers of unrestrained permissiveness, which can lead to debauchery, paedophilia [. . .] or the torture of others, were highlighted at the Stockholm World Conference. The protection of private life means the protection of a person's intimacy and dignity, not the protection of his baseness or the promotion of criminal immoralism.[67]

Pettiti's comments confirm Stychin's argument that at the heart of considerations in this case is 'the figure of the homosexual – sadomasochistic, polluted, addicted to his desires, self-destructive, and yet terrifyingly seductive'.[68] The Court's refusal to extend the protection of Article 8 to the applicants in *Laskey* can be seen to be significantly influenced by an uncritical acceptance of ideas about the social and moral danger posed by this form of homosexual sex. Moran offers a scathing criticism of the judgment, arguing that it illustrates the limits of human rights to protect particular kinds of sexual subjects:

> human rights are not necessarily about inclusion and recognition of difference. Human rights may also be about the violence of exclusion and the denial of human rights. In that process, human rights is about ontological categorization: is the humanity of those who derive pleasure from the consensual giving and receiving of pain worthy of recognition? In this instance the Court has denied the humanity of those who so act.[69]

Laskey is a striking example of the failure of applicants to use the Court to performatively produce a homosexual subject who is worthy of protection by the Convention. In this instance, the discursive production of the homosexual subject reiterated an ontology of dangerousness in need of legal suppression.

65 Ibid.

66 C.F. Stychin, *Law's Desire: Sexuality and the Limits of Justice*.

67 *Laskey, Jaggard and Brown v the United Kingdom*, nos. 21627/93, 21628/93 and 21974/93, 19 February 1997, *Reports of Judgments and Decisions* 1997-I, Concurring opinion of Judge Pettiti.

68 C.F. Stychin, *Law's Desire: Sexuality and the Limits of Justice*, p. 139.

69 L.J. Moran, '*Laskey v the United Kingdom:* Learning the Limits of Privacy', *Modern Law Review* 61(1), 1998, 77–84 at 83.

The limits of the Court's approach: nature versus value

The Court's ontological construction of the homosexual as a specific and coherent type of human being with an essential and immutable 'personality' has never accorded homosexuality any explicit value. On the contrary, the Court's approach to homosexual 'nature' has been characterized, since *Dudgeon* onwards, by a strong form of moral ambivalence. In *Dudgeon*, the Court made it clear that, whilst it now regarded the regulation of male homosexual activities in private to be a violation of Article 8, 'some degree of regulation of male homosexual conduct' was necessary in a democratic society 'to protect particular sections of society as well as the moral ethos of society as a whole'.[70] Furthermore, whilst the Court stated that it was 'not concerned with making any value-judgment as to the morality of homosexual relations between adult males',[71] it also emphasized that decriminalization of such acts in private 'does not imply approval'.[72] A defining characteristic of the judgment in *Dudgeon* is that the Court acknowledged and did not seek to challenge the moral disapproval that homosexuality regularly attracts.

Nevertheless, as dissenting Judge Walsh regretfully noted, an important consequence of *Dudgeon* is that it did accord homosexual sex in private the moral value of being a 'human right':

> The judgment of the Court does not constitute a declaration to the effect that the particular homosexual practices which are subject to penalty by the legislation in question virtually amount to fundamental human rights. However, that will not prevent it being hailed as such by those who seek to blur the essential difference between homosexual and heterosexual activities.[73]

Despite the implicit value that the Court has accorded to homosexuality since *Dudgeon*, through its recognition of the homosexual as a subject of rights, it has nevertheless remained consistently ambivalent about the moral value of homosexuality. In contrast to other higher courts, the Court is remarkably silent on the value of homosexuality and has refrained from making any overtly positive statement about homosexual love, relationships or families. Consider the Court's recent judgment in *Alekseyev v Russia*, in which it upheld the applicant's complaint that refusal by the Mayor of Moscow for a permit to hold a 'gay rights' demonstration violated his right to freedom of assembly under Article 11 of the Convention:

70 *Dudgeon v the United Kingdom*, no. 7525/76, 22 October 1981, Series A no. 45, § 49.
71 Ibid., § 54.
72 Ibid., § 61.
73 Ibid., Partially dissenting opinion of Judge Walsh, § 20.

> The mayor of Moscow [. . .] considered it necessary to confine every mention of homosexuality to the private sphere and to force gay men and lesbians out of the public eye, implying that homosexuality was a result of a conscious, and antisocial, choice. However, they were unable to provide justification for such exclusion. There is no scientific evidence or sociological data at the Court's disposal, suggesting that the mere mention of homosexuality, or open public debate about sexual minorities' social status, would adversely affect children or 'vulnerable adults'. On the contrary, it is only through fair and public debate that society may address such complex issues as the one raised in the present case. Such debate, backed up by academic research, would benefit social cohesion by ensuring that representatives of all views are heard, including the individuals concerned.[74]

Whilst the Court relies upon its construction of the immutable character of the homosexual subject to dismiss the argument that homosexuality is a 'choice' that those who are 'vulnerable' can be persuaded to make, it remains silent about the moral value of homosexuality. Although there is a concern to promote 'fair debate' and ensure 'social cohesion', there is no explicit promotion of the idea that homosexual subjects have the same moral value as heterosexuals and, as such, should have access to the same universe of rights under the Convention.

Similarly, in *Schalk and Kopf v Austria*, which I discuss in Chapter 6, the Court would not accept the argument that same-sex couples should be granted the right to civil marriage under Article 12.[75] In its published judgment, there is a fundamental absence of any acknowledgement that homosexual subjects possess intrinsic value equal to heterosexuals. By contrast, consider the recent judgment by the Constitutional Court of South Africa in respect of same-sex marriage:

> The exclusion of same-sex couples from the benefits and responsibilities of marriage [. . .] is not a small and tangential inconvenience resulting from a few surviving relics of societal prejudice destined to evaporate like the morning dew. It represents a harsh if oblique statement by the law that same-sex couples are outsiders, and that their need for affirmation and protection of their intimate relations as human beings is somehow less than that of heterosexual couples. It reinforces the wounding notion that they are to be treated as biological oddities, as failed or lapsed human beings who do not fit into normal society, and, as such, do not qualify for the full moral concern and respect that our Constitution seeks to secure

74 *Alekseyev v Russia*, nos. 4916/07, 25924/08 and 14599/09, 21 October 2010, § 86.
75 *Schalk and Kopf v Austria*, no. 30141/04, 24 June 2010.

> for everyone. It signifies that their capacity for love, commitment and accepting responsibility is by definition less worthy of regard than that of heterosexual couples.[76]

This interpretation of the South African Bill of Rights stands in stark contrast to the Court's interpretation of the Convention. The Court's discourse on homosexuality shows none of the concern of the Constitutional Court of South Africa to consider homosexuals as subjects of moral value equal to heterosexuals. An important outcome of the Court's approach to homosexuality is that it can sustain the idea that homosexuals are of less moral worth and, as a consequence, limit the practical development of Convention rights for non-heterosexuals. In a rare moment of candidness, Judges Bratza, Fuhrmann and Tulkens, in their dissenting opinion in *Fretté v France* (in which the majority rejected the applicant's complaint about his refusal for authorization to adopt a child on the grounds of his sexual orientation), noted this problem in the Court's approach:

> It is not for the Court to take decisions (or pass moral judgment) instead of States in an area which is also a subject of controversy in many Council of Europe member States, especially as the views of the French administrative courts also seem to be divided. Neither is it for the Court to express preference for any type of family model. On the other hand [the judgment is] liable to take the protection of fundamental rights backwards.[77]

Although these judges accept the established principle that it is not for the Court to 'pass moral judgment' about homosexuality, they acknowledge that, in failing to do so, the Court frequently falters in respect of issues relating to sexual orientation and, because of this, human rights go 'backwards'. This shows that conceiving homosexuality to be the stable core of a human personality will not in itself promote the rights of sexual minorities but that sexual 'nature' must be explicitly imbued with moral, social and cultural value.

Conclusion: the social construction of homosexual nature

The question of whether sexual orientation is an immutable characteristic is, of course, the subject of a much wider debate than the one found in the case

76 *Minister of Home Affairs v Fourie (2005) & Lesbian and Gay Equality Project and Eighteen Others v Minister of Home Affairs (2005)*, 1 December 2005, ZACC 19, § 71.

77 *Fretté v France*, no. 36515/97, 26 February 2002, ECHR 2002-I, Joint partly dissenting opinion of Judge Sir Nicolas Bratza and Judges Fuhrmann and Tulkens, § 2(c).

law of the Court. It is a debate that is foundational to professional and lay discourse across a range of scientific, religious and political contexts. Some sociologists have argued that essentialist understandings of sexuality have been superseded in contemporary societies by conceptions of sexuality as fluid and plastic.[78] And for non-heterosexuals, living and experiencing their sexual identities and practices in the changing landscape of European societies, the Court's discourse may seem 'old-fashioned'. After three decades of 'queer theory', which has consistently argued that essentialist and universalist understandings delimit the possibilities under which sexuality can be lived, the reliance upon the concept of sexual personality may be regarded as inherently limited and limiting. It is for this reason that some argue that in place of the conception of sexual orientation as innate and immutable, the Court should protect sexual 'choice' and expand the possibilities that the Convention affords to individuals to choose a sexual life.[79] Even Wintemute (hardly an exponent of queer theory) argues that the 'immutable status argument is probably best abandoned because of its factual problems, its inability to encompass directly the actual choice of direction of conduct, and its potentially negative connotations'.[80]

However, in societies that remain chronically structured by the homosexual/heterosexual binary,[81] through which homosexuality is regarded as 'second rate' to heterosexuality, constructionist approaches are themselves problematic. This is not least because of their ability to support claims, as advanced by Judge Walsh in the early 1980s, that sexual orientation is voluntaristic and alterable. As MacDougall argues:

> there are real strengths to the essentialist position, in particular because it does not lend itself to the foible quality many judges assume about homosexuality. While a thoughtful understanding of the constructionist approach does not in fact lead to this conclusion, unfortunately judges (like many others) will search only for the essence of constructionism in which contingency will be construed to mean simply 'choice' and 'changeability'.[82]

78 See, for example: S. Roseneil, 'The Heterosexual/Homosexual Binary: Past, Present and Future', in D. Richardson and S. Seidman (eds.), *Handbook of Lesbian and Gay Studies*, London: Sage, 2002, 27–44. See also: A. Giddens, *The Transformation of Intimacy: Sexuality, Love and Eroticism in Modern Societies*, Cambridge: Polity Press, 1992.

79 For example: M. Grigolo, 'Sexualities and the ECHR: Introducing the Universal Sexual Legal Subject'.

80 R. Wintemute, *Sexual Orientation and Human Rights: The United States Constitution, the European Convention, and the Canadian Charter*, Oxford: Clarendon Press, 1995, p. 246.

81 P. Johnson, *Love, Heterosexuality and Society*, London: Routledge, 2005.

82 B. MacDougall, *Queer Judgments: Homosexuality, Expression, and the Courts in Canada*, Toronto: University of Toronto Press, 2000, p. 44.

Whilst essentialism has its own limitations (not least in the way that it can be turned back on homosexuals to support medical interventions that purport to 'cure' them), it offers, through the liberal humanistic framework of human rights, a way to articulate a form of humanness that requires permanent protection. Therefore, although essentialist ideas about homosexuality are intrinsically linked to a history of social, medical and legal denigration, the same conceptions offer a vital mode of resistance and challenge to social and legal hostility. Invoking the essentialist concept of 'the homosexual' allows the subject who embodies that 'name' to claim important rights. As Butler argues:

> One is not simply fixed by the name that one is called. In being called an injurious name, one is derogated and demeaned. But the name holds out another possibility as well: by being called a name, one is also, paradoxically, given a certain possibility for social existence, initiated into a temporal life of language that exceeds the prior purposes that animate that call.[83]

The performative process through which the Court has interpellated and given ontological shape to the homosexual subject has provided an important framework through which to expand Convention rights. As I demonstrate in Part III of the book, the Court's discursive construction of homosexuality should be seen as an 'enabling constraint' for non-heterosexuals, giving scope for freedoms in some areas and continuing to pose limitations in others.

83 J. Butler, *Excitable Speech: A Politics of the Performative*, p. 2.

Part II

Methods and morals

Chapter 3

Homosexuality in the judicial laboratory

Instruments, interpretations and evolutions

In this chapter, I consider the methods used by the Court to interpret the Convention in respect of complaints relating to homosexuality. The Convention specifies the range of substantive human rights available to individuals and provides the procedural rules under which the Court operates, but it does not set out or bind the Court to any interpretative framework. Whilst the Court's interpretation of the Convention is influenced by international law (in particular the Vienna Convention on the Law of Treaties 1969), it has developed a distinctive suite of methods in light of the 'special character' of the Convention.[1] The standard textual format adopted in all published judgments issued by the Court suggests that its decisions are the outcome of the stringent application of its methods. In reading a judgment by the Court, one has the impression that the function of its judges is to engage in the 'quality control'[2] of the application of its methods rather than in moral reasoning about human rights. Even in cases that feature strong dissent from a majority judgment, and where judges publish separate opinions in which they dispute the use of particular methods to reach certain interpretations of the Convention, the Court's judgments always strongly reify its methods.

The Court's application of its methods has often produced the criticism that it lacks coherence and consistency. For instance, Orakhelashvili argues that the Court's judgments show that it 'feels free to pick and choose between different methods of interpretation as if there was no order or hierarchy between these methods'.[3] Mowbray's defence of the Court's jurisprudence emphasizes its development of a 'creative' interpretative approach that is necessary to give effect to the substantive provisions of the Convention within the complex social, cultural

1 *Soering v the United Kingdom*, no. 14038/88, 7 July 1989, Series A no. 161, § 87.

2 B. Latour, *The Making of Law: An Ethnography of the Conseil d'Etat*, Cambridge: Polity Press, 2010, p. 218.

3 A. Orakhelashvili, 'Restrictive Interpretation of Human Rights Treaties in the Recent Jurisprudence of the European Court of Human Rights', *European Journal of International Law* 14(3), 2002, 529–568 at 567.

and legal environment of contemporary Europe.[4] There are those who claim, as I examine below, that the extent to which the Court's methods, rather than moral reasoning, determine its judgments produces a technocratic approach that is problematic in the adjudication of human rights complaints. However, as I argue below, the Court's strong reliance on method should not be understood as an indication of an absence of moral reasoning but, rather, as a means by which it persuades of its authority to be an institution capable of impartially evaluating and resolving complex moral disputes. Although the Court's appeal to method can be seen as a way of staving off criticism of 'activism', its judgments in respect of gay and lesbian rights are far from the result of 'mechanical jurisprudence'[5] and remain grounded in moral interpretations of the Convention.

Avoiding activism

The very essence of judicial practice is the reproduction of legal stability. As Latour argues, the judicial field – unlike the academic field – is characterized by the desire of the actors within it to reproduce the seamlessness of the epistemological constructions under which they work:

> unlike scientists, who dream of overturning a paradigm, of putting their names to a radical change, a scientific revolution or a major discovery, commissioners of the law invariably present their innovations as the expression of a principle that was already in existence, so that even when it deeply transforms the corpus of [. . .] law it is 'even more' the same than it was before.[6]

In a court that is comprised of judges who, inevitably, possess very different habitus (by virtue of the disparate social, cultural and legal contexts from which they originate), that has an overwhelming caseload and labours under a vast history of case law and precedent, the Court's methods are an important framework through which to sustain judicial consistency and legal stability. As Nicolas Bratza, former President of the Court, has recently stated:

> while it is important that the Court's case law should evolve to deal with new factual and legal situations, it is equally important that the Court should show respect for precedent and recognize the vital need for consistency. It is difficult to overstate the importance of legal certainty.[7]

4 A. Mowbray, 'The Creativity of the European Court of Human Rights', *Human Rights Law Review* 5(1), 2005, 57–79.

5 R. Pound, 'Mechanical Jurisprudence', *Columbia Law Review* 8(8), 1908, 605–623.

6 B. Latour, *The Making of Law: An Ethnography of the Conseil d'Etat*, p. 215.

7 N. Bratza, 'The Relationship Between the UK Courts and Strasbourg', *European Human Rights Law Review* 5, 2011, 505–512 at 511.

The Court's reliance on method is the central way that it attempts to convince contracting states that its judgments are built on 'legal certainty' rather than the collective or individual ideological interest of its judges. In attempting to demonstrate that judgments are the expression of legal principles rather than political interests, the Court uses its methods to eschew any notion that its decisions are the result of 'activism'.

I do not want to rehearse the long-standing and ongoing debate about whether judges are 'active' or 'passive'.[8] I take as axiomatic the view that the Court, in performing a supervisory function to ensure that contracting states uphold the rights outlined in the Convention, inevitably has to adjudicate on a wide range of emerging issues and, to use Hart's formulation, *make* law where none previously existed.[9] As White and Boussiakou argue, the 'open texture of many of the provisions of the Convention has required choices to be made by the Court in adding substance to the text of the Convention'.[10] A previous Secretary of the Commission has argued that '[t]hanks to this creative jurisprudence, the text of the Convention has constantly been adapted to the economic, political and social changes in our society'.[11] This recognizes that the Court's work necessitates an active interpretation of the Convention that is nevertheless attuned to the restraints of its supervisory role. As Mahonney argues:

> the dilemma of activism versus restraint is more apparent than real, in that activism and restraint are complementary components of the methodology of judicial review inherent in the very nature of the Convention as an international treaty intended to secure effective protection of human rights and fundamental freedoms.[12]

The need for a creative interpretation of the Convention makes it vital that judgments by the Court appear to be founded on legal principle rather than judicial interest. Recent empirical research of judicial work has provided important understandings of how legal judgments (much like scientific findings) are constructed in particular ways so that they appear to be the outcome of a disinterested and dispassionate form of reasoning. Sachs, for instance,

8 T. Bingham, 'The Judges: Active or Passive?', *British Academy Maccabean Lecture*, Cardiff, 27 October 2005.

9 H.L.A. Hart, *The Concept of Law*, Oxford: Oxford University Press, 1961.

10 R.C.A. White and I. Boussiako, 'Separate Opinions in the European Court of Human Rights', *Human Rights Law Review* 9(1), 2009, 37–60 at 42.

11 H.C. Krüger, 'European Convention on Human Rights: 50 Years of Growth', in Human Rights Information Bulletin, *The European Convention on Human Rights at 50*, Strasbourg: Council of Europe, 2000, p. 4.

12 P. Mahoney, 'Judicial Activism and Judicial Self-Restraint in the European Court of Human Rights: Two Sides of the Same Coin', *Human Rights Law Journal* 11, 1990, 57–88 at 59.

argues that whilst legal judgments are not a 'flabby subjective response dressed up in the false guise of objectivity',[13] neither do they 'emerge from the dispassionate placing of logical propositions in rationally ordered sequence'.[14] Judicial decisions, argues Sachs, involve three stages of production: discovery of facts, justification of reasoning and persuasion of judgment. Whilst persuasion relies on both facts and reasoning, it also depends upon 'the powerful mystique built up by the law over the ages'.[15] As Latour's legal ethnography demonstrates, a key aspect of this mystique is the appeal to legal method. Reliance on method, Latour argues, gives the appearance of scientific detachment:

> Most of the qualities that are commonly attributed to scientists are drawn from the micro-procedures invented by lawyers to produce their fragile ethos of disinterest. Indifferent to the outcome of a case, the distance established between the mind and the object that is being spoken about, the coldness and rigour of judgment – in short, everything that we associate with objectivity – belongs not to the world of the laboratory or of calculation, but to the judicial bench.[16]

The Court can be seen to use method not only as a way of achieving objective rigour but of convincing of its value-neutrality. Whilst, as I argued in the previous chapter, the Court has occasionally stated that its moral position on homosexuality is neutral – in *Dudgeon v the United Kingdom*, the Court claimed that it was 'not concerned with making any value-judgment as to the morality of homosexual relations between adult males'[17] – such explicit expressions are rare. Rather, the Court relies upon its method to implicitly demonstrate that its judges are more 'passive arbiters' than 'active shapers'[18] of the Convention.

In elevating the importance of its 'tools' as the basis for its decisions, the Court has attracted the criticism that it is failing in its 'duty to discover and give effect to the morally best understanding of human rights'.[19] This criticism rests on an understanding of the Court's reliance upon method as evidence of a deferment of moral interpretation. This reiterates the common but mistaken view that the application of method (scientific or legal) is evidence of moral and political neutrality. Yet, as several decades of feminist epistemology and methodology have demonstrated, methods are always

13 A. Sachs, *The Strange Alchemy of Life and Law*, Oxford: Oxford University Press, 2009, p. 50.
14 Ibid., p. 47.
15 Ibid., pp. 55–56.
16 B. Latour, *The Making of Law: An Ethnography of the Conseil d'Etat*, p. 236.
17 *Dudgeon v the United Kingdom*, no. 7525/76, 22 October 1981, Series A no. 45, § 54.
18 N. Fielding, 'Judges and Their Work', *Social and Legal Studies* 20(4), 2011, 97–115 at 98.
19 G. Letsas, *A Theory of Interpretation of the European Convention on Human Rights*, Oxford: Oxford University Press, 2007, p. xi.

conceived and applied in respect of moral and political standpoints.[20] And, as many legal scholars have argued, the choice and application of interpretative method will be significantly influenced by the ideological commitments of individual judges.[21] Whilst the Court relies upon method to approximate coherence and consistency across its case law, this should not be understood to express a form of moral disinterest or impartiality. Rather, as I will explore through a consideration of three of the Court's methods – the margin of appreciation doctrine; consensus analysis; and the living instrument principle – methods are always subservient to the Court's moral interpretation of the Convention. Because moral interpretation determines the application of method, rather than vice versa, methodological discontinuities appear in the fabric of the Court's case law as a result of the different moral positions adopted by judges. These discontinuities demonstrate the fiction of the scientific positivism that law often aspires to and the moral basis of all legal adjudication. What becomes vital in respect of the development of lesbian and gay human rights, therefore, is the moral policy of the Court in respect of homosexuality.

The margin of appreciation

The margin of appreciation is one of the key methods used by the Court in its review of complaints. It has been described as the 'space for manoeuvre' that the Court will grant to a contracting state to fulfil its obligations under the Convention.[22] In respect of the qualified rights of the Convention (Articles 8–11), a state's margin of appreciation will be determined by the Court's assessment of the legality, legitimacy and necessity of any restriction by a public authority. However, both the concept and practical application of the margin of appreciation have been the subject of sustained criticism. For example, Singh argues that although the margin of appreciation 'has been variously described, in the literature and in the Strasbourg jurisprudence, as a "concept", a "doctrine" and a "principle" ', it is 'far from being a doctrine or principle capable of abstract definition and concrete application'.[23] Rather, Singh states, the margin of appreciation is 'a conclusory label which only serves to obscure the true basis on which a reviewing court decides whether or

20 See, for example: S. Harding, 'Is There a Feminist Method?', in N. Tuana (ed.), *Feminism and Science*, Bloomington: Indiana University Press, 1989.

21 A. Volokh, 'Choosing Interpretative Methods: A Positive Theory of Judges and Everyone Else', *New York University Law Review* 83, 2008, 769–846.

22 Council of Europe, 'The Margin of Appreciation', available HTTP: <http://www.coe.int/t/dghl/cooperation/lisbonnetwork/themis/ECHR/Paper2_en.asp> (accessed 18 February 2012).

23 R. Singh, 'Is There a Role for the "Margin of Appreciation" in National Law After the Human Rights Act?', *European Human Rights Law Review* 1(4), 1999, 15–22 at 20–21.

not intervention in a particular case is justifiable'.[24] Lord Lester of Herne Hill argues that the 'concept of the margin of appreciation has become as slippery and elusive as an eel' and that it is used by the Court 'as a substitute for coherent legal analysis of the issues at stake'.[25] And Kratochvíl calls the margin of appreciation 'black box magic'.[26]

The concept of the margin of appreciation has a long history in the jurisprudence of the Court and was developed as a method for negotiating the Court's subsidiary role. In *Handyside v the United Kingdom*, the Court stated that 'the machinery of protection established by the Convention is subsidiary to the national systems safeguarding human rights' and that the Convention 'leaves to each Contracting State, in the first place, the task of securing the rights and liberties it enshrines'.[27] The Court went on to state that the margin of appreciation doctrine was a recognition that, by 'reason of their direct and continuous contact with the vital forces of their countries, State authorities are in principle in a better position than the international judge to give an opinion' on the nature of the restriction of rights that may be necessary in a democratic society.[28] As a consequence of this, the Court leaves variable margins (often referred to by the size of their width) to contracting states in respect of a range of issues. However, because states are not given 'an unlimited power of appreciation', the Court has continually stressed that the 'domestic margin of appreciation thus goes hand in hand with a European supervision'.[29]

Letsas distinguishes between a 'structural' and 'substantive' conception of the margin of appreciation.[30] The structural concept is used by the Court to determine, as outlined in the *Handyside* judgment, the extent of its authority to review the decisions of domestic courts. The substantive concept is used by the Court in its review of the fair balance between individual rights and the restriction of those rights by a contracting state. The structural concept is therefore concerned with the scope of the Court's powers, whilst the substantive concept is used as an interpretive method. The substantive use of the margin of appreciation has received sustained criticism. A key problem with it is that, as MacDonald argues, the Court often invokes the concept as the justification for its judgments and, in doing so, leaves its reasoning as a matter

24 Ibid.
25 Lord Lester of Herne Hill, 'Universality Versus Subsidiarity: A Reply', *European Human Rights Law Review* 1, 1998, 73–81 at 75.
26 J. Kratochvíl, 'The Inflation of the Margin of Appreciation by the European Court of Human Rights', *Netherlands Quarterly of Human Rights* 29(3), 2011, 324–357 at 354.
27 *Handyside v the United Kingdom*, no. 5493/72, 7 December 1976, Series A no. 24, § 48.
28 Ibid.
29 Ibid., § 49.
30 G. Letsas, *A Theory of Interpretation of the European Convention on Human Rights.*

of guesswork.[31] As Lord Lester argues: 'The problem with the Court's invocation of the margin of appreciation is that it removes the need for the Court to discern and explain the criteria appropriate to particular problems.'[32]

What Lord Lester sees as a 'problem' for analytic jurisprudence – a problem that has led scholars to attempt to catalogue the various ways in which the margin of appreciation has been applied and the hierarchy of rights that it has produced[33] – is actually what makes it most useful because the doctrine provides the Court with a highly malleable device through which to mandate its moral judgments. In 'applying' the margin of appreciation, the Court appears to draw upon a precision instrument that enables it to calculate the 'width' of the margin available to a state in each case. By using the margin in this way, the Court is able, as Bourdieu argues, to obscure the 'fuzzy logic' of its practical reasoning and, as a result, underwrite claims about its 'objectivity'.[34] Although the margin available to a state appears to be determined by the outcome of the application of method, it is, in fact, an expression of the moral reasoning of the Court. Because of this, in respect of matters relating to homosexuality, it is not surprising to find variations in how the doctrine is applied and the margin is determined.

Analysis of Strasbourg case law shows that what margin is available to a state to regulate homosexuality varies according to the moral position adopted by the Strasbourg organs. As I outlined in Chapter 1, the Commission granted contracting states a blanket margin until the early 1980s on the basis that it regarded homosexuality as antithetical to social morality and public health. In *Dudgeon v the United Kingdom*, the Court established the principle that, whilst the protection of morals afforded a state a certain margin of appreciation to regulate homosexuality, the width of the margin would now be determined by the nature of the sexual activities in question.[35] In designating adult consensual sexual practice a 'most intimate aspect of private life', the Court decided that a state had no margin available under Article 8 in which to regulate private homosexual acts between two consenting adults.[36] Central to the Court's decision in *Dudgeon* was, as I argued in Chapter 2, the cultivation of a particular ontological understanding of homosexuality as an immutable characteristic of human nature. The understanding of homosexuality as an

31 R. Macdonald, 'The Margin of Appreciation', in R.St.J. Macdonald, F. Matscher and H. Petzold (eds.), *The European System for the Protection of Rights*, Alphen aan den Rijn: Kluwer, 1993.

32 Lord Lester of Herne Hill, 'Universality Versus Subsidiarity: A Reply', at 78.

33 L.R. Helfer, 'Finding a Consensus on Equality: The Homosexual Age of Consent and the European Convention on Human Rights', *New York University Law Review* 65, 1990, 1044–1100.

34 P. Bourdieu, *Pascalian Meditations*, Cambridge: Polity Press, 2000.

35 *Dudgeon v the United Kingdom*, no. 7525/76, 22 October 1981, Series A no. 45.

36 Ibid., § 52.

aspect of 'personality' worthy of protection can be seen to have significantly determined the Court's use of the margin doctrine.

The close relationship in *Dudgeon* between the moral approach adopted by the Court and the application of the margin doctrine is demonstrated in the dissenting opinion of Judge Walsh who, holding moral views about homosexuality contrary to the majority, argued for the application of a wide margin:

> Adults, even consenting adults, can be corrupted and may be exploited by reason of their own weaknesses. In my view this is an area in which the legislature has a wide discretion or margin of appreciation which should not be encroached upon save where it is clear beyond doubt that the legislation is such that no reasonable community could enact.[37]

The view that homosexual sex constitutes a 'most intimate aspect of private life', rather than the exploitation and corruption of the weak, has been the basis for the Court progressively closing down the scope for any margin in respect of the criminalization of private and consensual sexual practices. In *Norris v Ireland*, for example, the government argued that

> the moral fibre of a democratic nation is a matter for its own institutions and the Government should be allowed a degree of tolerance in their compliance with Article 8 [. . .], that is to say, a margin of appreciation that would allow the democratic legislature to deal with this problem in the manner which it sees best.[38]

The Court stated that it was 'not convinced by this line of argument'[39] and that it did not accept the government's contention that a state's 'discretion in the field of the protection of morals is unfettered'.[40] Similarly, in *Sutherland v the United Kingdom*, the Court relied upon its conception of the intimate nature of private life to close the margin available to states to set different minimum ages for homosexual and heterosexual sexual activities: 'given that it impinges on a most intimate aspect of affected individuals' private lives, the margin of appreciation must be relatively narrow'.[41]

The influence of the Court's moral position in respect of homosexual sex and sexual orientation on its use of the margin doctrine can be seen throughout its case law. In *A.D.T. v the United Kingdom*,[42] for example, the Court's moral

37 Ibid., Partially dissenting opinion of Judge Walsh, § 21.
38 *Norris v Ireland*, no. 10581/83, 26 October 1988, Series A no.142, § 43.
39 Ibid., § 44.
40 Ibid., § 45.
41 *Sutherland v the United Kingdom*, no. 25186/94, Commission report, 1 July 1997, § 57.
42 *A.D.T. v the United Kingdom*, no. 35765/97, 31 July 2000, ECHR 2000-IX.

position was decisive in closing the margin of appreciation available to a state to criminalize private and consensual sexual activities between groups of men (and, as a result, reversing its previous judgment in *Johnson v the United Kingdom*[43]). In *A.D.T.*, the government drew a moral distinction between intimate, private (and therefore acceptable) homosexual activity between two men, and group (potentially public and therefore unacceptable) homosexual activity. The Court did not recognize this moral distinction to be a valid justification for interference with the applicant's rights:

> Given the narrow margin of appreciation afforded to the national authorities in the case, the absence of any public-health considerations and the purely private nature of the behaviour in the present case, the Court finds that the reasons submitted for the maintenance in force of legislation criminalizing homosexual acts between men in private, and *a fortiori* the prosecution and conviction in the present case, are not sufficient to justify the legislation and the prosecution.[44]

The key determinant of the margin of appreciation here is the Court's rejection of the government's claim that homosexual sexual practices involving groups of men are immoral. As I discussed in Chapter 2, although the Court rarely makes explicit its moral position about homosexuality, by closing the margin in this case it can be seen to implicitly attribute moral value to these sexual acts.

By contrast, in *Laskey, Jaggard and Brown v the United Kingdom*,[45] both the Commission and the Court granted the contracting state a broad margin of appreciation to regulate private sadomasochistic sexual practices. In reviewing complaints about the convictions of a group of men who had engaged in private sadomasochistic sexual practices, both the Commission and the Court argued that the interference with the applicants' private lives fell within a state's margin to implement policies to meet the pressing social need of protecting individuals from harm. However, there was considerable dissent to the use of the margin of appreciation in this way. In a dissenting opinion in the Commission, which is worth quoting at length, Mr. Loucaides and six others argued that the application of the margin in this way revealed arbitrariness and inconsistency:

> The majority found that the conviction of the applicants was not disproportionate and falls within the margin of appreciation to be accorded to

43 *Johnson v the United Kingdom*, no. 10389/83, Commission decision, 17 July 1986.
44 *A.D.T. v the United Kingdom*, no. 35765/97, 31 July 2000, ECHR 2000-IX, § 38.
45 *Laskey, Jaggard and Brown v the United Kingdom*, nos. 21627/93, 21628/93 and 21974/93, 19 February 1997, Reports of Judgments and Decisions 1997-I.

> the Government as regards the imposition of measures to protect its citizens from physical injury [. . .]
>
> However, in the present case the domestic courts do not refer to any permanent or serious harm or injury being caused in the course of the applicants' activities. Nor was it established that a real risk of such harm or injury existed in the circumstances of this case. The risk of activities getting out of hand could be met effectively by the existing provisions of the criminal law because in such a situation either there will be no consent or serious harm will be caused. While mention has been made of AIDS and the risk of infection from bloodletting activities in both domestic and Commission proceedings, this risk has not been substantiated. At any rate the risk of infection with the AIDS virus arises in lawful adult heterosexual and homosexual acts and cannot by itself be used as a ground for prohibiting private sexual activities.
>
> I attach particular importance to the fact that in the legal system of the respondent State activities which cause injury or are inherently dangerous to health are generally considered lawful by the mere fact that they are consented to. A typical example is the case of boxing which may cause more severe physical injury than the activities of the Applicants and where violence is glorified with the result that it may incite others to engage in it.
>
> On 15 October 1995 two professional boxers died as a result of a boxing match. It has not been shown that the sadomasochistic acts of the applicants risk to have comparable consequences.
>
> For the margin of appreciation of the State to be acceptable justification it must not be arbitrary or lead to inconsistencies. It appears that the treatment of activities which may cause physical injury by the legal system of the respondent State is not consistent. Apart from the example of boxing, one may refer also to cosmetic surgery and tattooing where consent is sufficient to preclude offences being brought.[46]

What Loucaides astutely and eruditely discerns is that the margin available to a state will be significantly influenced by the Court's moral orientation towards the activities in question. Loucaides shows that the 'weighty reasons' offered by states and accepted by the Court as justifications for interfering with Convention rights are themselves founded on moral judgments and that these require scrutiny. By using the margin of appreciation to bypass an elucidation of its own moral reasoning, the Court invites the charge of inconsistency.

46 *Laskey, Jaggard and Brown v the United Kingdom*, nos. 21627/93, 21628/93 and 21974/93, Commission report, 26 October 1995, Dissenting opinion of Mr. L. Loucaides joined by MM. S. Trechsel, H.G. Schermers, C.L. Rozakis, J-C.Geus, J. Mucha and E. Konstantinov.

Yet the Court (and the Commission) has often invoked the margin of appreciation as a mechanism to legitimize its judgments and circumvent the need to outline its moral reasoning. As Kratochvíl argues, there are a 'large set of cases where no width of the margin is identified and it is mentioned only in the conclusion' of a judgment.[47] For example, in *H.F. v Austria*, which concerned a complaint against differential minimum legal ages for sexual activity, the Commission did not engage in any analysis of the margin but stated in its conclusion that 'the State's margin of appreciation has not been overstepped and that, consequently, there is no appearance of a violation'.[48] Kratochvíl argues that 'by invoking the margin, the Court avoids giving clear arguments as to why it interpreted the obligation in a certain way' and that this works as a 'smoke screen' by giving the impression that the margin 'resolved the dispute'.[49]

In contrast, the Court has often rejected a defence offered by a contracting state that has relied upon the margin doctrine in place of a justification based on an analysis of proportionality. In *Smith and Grady v the United Kingdom*, for example, the state invoked its margin of appreciation in the sphere of 'national security' to justify its interference with the Article 8 rights of armed forces personnel suspected of being homosexual.[50] In a partly dissenting opinion, Judge Loucaides argued that 'the narrow margin of appreciation which is applied to cases involving intimate private-life matters is widened' where the pressing social need of national security is concerned and that 'the wider the margin of appreciation allowed to the State, the narrower should be the scope for interference by the Court'.[51] The majority of the Court disagreed, finding that the state could not rely on the margin of appreciation to 'frustrate the exercise by individual members of the armed forces of their right to respect for their private lives, which right applies to service personnel as it does to others within the jurisdiction of the State'.[52]

In its recent jurisprudence in respect of homosexuality, the Court's use of the margin has been erratic. This is demonstrated very clearly by two similar facts cases, *Fretté v France*[53] and *E.B. v France*,[54] in which the margin was

47 J. Kratochvíl, 'The Inflation of the Margin of Appreciation by the European Court of Human Rights', at 342.

48 *H.F. v Austria*, no. 22646/93, Commission decision, 26 June 1995.

49 J. Kratochvíl, 'The Inflation of the Margin of Appreciation by the European Court of Human Rights', at 336–367.

50 *Smith and Grady v the United Kingdom*, nos. 33985/96 and 33986/96, 27 September 1999, ECHR 1999-VI.

51 Ibid., Partly concurring, partly dissenting opinion of Judge Loucaides.

52 *Smith and Grady v the United Kingdom*, nos. 33985/96 and 33986/96, 27 September 1999, ECHR 1999-VI, § 89.

53 *Fretté v France*, no. 36515/97, 26 February 2002, ECHR 2002-I.

54 *E.B. v France* [GC], no. 43546/02, 22 January 2008.

utilized in the former but excluded from the latter. Applicants in both *Fretté* and *E.B.* complained that their refusal for authorization to adopt a child (which is available to all single adults over 28 years of age under Article 343 of the French Civil Code) was based on a consideration of their sexual orientation and that this constituted discrimination contrary to Article 14 of the Convention, taken in conjunction with Article 8. In both cases, the French government argued that a wide margin was available to it in order to determine adoption in the best interests of the child. In *Fretté*, the Court explicitly endorsed the state's margin and, by relying on a form of consensus analysis (which I examine below), found it had not violated the Convention. By contrast, in *E.B.*, the Court never considered the question of margin and, by relying on the living instrument doctrine (which I examine below), found that the state had violated the applicant's Convention rights.

Further discontinuities are revealed when the use of the margin in *Kozak v Poland*[55] is compared with its use in *Schalk and Kopf v Austria*.[56] In *Kozak*, the Court stated that, in respect of Article 14, where 'a difference of treatment is based on sex or sexual orientation, the margin of appreciation afforded to the State is narrow' and that 'if the reasons advanced for a difference in treatment were based solely on the applicant's sexual orientation, this would amount to discrimination under the Convention'.[57] Yet in *Schalk and Kopf*, the Court confirmed the state's margin to prohibit same-sex couples from contracting civil marriage.[58] This produced dissent in respect of excluding same-sex couples from marriage in the absence of a legal framework offering similar rights and benefits:

> the Court should have found a violation of Article 14 taken in conjunction with Article 8 of the Convention because the respondent Government did not advance any argument to justify the difference of treatment, relying in this connection mainly on their margin of appreciation [. . .] However, in the absence of any cogent reasons offered by the respondent Government to justify the difference of treatment, there should be no room to apply the margin of appreciation.[59]

Schalk and Kopf is a clear example of the Court relying on the substantive concept of the margin to obscure its moral reasoning (in this case about same-sex marriage) and upon the structural concept to defer to the authority of the state. As I explore in the next section, a key aspect of this structural use of the margin is the Court's reliance upon the method of consensus analysis.

55 *Kozak v Poland*, no. 13102/02, 2 March 2010.
56 *Schalk and Kopf v Austria*, no. 30141/04, 24 June 2010.
57 *Kozak v Poland*, no. 13102/02, 2 March 2010, § 92.
58 *Schalk and Kopf v Austria*, no. 30141/04, 24 June 2010.
59 Ibid., Joint dissenting opinion of Judges Rozakis, Spielmann and Jebens.

Consensus analysis

Determining a state's margin depends, in principle, upon a consideration of the importance of the Convention right in question (which, as I show in later chapters, has created a hierarchy of rights in respect of homosexuality), scrutiny of the argument offered by a state for restricting that right, and a review of European practice. The Court's comparison of European practice is a method that it often applies to assess the consensus within contracting states in respect of the issue in question. A lack of consensus among member states will usually be the basis for maintaining a state's margin, whereas the existence of consensus may provide the foundation for a dynamic interpretation of the Convention in order to develop a right. The Court relies, as Helfer argues, on three forms of consensus analysis: first, it considers statutory developments across contracting states to determine the level of convergence in legal standards; second, it considers expert opinion; and third, it assesses developments in public opinion.[60] However, the Court's judgments show that there is no consistent application of these three elements: often, one or more will be present in a published judgment, whereas at other times an analysis of consensus will be entirely absent.

Consensus analysis has been consistently criticized as a method for determining human rights standards. Letsas argues that 'judges who adjudicate on [Convention] rights have a duty to discover and give effect to the *morally best understandings of human rights*, irrespective of contracting states' current consensus'.[61] Whilst many would agree with this because, as Hodson argues, consensus analysis is 'clearly an unsatisfactory approach that leaves minorities vulnerable to majoritarian domination',[62] the method, as Wintemute argues, 'is probably a defensible result of the court's role, which is that of an international court interpreting a voluntary, international treaty'.[63] Dzehtsiarou argues that consensus analysis 'injects European context and predictability' into the Court's reasoning.[64] I argue that it does neither. Consensus analysis is a construct through which the Court legitimizes its moral interpretation and because of this, as its case law shows, its use is unpredictable and variable.

The Court's case law on homosexuality shows a highly capricious and frequently contested use of statutory, expert and public consensus analysis. Formally, the Court maintains a principle that a lack of consensus will result in a state being granted a wide margin of appreciation:

60 L.R. Helfer, 'Finding a Consensus on Equality: The Homosexual Age of Consent and The European Convention on Human Rights'.

61 G. Letsas, *A Theory of Interpretation of the European Convention on Human Rights*, p. XI.

62 L. Hodson, 'A Marriage By Any Other Name? Schalk and Kopf v Austria', *Human Rights Law Review* 11(1), 170–179 at 177.

63 R. Wintemute, *Sexual Orientation and Human Rights: The United States Constitution, the European Convention, and the Canadian Charter*, Oxford: Clarendon Press, 1995, p. 139.

64 K. Dzehtsiarou, 'European Consensus and the Evolutive Interpretation of the European Convention on Human Rights', *German Law Journal* 12(10), 2011, 1730–1745 at 1730.

> Where a particularly important facet of an individual's existence or identity is at stake, the margin allowed to the State will be restricted [. . .] Where, however, there is no consensus within the Member States of the Council of Europe, either as to the relative importance of the interest at stake or as to how best to protect it, the margin will be wider.[65]

In practice, however, the use of consensus analysis varies to such an extent that it cannot be regarded as causally determinative of the margin in any straightforward way. Consensus analysis is better understood, like the margin of appreciation itself, as a framework through which the Court legitimizes a particular moral understanding of homosexuality.

Judges in the Court use consensus analysis much like scientists who, as Gilbert and Mulkay argue, deploy claims about consensus to establish a particular view of the world that is appropriate for a particular occasion:

> scientists' consensus accounts are neither literal descriptions of an independent social reality, nor are they the necessary outcome of scientists' standardized interpretative procedures. They are, rather, the means by which scientists make available to us, and to their colleagues, versions of the state of collective belief which are appropriate for specific interpretative occasions.[66]

The Court's judgments show that consensus analysis is a device through which 'reality' is selectively represented in order to add weight to moral reasoning. The Court does not fabricate or 'make up' consensus but what counts as consensus is significantly influenced by the moral standpoints adopted by the judges sitting in each individual case.[67] As an epistemological construction, consensus analysis produces knowledge of reality in ways that are relational to, and dependent upon, the social position of those who 'apply' the method.[68] What is crucial for the development of gay and lesbian rights, therefore, is that the Court does not simply assess the existence of an

65 *S. and Marper v the United Kingdom*, nos. 30562/04 and 30566/04, 4 December 2008, § 102.

66 G.N. Gilbert and M.J. Mulkay, *Opening Pandora's Box: a Sociological Analysis of Scientists' Discourse*, Cambridge: Cambridge University Press, 1984, p. 139.

67 S. Harding, 'Whose Standpoint Needs the Regimes of Truth and Reality? Comment on Hekman's "Truth and Method: Feminist Standpoint Theory Revisited" ', *Signs: Journal of Women in Culture and Society* 22(2), 1997, 382–391.

68 Our comprehension of 'reality' is determined by, as Bourdieu argues, our 'habitus': the 'systems of schemes of perception, appreciation and action' that result from our position in, and embodiment of, social relations. Habitus, Bourdieu argues, 'generates practice immediately adjusted to [a social] order, which are therefore perceived, by their author and also by others, as "right" [. . .] without being in any way the product of obedience to an order in the sense of an imperative, to a norm or to legal rules'. P. Bourdieu, *Pascalian Meditations*, pp. 138–143.

'objective' reality but actively constructs representations of consensus in particular ways. Because the Court is an institution with considerable symbolic power it has, as Bourdieu and Wacquant argue, the power to both construct reality and legitimize it as 'true'.[69]

The use of consensus analysis to represent reality in order to mandate a judgment can be seen very clearly in *X. v Federal Republic of Germany*.[70] In this case, the Commission invoked the existence of a consensus relating to the protection of children to underpin its decision that legislation maintaining differential ages for homosexual and heterosexual sexual acts fell within a state's margin:

> The Commission is not unaware that the danger to which an adolescent is exposed as a result of homosexual relations with an adult is a subject of controversy in several countries. It also notes that several states have undertaken a study of the complete decriminalization of homosexuality and a committee of experts of the Council of Europe is studying this problem [. . .] The fact remains that the action of the German legislature was clearly inspired by the need to protect the rights of children and adolescents and enable them to achieve true autonomy in sexual matters. This need is broadly admitted in a large number of member states of the Council of Europe.[71]

The Commission's decision shows that it elevated the importance of a general consensus about the need to protect children above expert opinion and statutory arrangements in respect of homosexuality (which it stated were 'developing rapidly in this field').[72] In doing so, the Commission can be seen to use consensus as a device to legitimize its own moral reasoning about the need for a higher 'age of consent' for homosexual acts. However, in a subsequent decision in a similar facts case the Commission abandoned consensus altogether:

> on an issue such as the age of consent, what is important is not the balance struck in other European countries but the reasonable and objective nature of the arguments adduced in favour of the actual limit chosen. The Commission does not share the applicant's view, in this regard, that because the majority of European States have an age of consent that is fixed at eighteen or below, the age of twenty-one established by the

69 Bourdieu and Wacquant describe this form of symbolic power as 'the power to constitute the given by stating it, to act upon the world by acting upon representation of the world', which consequently 'creates a belief in the legitimacy of the words and of the person who utters them'. P. Bourdieu and L.J.D. Wacquant, *An Invitation to Reflexive Sociology*, Cambridge: Polity Press, 1992, p. 148.

70 *X. v Federal Republic of Germany*, no. 5935/72, Commission decision, 30 September 1975.

71 Ibid., p. 54.

72 Ibid., p. 55.

United Kingdom Government must therefore *not* be 'necessary in a democratic society'.[73]

These cases show the Commission using consensus in variable ways to ultimately reach the same decision to grant states a wide margin of appreciation.

When the Commission came to reverse its position on the issue of maintaining legal differences in the minimum ages for sexual acts, in *Sutherland v the United Kingdom*, it relied upon the existence of a consensus in statutory law and expert medical opinion to legitimize its decision:

> The Commission [. . .] considers it opportune to reconsider its earlier case law in the light of these modern developments and, more especially, in the light of the weight of current medical opinion that to reduce the age of consent to 16 might have positively beneficial effects on the sexual health of young homosexual men without any corresponding harmful consequences.[74]

This use of consensus in *Sutherland* generated considerable dissent. Two members of the Commission disputed the majority's interpretation of the available evidence and questioned the existence of a consensus:

> A number of States parties (sic) to the Convention still maintain different minimum ages for homosexual and heterosexual relations, sometimes as far as four years apart. According to the majority of the Commission 'equality of treatment in respect of age for consent is now recognised by the great majority of Member States of the Council of Europe' [. . .] Does that statement really reflect the present situation?[75]

However, the Commission and the Court have often advanced highly contestable interpretations of evidence to make claims about the existence of a consensus on a particular issue related to homosexuality. One explanation of this is that, in the absence of any systematic and transparent mechanism for collecting and interpreting evidence, the Court makes its decisions 'on the basis of the different data available to it'.[76] Because the Court rarely engages in its own fact-finding,[77] what is most often available to it is the selective evidence offered to it by

73 *X. v the United Kingdom*, no. 7215/75, Commission report, 12 October 1978, § 147.
74 *Sutherland v the United Kingdom*, no. 25186/94, Commission report, 1 July 1997, § 60.
75 Ibid., Dissenting opinion of MM. K. Herndl and I. Békés.
76 *Handyside v the United Kingdom*, no. 5493/72, 7 December 1976, Series A no. 24, § 50.
77 P. Leach, C. Paraskeva and G. Uzelac, *International Human Rights and Fact-Finding: An Analysis of the Fact-Finding Missions Conducted by the European Commission and Court of Human Rights*, London: Human Right and Social Justice Research Institute at London Metropolitan University, 2009.

competing parties. Yet the partiality of data available to the Court does not alone explain its interpretation of consensus. Rather, its use of available evidence to construct a view of consensus must be seen as subservient to its moral judgments. For example, in *G.W. v Federal Republic of Germany*, the Commission accepted the 'criminological expertise' presented by the German government as evidence of a consensus on the need to socially control homosexuality because of the dangers created by 'recidivism'.[78] In *Dudgeon v the United Kingdom*, by contrast, the Court accepted expert medical evidence presented by the applicant to dispute claims regarding the pathological nature of homosexuality.

On occasion, applicants have explicitly contested the Strasbourg organ's reliance upon particular forms of evidence to assert the existence of a consensus. For example, in *Johnson v the United Kingdom* the applicant complained that in a previous decision, the Commission:

> chose to ignore the recommendations of the Council of Europe's own criminological experts in this field, as expressed at the 15th Criminological Research Conference, and the views expressed by the Council of Europe's Parliamentary Assembly, in recommendation No. 924 (1981) concerning, *inter alia*, the minimum age of consent for homosexual acts. The Commission further ignored the views of all the English experts, medical, legal and sociological, expressed in their various evidences to the CLRC, and subsequently endorsed by the body, that the age of consent should be reduced to at least 18 for homosexual acts between males.
>
> [I]t is illogical that the Government, and the Commission, should rely on expert medical, psychological and sociological studies from the 1950s and 1960s to provide the basis for a finding that there is objective and reasonable justification for restricting rights under the Convention, yet should refuse to rely on studies of a similar expert nature from the 1970s and 1980s when these all concur that the extent of such restrictions is no longer necessary.[79]

The claim that the selective use of evidence is 'illogical' becomes less persuasive if one accepts that the Court determines its use of evidence in relation to its overall moral view. The deployment of particular evidence is a deliberate (and therefore logical) strategy of the Court, albeit one that produces variable results for complainants.

Consensus analysis remains a frequent basis for granting a state a margin in which to differentiate between individuals on the basis of sexual orientation. For example, in *Mata Estevez v Spain*, the Court upheld the right of the Spanish government to maintain pension laws that disadvantaged the surviving partner of a same-sex relationship because:

78 *G.W. v Federal Republic of Germany*, no. 1307/61, Commission decision, 4 October 1962.
79 *Johnson v the United Kingdom*, no. 10389/83, Commission decision, 17 July 1986.

> despite the growing tendency in a number of European States towards the legal and judicial recognition of stable *de facto* partnerships between homosexuals, this is, given the existence of little common ground between the Contracting States, an area in which they still enjoy a wide margin of appreciation.[80]

Similarly, in *M.W. v the United Kingdom*, in which the applicant complained about the difference in treatment between married heterosexual partners and unmarried same-sex partners in respect of social security benefits (prior to the introduction of civil partnership legislation in the United Kingdom), the Court stated that there was not 'sufficient consensus among the Contracting Parties to the Convention on the formal recognition of same-sex relationships that would have significantly narrowed the United Kingdom's margin of appreciation in this respect'.[81] And in *Schalk and Kopf v Austria*, the Court stated that, in respect of same-sex marriage:

> there is not yet a majority of States providing for legal recognition of same-sex couples. The area in question must therefore still be regarded as one of evolving rights with no established consensus, where States must also enjoy a margin of appreciation in the timing of the introduction of legislative changes.[82]

In contrast to these judgments, in which the Court used an absence of consensus to withhold Convention rights from same-sex partners, in *E.B. v France* the Court ignored the issue of consensus altogether to uphold the complaint of a female applicant who argued that she had been refused authorization to adopt a child on the grounds of her sexual orientation.[83] It is possible that the Court did not regard consensus analysis as relevant to *E.B.* given that it was reviewing a domestic law that explicitly granted access to everyone but, in practice, differentiated between people on the grounds of sexual orientation. However, the Court had relied on consensus analysis in its previous judgment in *Fretté v France* in order to reach the opposite conclusion to *E.B.*[84] The different approaches adopted in *E.B* and *Fretté* demonstrate that the selective use of this method is determined by, and not determinative of, the Court's moral reasoning.

80 *Mata Estevez v Spain* (dec), no. 56501/00, 10 May 2001, ECHR 2001-VI.

81 *M.W. v the United Kingdom* (dec), no. 11313/02, 23 June 2009.

82 *Schalk and Kopf v Austria*, no. 30141/04, 24 June 2010, § 105.

83 *E.B. v France* [GC], no. 43546/02, 22 January 2008.

84 *Fretté v France*, no. 36515/97, 26 February 2002, ECHR 2002-I. For a discussion of the use of consensus analysis in *Fretté* and *E.B.*, see: P. Johnson, 'Homosexuality, Freedom of Assembly and the Margin of Appreciation Doctrine of the European Court of Human Rights: *Alekseyev v Russia*', *Human Rights Law Review* 11(3), 2011, 578–593.

Alekseyev v Russia provides an insight into the malleability of consensus analysis and demonstrates how it is used in different ways to legitimize the Court's decisions. On the one hand, in order to rebuff a claim by the Russian government that no consensus existed across contracting states in respect of the treatment of homosexuals, the Court stated that there 'is ample case law reflecting a long-standing European consensus' on matters relating to homosexuality.[85] In respect of the complaint in question, which concerned the right to assembly, the Court went on to make a highly contestable empirical claim about European consensus:

> There is no ambiguity about the other member States' recognition of the right of individuals to openly identify themselves as gay, lesbian or any other sexual minority, and to promote their rights and freedoms, in particular by exercising their freedom of peaceful assembly.[86]

The Court can be seen to use this claim about the existence of a consensus to justify its decision to narrow the state's margin. However, on the other hand, the Court stated that the existence of a consensus was of no relevance to the case 'because conferring substantive rights on homosexual persons is fundamentally different from recognizing their right to campaign for such rights'.[87] By invoking a hierarchy of rights in this way, the Court dispensed with the issue of consensus in closing the state's margin. Whilst the distinction between conferring substantive rights and recognizing a right to campaign for substantive rights is problematic for homosexuals who seek universal access to Convention rights – because it establishes a hierarchy in which some rights may be granted 'in principle' while other rights demand the support of a European majority – it shows that the Court will bypass consensus in respect of what it believes to be fundamental rights. Consensus analysis – although seemingly inconsistent and illogical if conceived as a method in the scientific sense – is a discursive device that is invoked by the Court to legitimize its reasoning. If understood this way, consensus analysis is less a method that 'serves to anchor the court in legal, political and social reality on the ground'[88] and more a process through which reality is constructed to mandate the Court's decisions.

85 *Alekseyev v Russia*, nos. 4916/07, 25924/08 and 14599/09, 21 October 2010, § 83.
86 Ibid., § 84.
87 Ibid.
88 R. Wintemute, 'Consensus is the Right Approach for the European Court of Human Rights', *The Guardian*, Thursday 12 August 2010.

A living instrument to be interpreted in the light of present-day conditions

A central aspect of the Court's judicial function is to engage in a dynamic or evolutive interpretation of the Convention in order to realize its teleological aims. The Preamble of the Convention specifies that contracting states have committed themselves to achieving the greater unity of European nations through the 'maintenance and further realization' of human rights. The scope of the Convention in furthering human rights has been the subject of much debate both within and outside the Court. In *Golder v the United Kingdom*, the Court engaged in expansive discussion of the 'object and purpose' of the Convention and, in a separate opinion, Judge Sir Gerald Fitzmaurice strongly advocated the adoption of a 'cautious and conservative interpretation'.[89] Fitzmaurice's plea for a restrictive interpretation of the Convention was, he claimed, based on the recognition that contracting states voluntarily subscribe to a system that makes 'heavy inroads on some of the most cherished preserves of governments in the sphere of their domestic jurisdiction'.[90] Baroness Hale of the Supreme Court of the United Kingdom has more recently urged the same cautious approach to the development of 'delicately nuanced' human rights issues:

> As a supporter of the Convention and the work of the Strasbourg Court, my plea to them is to accept that there are some natural limits to the growth and development of the living tree. Otherwise I have a fear that their judgments, and those of the national courts which follow them, will increasingly be defied by our governments and Parliaments.[91]

The idea of 'natural limits' to the development of human rights, or of practising deference to contracting states, is an anathema to those who view the Convention as a set of fundamental moral principles from which governments should not be able to hide. As Heinze argues, claims that the development of some rights requires a 'delicate' or 'cautious' approach are often foundational to suppressing the expansion of homosexual rights under the Convention.[92] Yet, because the text of the Convention is open to considerable interpretation and dispute, and because human rights claims have significantly evolved in

89 *Golder v the United Kingdom*, no. 4451/70, 21 February 1975, Series A no. 18, Separate opinion of Judge Sir Gerald Fitzmaurice, § 39.

90 Ibid., § 38.

91 Baroness Hale of Richmond, 'Beanstalk or Living Instrument? How Tall Can the ECHR Grow?', Bernard's Inn Reading 2011, available HTTP: <http://www.supremecourt.gov.uk/docs/speech_110616.pdf> (accessed 18 February 2012).

92 E. Heinze, 'Sexual Orientation and International Law: A Study in the Manufacture of Cross-Cultural "Sensitivity" ', *Michigan Journal of International Law* 22, 2001, 283–309.

the time since the original drafters created it, it is inevitable that the Court must adopt an evolutive approach when using this 'constitutional instrument of European public order in the field of human rights'.[93]

The method that the Court uses to structure its dynamic and evolutive interpretation was developed in *Tyrer v the United Kingdom*, in which the Court stated that the Convention is a 'living instrument' that 'must be interpreted in the light of present-day conditions'.[94] In conceiving the Convention in this way, the Court mandated its authority to engage in hermeneutic analysis of the Convention's text and to consider the changing social, cultural and legal contexts of European societies when doing so. This was clearly demonstrated in *Enhorn v Sweden*, which concerned restrictions placed upon the rights of those with AIDS, when Judge Costa argued that 'Aids was unknown when the Convention came into force, but the Convention is a living instrument which must be interpreted in the light of present-day conditions of living (and – alas! – dying)'.[95] The living instrument doctrine is a method ostensibly designed to allow the Court to update its case law in respect of changes that the original drafters of the Convention could not foresee or conceive. What remains contentious, however, is the extent to which the Court actually reflects present-day conditions or, by contrast, seeks to interpret the Convention in order to change and establish new conditions. The living instrument doctrine can be used to endorse both judicial conservatism (by grounding evolutive interpretation in consensus analysis) and judicial activism (by providing a mechanism to expand the positive obligations of contracting states). In respect of complaints relating to homosexuality, the Court has used the living instrument doctrine in both ways.

Conservative uses of the living instrument doctrine by the Court in cases relating to homosexuality can be found in judgments that both uphold and reject applicants' complaints. In *L. and V. v Austria*,[96] for example, the Court found in favour of the applicants' complaint that Article 209 of the Austrian Criminal Code, which maintained differential minimum ages for homosexual and heterosexual sexual acts, violated their rights under Article 14 taken in conjunction with Article 8. In its judgment, which reversed the decision of the Commission in a similar facts case eight years earlier,[97] the Court invoked the living instrument doctrine in order to interpret the law in light of modern-day conditions. However, given that Austria's Constitutional Court had

93 *Chrysostomos, Papachrysostomou and Loizidou v Turkey*, nos. 15299/89, 15300/89 and 15318/89, Commission decision, 4 March 1991, § 22.

94 *Tyrer v the United Kingdom*, no. 5856/72, 25 April 1978, Series A no. 26, § 31.

95 *Enhorn v Sweden*, no. 56529/00, 25 January 2005, ECHR 2005-I, Concurring opinion of Judge Costa, § 6.

96 *L. and V. v Austria*, nos. 39392/98 and 39829/98, 9 January 2003, ECHR 2003-I.

97 *H.F. v Austria*, no. 22646/93, Commission decision, 26 June 1995.

already invalidated Article 209, and that it had been subsequently repealed by Parliament, the Court's use of the living instrument doctrine can ultimately be seen as conservative. A more recent example of a conservative use of the doctrine can be found in *Schalk and Kopf v Austria*, in which the Court relied on consensus analysis of statutory provisions across contracting states to reject the applicants' claim that Article 12 should be read in light of the present-day existence of same-sex relationships in order to grant same-sex partners access to civil marriage:

> Although [. . .] the institution of marriage has undergone major social changes since the adoption of the Convention, the Court notes that there is no European consensus regarding same-sex marriage. At present no more than six out of forty-seven Convention States allow same-sex marriage.[98]

This is an example of the Court's reluctance to use the living instrument doctrine to introduce new positive obligations across contracting states in order to challenge the heteronormativity of present-day conditions.

By contrast, the Court has used the living instrument doctrine in order to creatively interpret the Convention to challenge a heteronormative consensus. For example, in *E.B. v France*, the Court explicitly relied upon the living instrument doctrine to hold that the differential treatment of individuals seeking authorization to adopt a child on the grounds of sexual orientation constituted discrimination under the Convention. Whilst *E.B.* does not expressly grant homosexuals the right to adopt, Judge Costa stated that the judgment did advance an important general principle:

> the message sent by our Court to the States Parties is clear: a person seeking to adopt cannot be prevented from doing so merely on the ground of his or her homosexuality. This point of view might not be shared by all, for good or not so good reasons, but – rightly or wrongly – our Court, whose duty under the Convention is to interpret and ultimately apply it, considers that a person can no more be refused authorization to adopt on grounds of their homosexuality than have their parental responsibility withdrawn on those grounds.[99]

The message *is* very clear, but there is no explicit discussion in the judgment of the present-day conditions that underpinned the use of the living instrument doctrine. In the absence of any evidence supporting a consensus across

98 *Schalk and Kopf v Austria,* no. 30141/04, 24 June 2010, § 58.
99 *E.B. v France* [GC], no. 43546/02, 22 January 2008, Dissenting opinion of Judge Costa joined by Judges Türmen, Ugrekhelidze and Jočienė, § 3.

contracting states in respect of the adoption of children by homosexual applicants, the Court's use of the living instrument doctrine must be seen as a vehicle to advance its own moral judgment. Similarly, in *Kozak v Poland*, the Court upheld the complaint of an applicant in respect of legislation that prohibited the surviving partner of a same-sex relationship from succeeding to a housing tenancy following the death of his partner.[100] In response to the Polish government's claim that the difference in treatment was a necessary measure to protect the 'traditional' family, the Court stated that:

> in pursuance of that aim a broad variety of measures might be implemented by the State [. . .] Also, given that the Convention is a living instrument, to be interpreted in the light of present-day conditions [. . .], the State, in its choice of means designed to protect the family and secure, as required by Article 8, respect for family life must necessarily take into account developments in society and changes in the perception of social, civil-status and relational issues, including the fact that there is not just one way or one choice in the sphere of leading and living one's family or private life.[101]

The Court used the living instrument doctrine in *Kozak* to compel the state to change legislation in light of changing perceptions about 'the family'. However, in the absence of any analysis or evidence of these changing perceptions, the Court can again be seen to use the doctrine in an active sense to advance its own moral view of the right in question. It is judgments like *E.B.* and *Kozak* that elicit hostility from those who argue that the Court uses the living instrument doctrine as a 'banner' to illegitimately impose its view of a European public order.[102] Such a criticism fails to recognize that when the Court pursues a conservative interpretation of the Convention, it also imposes a moral view that, because it accords with majority opinion, does not provoke the equivalent level of complaint.

The Court's use of the living instrument doctrine will appear as grossly inconsistent and incoherent if it is understood as a positivistic method that is applied to enable the Court to reach the 'correct' judgment. It is better understood as a framework through which the Court legitimizes its role as interpreter of the Convention and underwrites its moral reasoning. In *Kozak*, the use of the doctrine was largely superfluous, given that the judgment followed the more general development of the Court's Article 14 jurisprudence. However, the use of the doctrine provided the Court with the opportunity to appeal to a particular conception of social reality (the reality of discrimination

100 *Kozak v Poland*, no. 13102/02, 2 March 2010.

101 Ibid., § 98.

102 Lord Hoffmann, 'The Universality of Human Rights', *Law Quarterly Review* 125, 2009, 416–432.

that is recognized by homosexual men and woman) to add weight to its moral interpretation of the Convention. That the doctrine is used in this way shows that it is subservient to, rather than productive of, the decision making of sitting judges in the Court.

Conclusion

In the ongoing debates about the relative merits of judicial formalism and activism, and about the appropriate role of judges as the 'appliers' or 'creators' of law, the Strasbourg Court attracts considerable attention. Those hostile to the Court depict its judges as unelected tyrants who progressively expand their power in order to impose a European public order and erode the legal sovereignty of nation states. Although such a view provides a comfortable myth for conservative politicians who, as Kirby argues, 'are contemptuous of fundamental human rights and jealous of any source of lawmaking power apart from their own',[103] it belies the fact that European nations themselves established, ratified and expanded the provisions of the Convention. In doing so, contracting states recognized that a judicial system was necessary to carry out a supervisory function in order to give the Convention effect. The Court cannot, therefore, perform a declaratory function or conform to legal positivism, but must engage in active interpretation of the Convention in light of the changing human rights claims that come before it. As the Court has stated, it is of 'crucial importance that the Convention is interpreted and applied in a manner which renders its rights practical and effective, not theoretical and illusory'.[104] A passive orientation to the Convention is both impossible and undesirable: 'A failure by the Court to maintain a dynamic and evolutive approach would risk rendering it a bar to reform or improvement'.[105] 'Effectiveness,' Judge Costa has argued, 'is the golden thread running through the fabric of the Strasbourg case law' and this requires that 'formalism or legalism is put aside'.[106]

However, like all legal institutions, the Court's aspiration to 'legal certainty, foreseeability and equality before the law' is at the heart of its jurisprudence.[107] In an attempt to achieve this, the Court has developed methods to maintain coherence and consistency in its case law. Whilst the Court's methods often appear to constrain its interpretation of the Convention – those frustrated by the Court's lack of development in the area of gay and lesbian rights, for

103 M. Kirby, *Judicial Activism: Authority, Principle and Policy in the Judicial Mind*, London: Sweet and Maxwell, 2004, p. 10.

104 *Scoppola v Italy (no. 2)* [GC], no. 10249/03, 17 September 2009, § 104.

105 Ibid.

106 J-P. Costa, 'On the Legitimacy of the European Court of Human Rights' Judgments', European Constitutional Law Review 7, 2011, 173–182 at 177.

107 *Scoppola v Italy (no. 2)* [GC], no. 10249/03, 17 September 2009, § 104.

instance, may see it as shackled by its adherence to legal principles – its methods are better understood as a framework through which the Court legitimizes its moral judgments. The Court's methods do not, therefore, determine its judgments but are devices through which it endorses its reasoning and objectives. This does not mean that method provides a 'smokescreen' for whimsical judgments based on the ideological interests of individual judges. But it does recognize that the Court pursues particular policy agendas and uses its methods to mandate these. As Arai-Takahashi argues: 'Evolutive interpretation and the margin of appreciation represent diametrically opposed directions of judicial policy, and the comparative method works, as it were, as a bridge between them.'[108]

As I argued in Part I of this book, the Court has adopted a particular ontological understanding of homosexuality and this has underpinned the progressive development of its case law through which it has narrowed the margin of appreciation available to states in respect of certain discriminatory practices. An evolutive approach to interpreting the Convention has been a vital foundation on which the Court has engaged in creative forms of reasoning that effectively challenge heteronormative consensus. The Court's methods have not, therefore, precluded it from issuing strong condemnations of practices that maintain inequalities on the ground of sexual orientation. However, when the Court is hesitant to challenge a prevailing heteronormative consensus, it continues to rely upon the margin of appreciation doctrine in order to mandate its decisions. As I explore throughout Part III of this book, this maintains significant gaps in the protection available to homosexuals under the Convention.

108 Y. Arai-Takahashi, *The Margin of Appreciation Doctrine and the Principle of Proportionality in the Jurisprudence of the ECHR*, Oxford: Hart Publishing, 2001, p. 199.

Part III

Existing jurisprudence and potential future developments

Chapter 4

'An essentially private manifestation of the human personality'

The limitations of Article 8

Article 8 of the Convention provides that:

1 Everyone has the right to respect for his private and family life, his home and his correspondence.
2 There shall be no interference by a public authority with the exercise of this right except such as is in accordance with the law and is necessary in a democratic society in the interests of national security, public safety or the economic well-being of the country, for the prevention of disorder or crime, for the protection of health or morals, or for the protection of the rights and freedoms of others.

Article 8 has been the powerhouse for contesting and developing the scope of human rights available to gay men and lesbians under the Convention since the Strasbourg organs first began to consider individual petitions in the 1950s. It continues to be the most frequently and successfully used article of the Convention in applications made to the Court in cases concerning sexual orientation. Across a wide range of complaints, the Court has utilized the 'private life' limb of Article 8 to review a diverse number of issues relating to homosexuality, including: sexual practices, parent–child relationships, housing tenure, employment and immigration. As I explore in the following chapter, Article 8 has also provided the foundation for a wide range of successful complaints that have challenged discrimination under Article 14 of the Convention. In this chapter, whilst acknowledging the phenomenal success of complaints brought under Article 8 and their importance in the evolution of lesbian and gay rights, I want to focus on the limitations that its use has imposed on the realization of universal Convention rights for homosexuals. My aim is not, therefore, to provide an exhaustive study of Article 8 in respect of homosexuality, but to consider why the continued focus on private life is problematic in contemporary European societies where homosexuals seek full sexual citizenship[1] and, as Stychin argues,

1 J. Weeks, 'Sexual Citizenship', *Theory, Culture and Society*, 15(3–4), 1999, 35–52.

are attempting to 'construct meaningful categories of belonging' that 'challenge and undermine the fixity of boundaries' through which they have hitherto been excluded.[2]

The Court's approach to private life

The Court's interpretation of the right to respect for private life established by Article 8 of the Convention has attracted criticism that it lacks clarity and discipline.[3] This is principally the result of the very broad and flexible interpretation adopted by the Court. From the earliest days of the Convention, the Strasbourg organs have determined that a wide range of issues fall within the ambit of private life[4] and that the concept extends beyond matters relating to the secrecy of personal information. Whilst the Convention organs have never attempted to provide a definitive definition of private life, Moreham has identified that the Court's jurisprudence is structured around a consideration of five distinct areas: physical and psychological integrity; collection and disclosure of information; living environment; identity; and personal autonomy.[5] It is the theme of personal autonomy that has been the most fruitful in developing the right to respect for private life in matters relating to homosexuality. This is essentially because the Commission established that the right to respect for private life includes the right to develop autonomous human relationships:

> For numerous anglo-saxon and French authors the right to respect for 'private life' is the right to privacy, the right to live, as far as one wishes, protected from publicity [. . .] In the opinion of the Commission, however, the right to respect for private life does not end there. It comprises also, to a certain degree, the right to establish and to develop relationships with other human beings, especially in the emotional field for the development and fulfillment of one's own personality.[6]

The Court subsequently legitimized this view:

2 C.F. Stychin, *Governing Sexuality: The Changing Politics of Citizenship and Law Reform*, Oxford: Hart, 2003, p. 23.

3 D.J. Harris, M. O'Boyle, E.P. Bates and C.M. Buckley, *Law of the European Convention on Human Rights*, Oxford: Oxford University Press, 2009.

4 See: G. Cohen-Jonathan, 'Respect for Private and Family Life', in R.St.J. Macdonald, F. Matscher and H. Petzold (eds.), *The European System for the Protection of Rights*, Alphen aan den Rijn: Kluwer, 1993.

5 N.A. Moreham, 'The Right to Respect for Private Life in the European Convention on Human Rights: A Re-examination', *European Human Right Law Review* 1, 2008, 44–79.

6 *X. v Iceland*, no. 6825/74, Commission decision, 18 May 1976, p. 87.

> The Court does not consider it possible or necessary to attempt an exhaustive definition of the notion of 'private life'. However, it would be too restrictive to limit the notion to an 'inner circle' in which the individual may live his own personal life as he chooses and to exclude therefrom entirely the outside world not encompassed within that circle. Respect for private life must also comprise to a certain degree the right to establish and develop relationships with other human beings.[7]

Article 8 imposes both negative and positive obligations on contracting states. To assess the scope of negative obligations the Court, in common with its approach to all of the qualified rights contained in Articles 8–11 of the Convention, applies a two-stage test in its review of any complaint: first, the Court assesses whether the complaint falls within the ambit of one of the rights specified in Article 8(1); and, second, it considers if there has been an interference with a right. In respect of this second consideration, the Court asks three questions: was any interference with the right in accordance with the law; did it pursue one or more of the legitimate aims set out in Article 8(2); and was it necessary in a democratic society? Any interference will be considered necessary in a democratic society if it addresses a pressing social need and, in doing so, is proportionate and the reasons given to justify it are relevant and sufficient. The Court will allow a contracting state a margin of appreciation to assess what interference is considered necessary but the breadth of this margin will vary in respect of a number of factors, which include: the nature of the right in question; its importance for the individual; the nature of the interference; and the object pursued by the interference. Crucially, as the Court has recently stated, 'the margin will tend to be narrower where the right at stake is crucial to the individual's effective enjoyment of intimate or key rights' and will be restricted where 'a particularly important facet of an individual's existence or identity is at stake', but where 'there is no consensus within the Member States of the Council of Europe, either as to the relative importance of the interest at stake or as to how best to protect it, the margin will be wider'.[8]

The Court has also determined that Article 8 creates a number of positive obligations for contracting states and has emphasized their importance in respect of the most intimate aspects of private life:

> The Court further reiterates that, while the essential object of Article 8 is to protect the individual against arbitrary interference by the public authorities, it does not merely compel the State to abstain from such interference: in addition to this negative undertaking, there may be

7 *Niemietz v Germany*, no. 13710/88, 16 December 1992, Series A no. 251-B, § 29.

8 *S. and Marper v the United Kingdom*, nos. 30562/04 and 30566/04, 4 December 2008, § 102.

> positive obligations inherent in an effective respect for private or family life. These obligations may involve the adoption of measures designed to secure respect for private life even in the sphere of the relations of individuals between themselves [. . .] However, the boundaries between the State's positive and negative obligations under Article 8 do not lend themselves to precise definition. The applicable principles are nonetheless similar. In determining whether or not such an obligation exists, regard must be had to the fair balance which has to be struck between the general interest and the interests of the individual [. . .] For the balancing of the competing interests, the Court has emphasised the particular importance of matters relating to a most intimate part of an individual's life.[9]

The expansive interpretation of private life and the lack of precise limits on positive obligations have led, as Warbick argues, to some of the Court's boldest judgments, which have taken it 'not only into jurisprudential complexity but political controversy'.[10] This has certainly been the case in matters relating to homosexuality where the Court has creatively interpreted the 'private life' aspect of Article 8 in respect of a wide range of issues.

Protecting sexual privacy

A common story told about the evolution of gay and lesbian human rights under the Convention is that they are the outcome of a progressive series of applications to Strasbourg which, beginning in the 1950s with the demand for the recognition of 'sex rights' under Article 8, developed after the success of *Dudgeon v the United Kingdom*[11] in the early 1980s into a broader campaign for 'love rights' and 'citizenship rights' under the other substantive provisions.[12] However, as I argued in Chapter 1, whilst the earliest complaints from homosexuals did relate to the criminalization of private sexual acts, a wide range of other issues, including same-sex love and freedom of expression, were present. Furthermore, applicants relied upon a wide range of Convention articles to support their complaints. It was actually the Commission, rather than applicants, who took the lead in channelling complaints relating to homosexuality under the private life provisions of Article 8. In doing so, the Strasbourg organs focused their attention solely on interferences created with private sexual acts and routinely ignored the other issues raised by applicants.

9 *Van Kück v Germany*, no. 35968/97, 12 June 2003, ECHR 2003-VII, § 70–71.
10 C. Warbick, 'The Structure of Article 8', *European Human Rights Law Review* 1, 1998, 32–44 at 33.
11 *Dudgeon v the United Kingdom*, no. 7525/76, 22 October 1981, Series A no. 45.
12 See, for example: R. Wintemute, ' "From Sex Rights" to "Love Rights": Partnership Rights as Human Rights', in N. Bamforth (ed.), *Sex Rights: The Oxford Amnesty Lectures 2002*, Oxford: Oxford University Press, 2005.

However, given that in its first consideration of homosexuality in 1955[13] the Commission had established that homosexual sexual activities fell within the ambit of private life, it is unsurprising that applicants focused attention on the private nature of their sexual activities in their complaints. They did so as a way of persuading the Court that any interference with sexual acts was a violation of their Article 8 rights. In *X. v the United Kingdom*, for example, the applicant argued that his relationship with another man 'could not have been more private until the police interfered' and, as a consequence, he 'was dragged from his home by the police and locked up; his home was ransacked and he was interrogated'.[14] The applicant's complaint against this interference hinged on the claim that he had attempted to maintain a strictly private homosexual relationship and that it was only as a result of a police investigation that aspects of this relationship entered the public domain. This complaint was, as I noted in Chapter 1, unsuccessful and the Commission upheld the state's claim that the prosecution of the applicant was a legitimate measure designed to meet the aim of protecting the rights and freedoms of others, and was necessary in a democratic society.

It is somewhat ironic that when the Strasbourg organs decided to extend the protection of Article 8 to private homosexual sex in *Dudgeon v the United Kingdom*, the applicant had not been subject to arrest or prosecution for any homosexual acts. Rather, the complaint concerned the potential effect of criminal law upon the private life of the applicant who, having been visited by the police, was informed that 'the criminal law was to be enforced'.[15] The applicant, a resident of Northern Ireland, feared potential prosecution under sections 61 and 62 of the Offences Against the Person Act 1861 (which criminalized buggery and attempted buggery); section 11 of the Criminal Law Amendment Act 1885 (which criminalized gross indecency); and the common law, which criminalized the corruption of public morals and conspiracy to outrage public decency. Unlike in England and Wales, all male homosexual acts were prohibited in Northern Ireland and an attempt to introduce legislation to establish partial decriminalization – in the draft Homosexual Offences (Northern Ireland) Order 1978 – had failed because a 'substantial body of opinion there (embracing a wide range of religious as well as political opinion) is opposed to the proposed change'.[16] The applicant claimed that, because of the existence of the criminal law, 'as a homosexual he had suffered injurious infringements in respect of his private life'.[17]

13 *W.B. v Federal Republic of Germany*, no. 104/55, Commission decision, 17 December 1955.
14 *X. v the United Kingdom*, no. 7215/75, Commission decision, 7 July 1977, pp. 41–42.
15 *Dudgeon v the United Kingdom*, no. 7525/76, Commission decision, 3 March 1978, p. 119.
16 *Dudgeon v the United Kingdom*, no. 7525/76, Commission report, 13 March 1980, § 38.
17 *Dudgeon v the United Kingdom*, no. 7525/76, Commission decision, 3 March 1978, p. 120.

In their defence of the criminal law in *Dudgeon*, the United Kingdom government invoked the Commission's previous decisions to argue that, whilst the criminalization of homosexual acts did interfere with private life, such interference was necessary in a democratic society and within a state's margin of appreciation. The government claimed that criminalizing male homosexual acts pursued two legitimate aims: the protection of the rights and freedoms of others, and the protection of morals. Although these two aims were accepted by the Commission, the Court stated that the government's aim to safeguard the moral interests and welfare of certain individuals or classes of individuals (who, it was claimed, were in need of special protection for reasons such as lack of maturity, mental disability or being in a state of dependence) amounted to one aspect of an overall attempt to protect morals. This was decisive since it allowed the Court to establish that the central question in *Dudgeon* was whether the interference with the applicant's private life was necessary in a democratic society to meet the pressing social need of protecting morals.

In *Handyside v the United Kingdom*, the Court had established that a wide margin of appreciation was available to a contracting state in order to protect morals.[18] In *Dudgeon*, the Court stressed that whilst the aim of the state in restricting a right was relevant to determining its margin, so too was the nature of the activities in question. The Court stated that homosexual sexual activities constitute 'a most intimate aspect of private life'[19] and 'an essentially private manifestation of the human personality'[20] and, in view of this, that particularly serious reasons must exist to justify any interference as necessary in a democratic society. The Court also stressed that in determining whether any interference was proportionate to the legitimate aim pursued, it must consider the two important hallmarks of tolerance and broadmindedness that characterize democratic societies.[21] The government's defence of the legal prohibition of male homosexual sex acts was that it was a necessary measure to meet the pressing social need of protecting vulnerable members of society from moral corruption and was a proportionate response in light of the strong moral opposition to homosexuality in the community. The Court regarded this argument as insufficient to justify the criminalization of private homosexual acts:

> It cannot be maintained [. . .] that there is a 'pressing social need' to make such acts criminal offences, there being no sufficient justification provided by the risk of harm to vulnerable sections of society requiring protection

18 *Handyside v the United Kingdom*, no. 5493/72, 7 December 1976, Series A no. 24.
19 *Dudgeon v the United Kingdom*, no. 7525/76, 22 October 1981, Series A no. 45, § 52.
20 Ibid., § 60.
21 Ibid., § 53.

> or by the effects on the public. On the issue of proportionality, the Court considers that such justifications as there are for retaining the law in force unamended are outweighed by the detrimental effects which the very existence of the legislative provisions in question can have on the life of a person of homosexual orientation like the applicant. Although members of the public who regard homosexuality as immoral may be shocked, offended or disturbed by the commission by others of private homosexual acts, this cannot on its own warrant the application of penal sanctions when it is consenting adults alone who are involved.[22]

There was considerable dissent to the majority judgment in *Dudgeon*. Judge Zekia argued that it was 'odd and perplexing [. . .] to underestimate the necessity of keeping a law in force for the protection of morals held in high esteem by the majority of people' when legalizing 'homosexual activities in private by adults is very likely to cause many disturbances in the country in question'.[23] Judge Walsh, following Lord Devlin,[24] rejected the view that a sphere of private morality is separable, and protectable, from social morality if, in the course of an individual's private moral conduct, he or she threatens the moral values of society as a whole:

> If it is accepted that the State has a valid interest in the prevention of corruption and in the preservation of the moral ethos of its society, then the State has a right to enact such laws as it may reasonably think necessary to achieve these objects. The rule of law itself depends on a moral consensus in the community and in a democracy the law cannot afford to ignore the moral consensus of the community, whether by being either too far below it or too far above it, the law is brought into contempt. Virtue cannot be legislated into existence but non-virtue can be if the legislation renders excessively difficult the struggle after virtue. Such a situation can have an eroding effect on the moral ethos of the community in question. The ultimate justification of law is that it serves moral ends. It is true that many forms of immorality which can have a corrupting effect are not the subject of prohibitory or penal legislation. However, such omissions do not imply a denial of the possibility of corruption or of the erosion of the moral ethos of the community but acknowledge the practical impossibility of legislating effectively for every area of immorality. Where such legislation is enacted it is a reflection of the concern of the 'prudent legislator'.[25]

22 Ibid., § 60.
23 Ibid., Dissenting opinion of Judge Zekia, § 3.
24 P. Devlin, *The Enforcement of Morals*, Oxford: Oxford University Press, 1965.
25 *Dudgeon v the United Kingdom*, no. 7525/76, 22 October 1981, Series A no. 45, Partially dissenting opinion of Judge Walsh, §14.

Yet the majority's view, which can be seen to express a Millian/liberal approach to sexuality similar to that proposed by H.L.A. Hart[26] and the 'Wolfenden Report',[27] was that the legal regulation of homosexual activities, where they are strictly separated from the public sphere, is not necessary in a democratic society to protect social morality. The importance of the judgment in *Dudgeon* cannot be underestimated. Not only did it force the United Kingdom to partially decriminalize private male homosexual acts in Northern Ireland, but this also produced a 'domino effect' resulting in partial decriminalization in Guernsey, Jersey, the Isle of Man, Gibraltar and Bermuda.[28] The judgment also underpinned decisions by the Court in similar facts cases originating in Cyprus[29] and Ireland.[30] The judgment was given significant endorsement by Recommendation 924 of the Parliamentary Assembly of the Council of Europe, which urged 'those member states where homosexual acts between consenting adults are liable to criminal prosecution, to abolish those laws and practices'.[31]

The limits of private life

In *Dudgeon*, the Court – as Moran argues – made the unprecedented judgment that not only should consensual adult homosexual acts in private be free from interference but, additionally, the freedom to engage in such acts constituted a human right.[32] In designating the private manifestation of homosexual sexuality to be a most intimate aspect of private life, the Court can be seen to have taken a significant step away from the idea, exemplified by Wolfenden, that the decriminalization of private homosexual behaviour represented a grudging democratic tolerance for private sexual acts publicly regarded as immoral.[33] Instead, the judgment implicitly conveys the idea that private sexual intimacy, regardless of sexual orientation, is of significant value to the individual and is worthy of protection. However, whilst the Court established that the criminalization of consensual homosexual acts between adults in

26 H.L.A. Hart, *Law, Liberty and Morality*, Oxford: Oxford University Press, 1963.

27 Home Office, *Report of the Committee on Homosexual Offences and Prostitution* (Cmnd. 247), London: Home Office, 1957.

28 R. Wintemute, *Sexual Orientation and Human Rights: The United States Constitution, the European Convention, and the Canadian Charter*, Oxford: Clarendon Press, 1995, p. 93.

29 *Modinos v Cyprus*, no. 15070/89, 22 April 1993, Series A no. 259.

30 *Norris v Ireland*, no. 10581/83, 26 October 1988, Series A no. 142.

31 Parliamentary Assembly of the Council of Europe, Recommendation 924, 1 October 1981. This recommendation also urged 'member states to apply the same minimum age of consent for homosexual and heterosexual acts'. The Commission and the Court did not follow this recommendation.

32 *Dudgeon v the United Kingdom*, no. 7525/76, 22 October 1981, Series A no. 45.

33 Home Office, *Report of the Committee on Homosexual Offences and Prostitution*.

private was unnecessary in a democratic society, it very explicitly set out strict limits for the protection available for such acts under Article 8.

The Court stated that whilst it was not necessary to regulate sexual acts involving 'consenting adults alone',[34] it was a 'legitimate necessity in a democratic society' to exercise 'some degree of control over homosexual conduct' to prevent the 'exploitation and corruption of those who are specially vulnerable by reason, for example, of their youth'.[35] In emphasizing the legitimacy and necessity of controlling homosexual conduct that does not take place between 'consenting adults alone', the Court gave support to the argument established by Wolfenden that homosexual conduct must be strictly segregated from the public sphere.[36] The protection the Court afforded to private acts in *Dudgeon*, therefore, provided little challenge to socially dominant ideas about homosexual men as deviant sexual predators intent on corrupting youth, or homosexuality being a 'germ' in need of domestic quarantine. In uncritically reiterating the view that exploitation and corruption may be the potential outcome of unregulated homosexual conduct in contexts where consenting adults are not alone – that is, outside of private dwellings and/or in the presence of (heterosexual) others – the Court's judgment implicitly legitimized the view that maintaining homosexuality in private was necessary.

The Court has consistently attempted to maintain a clear conceptual distinction between 'private' and 'public' manifestations of homosexuality when interpreting Article 8 in respect of complaints about sexual orientation discrimination. However, this has increasingly proved something of a challenge. For example, 10 years after *Dudgeon*, in a concurring opinion in *Modinos v Cyprus*, in which the Court upheld the applicant's complaint that the total prohibition on male homosexual acts by the Criminal Code of Cyprus violated the right to respect for private life, Judge Matscher demonstrated that he was still attempting to determine the precise scope of private life in relation to homosexual acts:

> In my view, Article 8 [. . .] will be infringed only where the law makes it a criminal offence for consenting adults to commit homosexual acts in private – and I would exclude from that rule a number of specific situations, for instance the abuse of a relationship in which one party is dependent on the other or carrying out such acts within a closed community, such as a boarding-school or a barracks, etc.[37]

34 *Dudgeon v the United Kingdom*, no. 7525/76, 22 October 1981, Series A no. 45, § 60.
35 Ibid., § 62.
36 Home Office, *Report of the Committee on Homosexual Offences and Prostitution*.
37 *Modinos v Cyprus*, no. 15070/89, 22 April 1993, Series A no. 259, Concurring opinion of Judge Matscher.

Even when homosexual conduct takes place in private domestic homes, the Court has shown that not all sexual acts qualify for protection under Article 8. In *Laskey, Jaggard and Brown v the United Kingdom*, which concerned the prosecution of a group of men engaged in consensual sadomasochistic sexual activities, the Court rejected the applicants' complaint that their convictions for assault and wounding constituted an interference with their right to respect for their private life. In their report, the Commission had stressed that, whilst 'sexual orientation and practice are of a highly personal nature and concern a most intimate aspect of private life',[38] the sexual practices in question could not be regarded as 'private'. Emphasizing that 'the conduct in question in these cases was, on any view, of an extreme nature', the Commission also stressed that there 'was also an aspect of organization'[39] involved:

> the Commission recalls for example that a significant number of people were involved, that rooms in various locations were specially equipped and that while the conduct was private in essence, it came to light through videos which were being disseminated. It was not a question of the State trespassing into a private bedroom. The Commission does not consider that the prosecution of the applicants can be considered as heralding an invasion into the private lives of people generally or as being particularly aimed at homosexuals.[40]

Several members of the Commission were not satisfied with this justification for interfering with sexual practices that are 'private in essence' and expressed grave concern about the legitimacy it gave to investigations into the 'bedrooms' of all individuals:

> If we accept that the interference in question is legitimate we inevitably open the way to Governments to intrude into persons' bedrooms to investigate allegations, for example, that spouses engage in sado-masochistic activities. Strong good reasons are necessary for such a course which in my opinion are lacking.[41]

The Court not only adopted the majority view of the Commission but went on to question whether the sexual activities actually fell within the ambit of Article 8:

38 *Laskey, Jaggard and Brown v the United Kingdom*, nos. 21627/93, 21628/93 and 21974/93, Commission report, 26 October 1995, § 55.

39 Ibid., § 62.

40 Ibid.

41 Ibid., Dissenting opinion of Mr. L. Loucaides joined by MM. S. Rrechsel, H.G. Schermers, C.L. Rozakis, J-C. Geus, J. Mucha and E. Konstantinov.

> a considerable number of people were involved in the activities in question which included, *inter alia*, the recruitment of new 'members', the provision of several specially equipped 'chambers', and the shooting of many videotapes which were distributed among the 'members' [and it] may thus be open to question whether the sexual activities of the applicants fell entirely within the notion of 'private life'.[42]

Whilst the Court ultimately accepted that the activities did fall within the scope of Article 8, it found, in view of the degree of organization involved in the activities, that the measures taken against the applicants were proportionate in meeting the legitimate aim of protecting health. In his concurring opinion, Judge Pettiti stated that the 'concept of private life cannot be stretched indefinitely', that not 'every aspect of private life automatically qualifies for protection under the Convention', and that the 'fact that the behaviour concerned takes place on private premises does not suffice to ensure complete immunity and impunity'.[43] He went on to state that the 'protection of private life means the protection of a person's intimacy and dignity, not the protection of his baseness or the promotion of criminal immoralism'.[44] Moran has criticized the Court's interpretation of private life for institutionalizing a moral order in which particular sexual practices are excluded from the protection of the Convention.[45] It is certainly the case that, in respect of homosexual sexual practices, the Strasbourg organs have consistently maintained a particular moral view about what types of activities can be regarded as private for the purposes of Article 8. For instance, the Commission found that the conviction of an Austrian man for showing a homosexual-themed pornographic video in a bar that he owned did not constitute a violation of his right to respect for private life.[46] Nor did it consider that the conviction of a prostitute for engaging in homosexual acts constituted an interference with private life.[47]

The public/private binary and the reproduction of the closet

A consequence of the Court's view that (some) homosexual acts are protectable under the Convention when they take place in private is its potential to

42 *Laskey, Jaggard and Brown v the United Kingdom*, nos. 21627/93, 21628/93 and 21974/93, Reports of Judgments and Decisions 1997-I, § 36.

43 Ibid., Concurring opinion of Judge Pettiti.

44 Ibid.

45 L.J. Moran, '*Laskey v the United Kingdom:* Learning the Limits of Privacy', *Modern Law Review* 61(1), 1998, 77–84.

46 *Reiss v Austria*, no. 23953/94, Commission decision, 6 September 1995.

47 *X. v Switzerland*, no. 11680/85, Commission decision, 10 March 1988.

reinforce the social relations of the 'closet'. Homosexuals gain access to privacy rights when they undertake to keep their sexual practices hidden from 'the public'. This is problematic because it reiterates the idea that maintaining a strict exclusion of expressions of homosexuality from the public sphere is both desirable and necessary. It perpetuates the social relations of the closet which, as Eve Sedgwick argues, provide the 'defining structure for gay oppression'[48] in contemporary societies by rendering homosexuality socially invisible and erasing it from public life:

> for many gay people [the closet] is still the fundamental feature of social life; and there can be few gay people, however courageous and forthright by habit, however fortunate in the support of their immediate communities, in whose lives the closet is not still a shaping presence.[49]

The 'shaping presence' of the closet can be seen throughout the Court's Article 8 jurisprudence in respect of homosexuality. In four sets of cases – concerning the criminalization of sexual activities in private involving more than two men, the deportation of migrants seeking asylum, prohibitions on homosexuality in the armed forces, and the adoption of children – the Court has been required to deal with complaints under Article 8 concerning issues that go beyond the rights of couples to engage in homosexual sexual acts in domestic homes. Nevertheless, in all of these cases the Court has consistently approached complaints using the framework established in *Dudgeon* and, relying on a binary separation between 'private' and 'public' manifestations of homosexuality, has reinforced the social relations of the closet.

For example, in *A.D.T. v the United Kingdom*, the Court reversed a previous decision[50] to hold that the conviction of the applicant for acts of gross indecency with up to four other men in his home constituted a violation of his Article 8 rights.[51] At the time the applicant was prosecuted the United Kingdom had partially decriminalized male homosexual acts in private if committed between two men over the age of 18 but continued to criminalize buggery and gross indecency in private when more than two persons took part or were present.[52] In its review, the Court placed significant emphasis on the fact that the applicant had 'gone to some lengths not to reveal his sexual orientation' to anyone and had 'repeated his desire for anonymity before the Court'.[53] The Court further stated that the 'applicant was involved in sexual activities with a restricted number of

48 E. Sedgwick, *Epistemology of the Closet*, Harmondsworth: Penguin, 1990, p. 71.
49 Ibid., p. 68.
50 *Johnson v the United Kingdom*, no. 10389/83, Commission decision, 17 July 1986.
51 *A.D.T. v the United Kingdom*, no. 35765/97, 31 July 2000, ECHR 2000-IX.
52 Section 1 Sexual Offences Act 1967.
53 *A.D.T. v the United Kingdom*, no. 35765/97, 31 July 2000, ECHR 2000-IX, § 25.

friends in circumstances in which it was most unlikely that others would become aware of what was going on', that there was no 'risk' of the activities entering the public domain, and that the 'activities were therefore genuinely "private"'. In view of this, the Court held that it must 'adopt the same narrow margin of appreciation as it found applicable in other cases involving intimate aspects of private life'.[54] Central to the Court's decision, therefore, was not the number of people involved in the acts but 'the purely private nature of the behaviour'.[55] The Court can therefore be seen to reproduce the social relations of the closet by emphasizing that homosexual acts are protectable under the Convention only if individuals ensure they are 'genuinely' and 'purely' private.

The same emphasis on maintaining a strict division between private and public life is acutely demonstrated by the Court's consideration of complaints brought by migrants seeking asylum. In *F. v the United Kingdom*, for example, the applicant, who was subject to deportation to Iran by the United Kingdom government, claimed that returning him to a state that operated a legal prohibition on all homosexual acts could not be regarded as proportionate. Whilst, as I explore in Chapter 8, the applicant invoked Articles 2 and 3 in respect of the risk of ill-treatment and torture he claimed would result from his return to Iran, the Court was not persuaded of the evidence offered and deemed these parts of the complaint inadmissible. This left the Court to consider the applicant's claim that the existence of laws criminalizing adult consensual homosexual acts in Iran violated an intimate aspect of his private life. This claim necessitated a consideration of the potential threat to the applicant's 'moral and physical integrity' – a form of integrity that the Court has established is encompassed by private life[56] but has rarely applied in cases relating to homosexuality. The Court found that since the applicant had not convincingly shown, in respect of his Article 2 and 3 claims, that he was at immediate risk of ill-treatment, his Article 8 claim was inadmissible:

> Insofar as it is apparent that he would live under a ban against homosexual adult consensual relations, which would in Contracting States disclose a violation of Article 8 of the Convention [. . .], the Court observes that its case law has found responsibility attaching to Contracting States in respect of expelling persons who are at risk of treatment contrary to Articles 2 and 3 of the Convention. This is based on the fundamental importance of these provisions, whose guarantees it is imperative to render effective in practice [. . .]. Such compelling considerations do not automatically apply under the other provisions of the Convention. On a purely pragmatic basis, it cannot be required that an expelling Contracting

54 Ibid., § 37.
55 Ibid., § 38.
56 *Bensaid v the United Kingdom*, no. 44599/98, 6 February 2001, ECHR 2001-I.

> State only return an alien to a country which is in full and effective enforcement of all the rights and freedoms set out in the Convention.[57]

In deeming the applicant's Article 8 claim inadmissible, the Court established the principle that, whilst an interference with private life will result from the deportation of a homosexual to a country that criminalizes homosexual sexual acts, repatriation can be justified as a proportionate response to meet a legitimate aim (the aim frequently cited in similar facts cases is the 'economic well-being of the country')[58] and does not constitute a violation of the Convention. Although 'sexual orientation and activity concern an intimate aspect of private life',[59] the Court does not interpret Article 8 to require contracting states to have a positive obligation to protect those seeking asylum from states who promote policies detrimental to their moral and physical integrity.[60] A key influence on the Court's reasoning in *F. v the United Kingdom* was the evidence produced by the United Kingdom government (obtained from the Canadian Immigration and Refugee Board) suggesting that 'discreet' homosexual practices were tolerated in Iran.[61] The Court accepted the argument that men

57 *F. v the United Kingdom* (dec), no. 17341/03, 22 June 2004, § 3.

58 Council of Europe, *Asylum and the European Convention on Human Rights*, Strasbourg: Council of Europe Publishing, 2010.

59 *Laskey, Jaggard and Brown v the United Kingdom*, nos. 21627/93, 21628/93 and 21974/93, 19 February 1997, Reports of Judgments and Decisions 1997-I, § 36.

60 In an outstanding application, lodged by an asylum-seeker complaining about deportation from the United Kingdom, the applicant claims that 'as a "butch" lesbian who dresses like a man, she would be at risk in Zimbabwe, not only from her family, but also from the wider community because of their attitude towards gays and lesbians'. Given the Court's case-law it seems likely that, unless the applicant can establish a successful case under Articles 2 or 3 of the Convention, any Article 8 complaint will fail. *D.B.N. v the United Kingdom*, no. 26550/10, Statement of facts, 11 May 2010.

61 *F. v the United Kingdom* (dec), no. 17341/03, 22 June 2004. This approach was formulated in *Z.B. v the United Kingdom* (no. 16106/90, Commission decision, 10 February 1990) in which the applicant complained about his deportation from the United Kingdom to Cyprus as the result of an overstay on his visa. The Commission would not accept the argument that deportation constituted an unjustified interference with his Convention rights because of the impossibility of his partner joining him in Cyprus due to the risks of prosecution and imprisonment for homosexual acts. A key aspect of the Commission's decision was its assessment of the risk posed by the applicant's deportation: 'while the evidence indicates that the applicant might at some stage in the future be subject to the risk of prosecution for homosexual acts it does not indicate that the risk is high'. The 'evidence' that underpinned the Commission's assessment was a judicial review from the English High Court in which it was argued that, if deported to Cyprus, 'it is not inevitable that [the applicant] will openly behave in a homosexual manner, nor is it inevitable that if he does so he will suffer as a result anything which would properly be described as persecution [. . .] Of course, on the evidence, if the Appellant were to indulge in certain types of homosexual activity he would risk prosecution [. . .] the risk of prosecution would be avoided by self-restraint'. The Commission implicitly endorsed the idea that the applicant could exercise 'restraint' over his sexual orientation in order to avoid prosecution for homosexual behaviours.

who maintained a strict separation of their homosexual identity and practices from the public sphere would be unlikely to encounter a threat to their physical or moral integrity amounting to a violation of the Convention. The Court has maintained this emphasis on 'discretion' when considering the risks posed to individuals repatriated to states that criminalize homosexual acts, although it has since been rejected by the Supreme Court of the United Kingdom.[62]

If in *F. v the United Kingdom*, the Court can be seen to emphasize the need for homosexuals to stay 'in' the closet, in two cases that concerned the prohibition on homosexuality in the UK armed forces the Court can be seen to stress the need to 'come out'. In *Smith and Grady v the United Kingdom*[63] and *Lustig-Prean and Beckett v the United Kingdom*,[64] both involving complaints by service personnel who had been subject to intrusive investigations and dismissal from work on the grounds of their sexual orientation, the Court reversed an earlier decision[65] and extended the protection of private life to the applicants. In its review, the Court shoehorned a range of complaints about the effects of the legal prohibition of homosexuality on the applicants' lives into a narrow discussion of privacy. In *Smith and Grady*, for example, the applicants brought their complaint under a range of Articles (including 3, 10 and 14) but the Court focused its attention solely on their Article 8 claim. The Court's judgment was that discharging the applicants from the armed forces on the sole basis of their sexual orientation interfered with their private life and, despite claims from the government that such interference was justified to prevent the significant and negative effect on morale created by the presence of homosexuals in the armed forces, that interference with a most intimate aspect of private life was not justifiable. However, a key aspect of the Court's reasoning was the 'especially grave'[66] impact of the interference with private life that was created by the 'exceptionally intrusive character' of investigations into the applicants' sexual orientation.[67] The Court stated that:

> While the applicants' administrative discharges were a direct consequence of their homosexuality, the Court considers that the justification

62 In *H.J. (Iran) & H.T. (Cameroon) v Secretary of State for the Home Department* ([2010] UKSC 31) the Supreme Court unanimously rejected the idea that 'discretion' is an appropriate basis for assessing the risk faced by gay men and lesbians returned to nation states that criminalize homosexual acts. The Supreme Court stated that the words 'discreet' and 'discretion' are euphemisms for 'concealment' and that expecting gay men and lesbians to conceal their sexualities is unacceptable and objectionable.

63 *Smith and Grady v the United Kingdom*, nos. 33985/96 and 33986/96, 27 September 1999, ECHR 1999-VI.

64 *Lustig-Prean and Beckett v the United Kingdom*, no. 31417/96 and 32377/96, 27 September 1999.

65 *B. v the United Kingdom*, no. 9237/81, Commission decision, 12 October 1983.

66 *Smith and Grady v the United Kingdom*, nos. 33985/96 and 33986/96, 27 September 1999, ECHR 1999-VI, § 90.

67 Ibid., § 91.

> for the investigations into the applicants' homosexuality requires separate consideration in so far as those investigations continued after the applicants' admissions of homosexuality.[68]
>
> In such circumstances, the Court considers that the Government have not offered convincing and weighty reasons justifying the continued investigation of the applicants' sexual orientation once they had confirmed their homosexuality to the air force authorities.[69]

Similarly, in *Lustig-Prean and Beckett v the United Kingdom*, the Court stated:

> that the Government has not offered convincing and weighty reasons justifying the continued investigation of the applicants' sexual orientation once they had confirmed their homosexuality to the naval authorities.[70]

In both *Smith and Grady* and *Lustig-Prean and Beckett*, a central factor determining the success of the applicants' Article 8 complaint about the investigation of their sexual orientation was their readiness to 'confirm' they were homosexuals. In other words, it was their willingness to 'come out' of the closet that persuaded the Court that the investigations into their private life were unnecessary. This is clear because, although a blanket ban against homosexuals serving in the armed services was found to be a violation of the applicants' Article 8 rights, the Court remained equivocal about the violation created by the investigations. The Court did not rule, for instance, that investigations into sexual orientation interfere with Article 8 rights *per se* but, rather, that there was disproportionate interference once the applicants had 'confirmed' their homosexuality. Ironically, then, gaining access to the rights associated with private life depended upon the applicants coming out of the closet.[71]

68 Ibid., § 106.

69 Ibid., § 110.

70 *Lustig-Prean and Beckett v the United Kingdom*, no. 31417/96 and 32377/96, 27 September 1999, § 103.

71 It follows from this that where a public authority requires knowledge of sexual orientation and where individuals do not confirm their homosexual identity and/or practice, investigations by contracting states might be deemed both legitimate and proportionate. Bamforth argues that *Norris v Ireland* (no. 10581/83, 26 October 1988, Series A no. 142), in which the Court held that a criminal law prohibiting homosexual sex violated the Article 8 rights of the applicant even though he had never been subject to any police investigation, establishes that the mere existence of a law that allows investigations into sexual orientation contravenes Convention rights. However, it does not follow from *Norris* that all investigations into an individual's sexual orientation will be deemed a violation of Article 8. *Norris* relates to the interference with private sexual activity and not with, as I explore below, civil contexts in which the disclosure of sexual orientation is deemed necessary by public authorities. See: N. Bamforth, 'Sexual Orientation Discrimination after *Grant v South-West Trains*', *Modern Law Review* 63, 2000, 694–720.

Yet when homosexuals do come out, the Court is not always willing to recognize that the discrimination resulting from this constitutes a violation of the Convention. This was certainly the case in *Fretté v France*, which concerned a complaint about the refusal of an application for authorization to adopt a child on the grounds of sexual orientation.[72] The applicant claimed that a policy of refusing homosexuals authorization to adopt forced him to 'choose between denying his sexual orientation or being penalized' and, as a consequence, meant that he could either seek to become a parent or remain 'true to his sexual orientation'.[73] The Court stated that the applicant's 'avowed homosexuality' was the decisive factor that determined the refusal of his application[74] but that, in pursuing a legitimate aim, and in the absence of a European consensus on adoption by homosexual parents, this did not constitute a violation of Article 8. Aside from the specific issue of the adoption of children, the judgment reveals the general limitations of the protection available to homosexuals under the private life component of Article 8. Whilst Article 8 provides protection from invasive policies that interfere with the capacity to freely engage in consensual homosexual relationships, other forms of discriminatory treatment, as I discuss in the next chapter, may fall outside of its scope. Indeed, as Judge Costa stated in his partly concurring opinion, there is wide debate about whether the form of discrimination experienced by Mr. Fretté actually relates to private life:

> The rejection of Mr. Fretté's application for authorization was not in itself a violation of his private life [. . .] Might it legitimately be said that the very reasons for the negative response constituted an interference in his private life in that they stigmatized a certain choice of lifestyle? There may be some hesitation on this point but ultimately I do not believe it can be true [. . .] Whether the authorities were right or wrong is another question, but in any event their decision does not seem to me to affect the right to respect for private and/or family life within the meaning of Article 8.[75]

In Judge Costa's view, the discrimination experienced by the applicant did not affect his private life because it did not, in essence, interfere with an intimate aspect of his existence – it did not inhibit the 'private manifestation of the human personality'. If the concept of private life is used to consider sexual orientation within the terms suggested by Judge Costa, then a fundamental distinction is made between forms of sexual orientation discrimination that

72 *Fretté v France*, no. 36515/97, 26 February 2002, ECHR 2002-I.
73 Ibid., § 28.
74 Ibid., § 32.
75 Ibid., Partly concurring opinion of Judge Costa joined by Judges Jungwiert and Traja.

relate to the private and public spheres. Judge Costa suggests that forms of discrimination like that experienced by Mr. Fretté do not violate Article 8 because they do not relate to an intimate aspect of private life. However, given that it was the very mention of homosexuality – which Judge Costa said Mr. Fretté had 'courageously revealed during the inquiries carried out as part of the authorization procedure'[76] – that resulted in the refusal for authorization to adopt a child, the treatment experienced by the applicant must be seen to have a fundamental impact upon his private life. The policy of the adoption authorities interfered with Mr. Fretté's private life because it provided him with a stark choice: he could conceal this aspect of his 'human personality' and, in doing so, gain access to adopting a child (although, in light of the armed forces' judgments discussed above, had Mr. Fretté chosen this course of action then an investigation into his private life by the public authorities may have been regarded as legitimate and necessary by the Court until he 'confirmed' his homosexuality) or publicly reveal his sexual orientation and suffer discrimination. In *E.B. v France*, the Court overturned its judgment in *Fretté* and, as I have argued elsewhere, provided a rare challenge to the heteronormativity of the public sphere in which gay men and lesbians are often required to conceal their sexual identity and practices.[77]

A key problem with the Court's interpretation of the private life provisions of Article 8 in respect of homosexuality is its tendency to reproduce the conceptual apparatus of the closet. Sexual orientation is imagined as a form of private practice that is protectable when it is segregated from wider social life. Whilst the Court can only deal with the complaints that come before it, its fixation on private life has frequently resulted in its refusal to consider complaints brought under other articles and this, in turn, has encouraged applicants to rely on the private life provisions of Article 8. Instead of dealing with the issue of 'group sex' as a right to association, of discharge from the armed services as a matter of degrading treatment or freedom of expression, and of the refusal for authorization to adopt a child as a violation of family life, the Court has consistently maintained that all of these issues concern 'privacy'. In contrast to Lord Mustill's argument that the Court forces issues under the private life provisions of Article 8 because the Convention lacks appropriate provisions to address the range of complaints that come before it,[78] the Court can be seen to focus on private life because of its ontological conception of homosexuality as an 'essentially private' phenomenon.

76 Ibid.

77 P. Johnson, 'Heteronormativity and the European Court of Human Rights', *Law and Critique*, 23(1), 2012, 43–66.

78 *R v Brown* [1994] 1 AC 212.

The political consequences of the Court's interpretation of private life

A problematic consequence of the Court's strong reliance on a public/private binary when reviewing complaints relating to homosexuality is the legitimacy it lends to a conceptual framework that contracting states continue to use to justify mechanisms of social control designed to suppress the leakage of homosexuality into the public sphere. An example of this can be seen in the decision by the President of Latvia, in 2005, to sign an amendment to Article 110 of the Latvian Constitution to explicitly define marriage as 'the union between a man and a woman' (a direct result of parliamentary efforts to enforce legal discrimination in marriage on the grounds of sexual orientation), which she justified with recourse to a distinction between private and public rights:

> The debates which took place in the Saeima [the Latvian parliament] when discussing this amendment, in my view, very often demonstrated very explicit intolerance and explicit homophobia, which I believe, in a democratic nation neither should be [expected or] encouraged. People can have their own religious beliefs, their own understanding of what is sin and what is not, what is appropriate and what is not appropriate behaviour. However, as a president, I would like to remind, that in a democratic nation as we are, a private life is separated from a public sphere and what people do in their intimacy is no one's business, unless it contradicts our[s] [. . .] I would like to remind everyone, that we want to see our nation where democracy, in its most deepest and true expression, prevails, which means each and everyone is equally valued as a human being, before the state and not only before the God. Everyone is equal in their rights [. . .] We all want to enjoy freedom provided by our constitution and our democracy. Please, let us be tolerant towards other people's freedom of choice![79]

The 'freedom of choice', the rights that we are all 'equal in', and the 'tolerance' required to ensure these, are presented here in relation to 'private manifestations' of homosexuality. It is on the basis of extending 'freedom' and 'equality' to homosexuals through a 'tolerance' of private sexuality that a claim is made to the limits of these rights in relation to the public sphere. By making the private sphere ('what people do in their own intimacy') separate from the public sphere, the Latvian President also reiterated the heteronormativity of

79 V. Vike-Freiberga, 'Statement By the President of Latvia Regarding Her Decision To Sign a Constitutional Amendment Defining Marriage as a Union of a Man and a Woman', 21 December 2005, available HTTP: <http://www.ilga-europe.org/europe/guide/country_by_country/latvia/latvian_president_signs_homophobic_constitutional_amendment> (last accessed 20 February 2012).

the public sphere where, it is claimed, homosexuality becomes 'our' business and provides a legitimate basis for discriminating against homosexuals in civil society. Whilst there has been some evolution in the Court's approach, it continues to operate a similar public/private binary in its conception of homosexuality. In *Alekseyev v Russia*, for example, whilst the Court made the decision to uphold the applicant's complaint about a refusal to permit a public assembly for the purposes of holding a 'gay pride' event, it went to great lengths to stress that the event would not 'involve any graphic demonstration of obscenity', 'nudity' or 'sexually provocative behaviour' that might 'criticize public morals or religious views'.[80] Although, as I discuss in Chapter 7, *Alekseyev* is a significant judgment that evolves Convention rights for homosexuals, it still maintains the idea that there are aspects of 'homosexual conduct' that must be separated from the public sphere in order to protect the 'morals' and 'views' of the heterosexual majority.

A result of the Court's maintenance of a public/private binary when adjudicating complaints in respect of homosexuality is its reproduction of the social relations of the closet in which those who 'come out' continue to suffer forms of discrimination. On the one hand, coming out of the closet is the basis for asserting a human right to have one's 'avowed' private life protected, while on the other hand, coming out continues to render individuals excluded from the civil institutions that they wish to be 'in'. As Fuss argues, to come out confirms one's status as an outsider and places one in the realm of social exclusion and civil deprivation that outsiderhood imposes.[81] It is perhaps for this reason that the applicants in *N.N. and T.A. v Belgium*, a homosexual couple whose love letters had been disclosed in an application for divorce by the wife of *T.A.*, complained about a violation of their right to respect for correspondence under Article 8.[82] Homosexuals are acutely aware of the social vulnerabilities created by outsider status in contracting states where, although the statutory criminalization of homosexual sex has been abolished, there remain strong social and cultural relations of homophobic discrimination. Such relations will determine, to varying degrees, the interaction between individuals and the legal and civil institutions of nation states, and potentially limit the 'public' demands that homosexuals can make for the protection of 'private' life. Conceiving sexual orientation as a discrete aspect of human existence that is protectable when it is detached from the public sphere does not address this continuing discrimination.

80 *Alekseyev v Russia*, nos. 4916/07, 25924/08 and 14599/09, 21 October 2010, § 82.

81 Fuss, D., 'Inside/Out', in D. Fuss (ed.), *Inside/Out: Lesbian Theories, Gay Theories*, New York: Routledge, 1991.

82 *N.N. and T.A. v Belgium*, no. 65097/01, 13 May 2008.

Family life

One of the key consequences of the Court's fixation on private life in matters relating to homosexuality has been its underdevelopment of the 'family life' limb of Article 8. The systematic failure of the Court to consider a wide range of issues relating to same-sex relationships under family life has not been accidental. Rather, it is the direct result of the Court's deliberate reading of Article 8 to separate the rights associated with 'private' and 'family' life. There are two ways of understanding why the Court has pursued this interpretation of Article 8. On the one hand, the Court's interpretative approach has allowed it to challenge the view that the phrase 'private and family life' establishes a right to a sphere of existence that is defined by familial relationships. This has been important because, in contemporary European societies where conceptions of 'the family' are hegemonically heteronormative, the Court has established that the right to a sphere of sexual privacy exists outside of familial relationships. In doing so, the Court has moved beyond the interpretation of Article 8 offered in *Dudgeon v the United Kingdom* by Judge Walsh in which sexual privacy is imagined to be protectable only when it is established within heterosexual family formations:

> It is to be noted that Article 8 [. . .] of the Convention speaks of 'private and family life'. If the *ejusdem generis* rule is to be applied, then the provision should be interpreted as relating to private life in that context as, for example, the right to raise one's children according to one's own philosophical and religious tenets and generally to pursue without interference the activities which are akin to those pursued in the privacy of family life and as such are in the course of ordinary human and fundamental rights. No such claim can be made for homosexual practices.[83]

The Court's reading of Article 8 has generally avoided this heteronormative interpretation by giving private life autonomy (something that would not be possible if, like the African Charter on Human and Peoples' Rights, the Convention omitted private life in its articles on the family). On the other hand, by siphoning issues relating to homosexuality into the 'private life' limb of Article 8, the Court can be seen to have maintained a strongly heteronormative conception of family life. Whilst the Court has creatively evolved its jurisprudence to establish that 'the institution of the family is not fixed, be it historically, sociologically or even legally'[84] in order to take account of a range of family formations, it has maintained the view that the family is a

83 *Dudgeon v the United Kingdom*, no. 7525/76, 22 October 1981, Series A no. 45, § 52, Partially dissenting opinion of Judge Walsh, § 23.

84 *Mazurek v France*, no. 34406/97, 1 February 2000, ECHR 2000-II, § 52.

heterosexual institution.[85] As Hart argues, although the Court has dealt with a range of issues relating to the biological, social, legal and symbolic relationships that together comprise 'a family',[86] it has been reluctant to acknowledge that these involve homosexual relationships.

The aversion of the Strasbourg organs to recognizing same-sex relationships under the family life provisions of Article 8 has been the result of a pervasive 'heterosexual imaginary'[87] in its conceptualization of the family. Decades of decisions and judgments show that, because the family has been conceived in strictly heterosexual terms, considering homosexual relationships under the family life provisions of Article 8 was impossible. For example, a separate opinion annexed in the Commission's report in *X. v the United Kingdom* by Mr. Opsahl demonstrates the extent to which considering a homosexual relationship as 'a family' was inconceivable.[88] The case concerned a complaint about the higher minimum age for homosexual sexual acts in the United Kingdom, which, Mr. Opsahl stated, created a 'minor' interference with the applicant's private life. Mr. Opsahl reasoned that because the applicant was over the threshold of the minimum age, as long as he obeyed the law, he could engage in homosexual sex with others over the minimum age. Mr. Opsahl compared the applicant's situation with his sexual partner who, being under the minimum age, suffered a 'much more significant interference' because he was denied the right to engage in any homosexual sex. Mr. Opsahl bemoaned the fact that the Commission could not consider the issue of the interference with the applicant's partner's rights because the Convention offered no way of considering a complaint in respect of a 'common private life'.[89] Yet, what Mr. Opsahl and his colleagues in the Commission could have considered, in order to capture the full effect of the interference, was the applicant's right to private *and* family life. That it didn't occur to them to do this demonstrates the hegemony of a heteronormative understanding of the family, which made considering a relationship between the two men under the 'family life' limb of Article 8 unthinkable.

Despite a changing European social landscape, in which non-heterosexual familial relations have become increasingly established (with and without the

85 For a discussion of the Court's evolution of the concept of 'family life' under Article 8, see: L. Hodson, 'Ties That Bind: Towards a Child-Centred Approach to Lesbian, Gay, Bi-Sexual and Transgender Families under the ECHR', *International Journal of Children's Rights* (in press), 2012.

86 L. Hart, 'Individual Adoption by Non-Heterosexuals and the Order of Family Life in the European Court of Human Rights', *Journal of Law and Society*, 36(4), 2009, 536–557.

87 C. Ingraham, 'The Heterosexual Imaginary: Feminist Sociology and Theories of Gender', in S. Seidman (ed.), *Queer Theory/Sociology*, Oxford: Blackwell, 1996.

88 *X. v the United Kingdom*, no. 7215/75, Commission report, 12 October 1978, Separate opinion of Mr. Opsahl.

89 Ibid., p. 49a.

support of domestic legislation), the Court has been reluctant to regard homosexual relationships as falling within the ambit of family life. While sociologists and anthropologists have described the development of 'families of choice'[90] in contemporary societies, the Court has maintained a very restrictive heteronormative view. In *E.B. v France*, for example, whilst the applicant claimed that her refusal for authorization to adopt a child constituted a violation of her right to family life, since it concerned an attempt to create a familial relationship with a child, the Court focused only on the interference with her private life.[91] In *Mata Estevez v Spain*, the Court would not recognize the applicant's complaint that, following the death of his male partner, a refusal to award him a survivor's pension that was available to the surviving partner of a heterosexual marriage amounted to discriminatory treatment that infringed his right to respect for his private and family life:

> As regards establishing whether the decision in question concerns the sphere of 'family life' within the meaning of Article 8 § 1 of the Convention, the Court reiterates that, according to the established case law of the Convention institutions, long-term homosexual relationships between two men do not fall within the scope of the right to respect for family life protected by Article 8 of the Convention [. . .] The Court considers that, despite the growing tendency in a number of European States towards the legal and judicial recognition of stable *de facto* partnerships between homosexuals, this is, given the existence of little common ground between the Contracting States, an area in which they still enjoy a wide margin of appreciation [. . .] Accordingly, the applicant's relationship with his late partner does not fall within Article 8 in so far as that provision protects the right to respect for family life.[92]

In this case, the Court relied upon consensus analysis to legitimize its view that homosexual partnerships do not constitute a form of family life recognizable under the Convention.[93] However, in previous decisions by both the Commission and the Court, no use was made of consensus analysis to mandate the Strasbourg organ's own heteronormative interpretation of family life. For

90 See: K. Weston, *Families We Choose: Lesbians, Gays, Kinship*, Irvington, NY: Columbia University Press, 1998. See also: J. Weeks, B. Heaphy and C. Donovan, *Same Sex Intimacies: Families of Choice and Other Life Experiments*, London: Routledge, 2001.

91 *E.B. v France* [GC], no. 43546/02, 22 January 2008.

92 *Mata Estevez v Spain* (dec), no. 56501/00, 10 May 2001, ECHR 2001-VI.

93 In their concurring opinion in *J.M. v the United Kingdom* (no. 37060/06, 28 September 2010), Judges Garlicki, Hirvelä and Vučinić stated that the judgment in *Mata Estevez v Spain* to exclude homosexual relationships from family life was wrong: 'Judicial self-restraint is often a virtue, but not in cases in which courts should admit their own mistakes. It cannot be excluded that the Court was wrong already in Mata Estevez.'

example, in *X. and Y. v the United Kingdom*, which concerned the deportation of one of the applicants who was in a same-sex relationship with the other, the Commission made the unilateral statement that: 'Despite the modern evolution of attitudes towards homosexuality [. . .] the applicants' relationship does not fall within the scope of the right to respect for family life ensured by Article 8.'[94] Such a view has remained axiomatic in similar facts cases and applicants seeking redress for enforced deportation have been unsuccessful in advancing the claim that their same-sex 'stable relationship is comparable with family life and merits similar protection as private life under Article 8'.[95]

For example, in *C. and L.M. v the United Kingdom*, the two applicants, a mother and her child, complained that their deportation interfered with their right to respect for family life in two respects: first, the mother's right to family life was violated by a failure to recognize the relationship between herself, her partner and her child as a *de facto* family unit; second, the child's right to family life was violated by a failure to recognize her best interests in growing up in a stable family composed of monogamous parents.[96] The Commission paid no attention to the issues raised regarding the best interests of the child, but focused exclusively on the question of whether a lesbian relationship fell within the ambit of family life. In stating that lesbian relationships do not constitute a family life under Article 8 the Commission stressed that giving 'priority and better guarantees to traditional established families, rather than other established relationships like a lesbian partnership', was within the margin of appreciation afforded to contracting states.[97] Furthermore, in *Kerkhoven, Hinke and Hinke v Netherlands*, the Commission established that the family life provisions of Article 8 do not impose any positive obligations on contracting states to grant parental rights to non-biological parents in a same-sex relationship.[98]

The importance placed by the Strasbourg organs on protecting the 'traditional' (heterosexual) family is apparent throughout its jurisprudence. For instance, in *S. v the United Kingdom*, the Commission found that, whilst the applicant was in a stable and cohabiting same-sex relationship, domestic legislation that excluded her from inheriting a secure housing tenancy from her deceased partner did not fall within the scope of family life:

> The Commission accepts that the treatment accorded to the applicant was different from the treatment she would have received if the partners

94 *X. and Y. v the United Kingdom*, no. 9369/81, Commission decision, 3 May 1983, p. 221.
95 *W.J. and D.P v the United Kingdom*, no. 12513/86, Commission decision, 13 July 1987.
96 *C. and L.M. v the United Kingdom*, no. 14753/89, Commission decision, 9 October 1989.
97 Ibid.
98 *Kerkhoven, Hinke and Hinke v Netherlands*, no. 15666/89, Commission decision, 19 May 1992.

> had been of different sexes. The Commission finds that the aim of the legislation in question was to protect the family, a goal similar to the protection of the right to respect for family life guaranteed by Article 8 [. . .] of the Convention [. . .] The Commission considers that the family (to which the relationship of heterosexual unmarried couples living together as husband and wife can be assimilated) merits special protection in society and it sees no reason why a High Contracting Party should not afford particular assistance to families.[99]

In *Karner v Austria*, the Court upheld the applicant's complaint against legislation that prohibited him from succeeding to a tenancy previously held by his deceased same-sex partner, although it explicitly sidestepped the issue of family life by stating that the case fell within the ambit of the right to respect for one's home.[100] Although *Karner* is a rare example of the Court not forcing a complaint relating to homosexuality into the private life limb of Article 8, it nevertheless focused on 'home' to avoid the issue of family life.

The heteronormative approach of the Strasbourg organs to family life continued unchanged until the Court gave its judgments in *Schalk and Kopf v Austria*[101] and *P.B. and J.S. v Austria*[102] in 2010. In both cases, the Court finally relinquished its trenchant view that same-sex partnerships do not fall under family life:

> The Court notes that [. . .] a rapid evolution of social attitudes towards same-sex couples has taken place in many member States [. . .] In view of this evolution the Court considers it artificial to maintain the view that, in contrast to a different-sex couple, a same-sex couple cannot enjoy 'family life' for the purposes of Article 8. Consequently the relationship of [. . .] a cohabiting same-sex couple living in a stable *de facto* partnership, falls within the notion of 'family life', just as the relationship of a different-sex couple in the same situation would.[103]

The Court has also recently declared admissible an application lodged by two women who, in a long-term relationship and co-parenting the biological child of one of the applicants, complained about the inability under French law of the non-biological parent to legally adopt the child. In declaring the complaint admissible under Article 8, the Court has stated that:

99 *S. v the United Kingdom*, no. 11716/85, Commission decision, 14 May 1986, § 7.
100 *Karner v Austria*, no. 40016/98, 24 July 2003, ECHR 2003-IX.
101 *Schalk and Kopf v Austria*, no. 30141/04, 24 June 2010.
102 *P.B. and J.S. v Austria*, no. 18984/02, 22 July 2010.
103 *Schalk and Kopf v Austria*, no. 30141/04, 24 June 2010, § 93–94.

> The [. . .] case concerns two people who have lived together since 1989 and entered into a civil partnership in 2002 which established contractual ties between them concerning the organisation of their life together [. . .] One of the partners is the biological mother of A., a child wished for by both partners and conceived by means of medically-assisted procreation using an anonymous donor. The applicants have raised A. since she was born and are jointly and actively involved in her upbringing, a fact acknowledged by the domestic courts. In these circumstances, the Court considers that the relationship between the applicants and A. amounts to 'family life' within the meaning of Article 8 of the Convention.[104]

This recent shift in the Court's interpretation of the family life limb of Article 8 is important since it opens the possibility of extending both positive and negative rights to homosexuals in respect of a wide range of issues. It has the potential to evolve rights for homosexuals under the Convention by considering complaints outside of the confines of private life. However, as I will discuss in the following Chapter and in Chapter 6, the Court's recognition that homosexual relationships fall within the ambit of family life does not guarantee access to a new range of rights. In *Schalk and Kopf v Austria*, for example, whilst the Court conceded that a same-sex couple formed a family unit that was analogous to a different-sex couple, it did not uphold the applicants' complaint that their exclusion from civil marriage constituted a violation of their right to respect for family life. Although some commentators have advanced a sanguine interpretation of the Court's evolution of family life in *Schalk and Kopf* – for example, by viewing it as a 'hidden but hopeful message' of the Court's intention to expand the rights of same-sex couples in respect of access to legal recognition for their partnerships[105] – the Court's overall case law encourages a more cautious analysis. As I explore in the next chapter, there are significant gaps in the Court's case law in respect of homosexual rights that result from what Bamforth describes as a haphazard and case-specific application of Article 8 when it is considered in conjunction with Article 14.[106]

Conclusion

The Court's interpretation of Article 8 has been decisive in fashioning a range of rights for homosexuals under the Convention. The private life limb of

104 *Gas and Dubois v France* (dec), no. 25951/07, 31 August 2010.

105 C. Baldwin, 'The European Court's Hidden But Hopeful Message on Same-Sex Marriage', *The Guardian*, 29 June 2010.

106 N. Bamforth, 'Families But Not (Yet) Marriages? Same-Sex Partners and the Developing European Convention "Margin of Appreciation" ', *Child and Family Law Quarterly* 23(1), 2011, 128–143.

Article 8 has been used to grant protection from discrimination in matters such as housing, employment and sexual relationships. Recognition that these issues fall within the scope of private life, and are protectable because of it, was not inevitable. As I argued in Chapter 1, whilst the Strasbourg organs have always regarded the criminalization of homosexual sex to interfere with private life, they maintained until the early 1980s that such interference was not a violation of the Convention. The Court's groundbreaking recognition in *Dudgeon v the United Kingdom* that the criminalization of consensual acts constitutes a violation of the right to respect for private life has provided a significant basis on which subsequent rights have been developed. Campaigning for the greater protection of private life has remained axiomatic to the political project of establishing full sexual citizenship for homosexuals.[107] Whilst there is every reason to be critical of the focus on private and family life that is inherent in contemporary sexual politics – particularly of the way that the demand for these 'domestic' rights reproduces a private/public binary through which homosexuals become privatized and heteronormative social relations are protected[108] – the right to respect for private life has provided an important 'building block' from which other human rights claims can be articulated. This is lacking in many jurisdictions outside of Europe where discrimination on the grounds of sexual orientation is understood to not constitute a violation of the right to private life. For example, although Article 37 of the Constitution of the Federal Republic of Nigeria duplicates the substance of Article 8(1) of the Convention and provides the right to respect for private life, Nigerian criminal law specifies a total prohibition on all homosexual sexual acts. Without the Court's interpretation of Article 8 in *Dudgeon*, a similar situation may still exist in contemporary European societies.

However, as I will explore in subsequent chapters, the Court's understanding of homosexuality, as an essentially private manifestation of human personality, has created severe limitations in the development of full Convention rights for homosexuals. The repetitive emphasis in the Court's judgments on homosexuality as a matter of private life has legitimized a framework in which the rights associated with the domestic sphere have been separated from the rights associated with social, public and institutional participation. This is a distinction that continues to be used to justify discriminatory practices on the grounds of sexual orientation in nation states across contemporary Europe. It is now common for those opposed to the expansion of gay and lesbian rights to concede that, whilst homosexuals have the right to be 'left alone' in private, limits should still be maintained in respect of

107 D. McGhee, 'Beyond Toleration: Privacy, Citizenship and Sexual Minorities in England and Wales', *The British Journal of Sociology* 55:3, 2004, 357–375.

108 D. Bell and J. Binnie, *The Sexual Citizen: Queer Politics and Beyond*, Cambridge: Polity Press, 2000.

access to social and public institutions.[109] Use of a private/public binary in this way is contrary to the essence of gay rights movements which, as Fairfield argues, are founded on the aim of replacing the 'philosophy of concealment' associated with sexual rights with one of 'equality and freedom' associated with civil rights.[110] The overall effect of the Court's approach to homosexuality is that, whilst it has socialized European societies in respect of a range of rights associated with private life, it has also legitimized the privatization of homosexuality. As I will argue in the following chapters, the Court's interpretation of Article 8 in respect of homosexuality has been a key aspect of its continuing failure to guarantee universal rights for homosexuals.

109 See: C.A. Ball, *The Morality of Gay Rights: An Exploration in Political Philosophy*, New York: Routledge, 2003.

110 P. Fairfield, *Public/Private*, Lanham: Rowman and Littlefield, 2005, p. 82.

Chapter 5

The anti-discrimination provisions of the Convention

Article 14 and Protocol 12

The Convention contains two provisions that prohibit discrimination and both are highly relevant to complaints relating to sexual orientation. Article 14 provides that:

> The enjoyment of the rights and freedoms set forth in this Convention shall be secured without discrimination on any ground such as sex, race, colour, language, religion, political or other opinion, national or social origin, association with a national minority, property, birth or other status.

Article 14 'complements the other substantive provisions of the Convention'[1] and prohibits discrimination in respect of the rights and freedoms guaranteed by the Convention. Article 14 is not, therefore, a general anti-discriminatory provision that can be used to address the differential treatment of sexual minorities across all areas of social life. However, used in conjunction with the private life limb of Article 8, Article 14 has provided an important mechanism through which to develop gay and lesbian human rights. Protocol 12, which came into force in 2005, extends the reach of Article 14 by providing, at Article 1:

1 The enjoyment of any right set forth by law shall be secured without discrimination on any ground such as sex, race, colour, language, religion, political or other opinion, national or social origin, association with a national minority, property, birth or other status.
2 No one shall be discriminated against by any public authority on any ground such as those mentioned in paragraph 1.

1 *E.B. v France* [GC], no. 43546/02, 22 January 2008, § 47.

The Court has, to date, issued only one judgment in respect of Protocol 12 but has determined that, in expanding the scope of protection to 'any right set forth by law', it 'introduces a general prohibition of discrimination'.[2]

During the development of Protocol 12, the Parliamentary Assembly of the Council of Europe argued that the enumeration of grounds in Article 1 on which discrimination is prohibited should include an explicit reference to sexual orientation because the specification of grounds is 'meant to list forms of discrimination which [the Convention] regards as being especially odious'.[3] The drafters decided not to include sexual orientation, stating that:

> The list of non-discrimination grounds in Article 1 is identical to that in Article 14 of the Convention. This solution was considered preferable over others, such as expressly including certain additional non-discrimination grounds (for example, physical or mental disability, sexual orientation or age), not because of a lack of awareness that such grounds have become particularly important in today's societies as compared with the time of drafting of Article 14 of the Convention, but because such an inclusion was considered unnecessary from a legal point of view since the list of non-discrimination grounds is not exhaustive, and because inclusion of any particular additional ground might give rise to unwarranted *a contrario* interpretations as regards discrimination based on grounds not so included.[4]

In this chapter, I will consider the anti-discrimination provisions of the Convention in respect of gay and lesbian rights. I will explore the ways in which Article 14 has been invoked by applicants, and interpreted by the Court, to expand the human rights available to homosexuals under the Convention. I will also consider current limitations in the Court's approach to Article 14 that produce significant gaps in the protection available to lesbians and gay men. In the absence of any case law relating to Protocol 12, I will consider how its more expansive anti-discriminatory provisions may be used in the future to further enhance rights for homosexuals under the Convention.

2 *Sejdić and Finci v Bosnia and Herzegovina* [GC], nos. 27996/06 and 34836/06, 22 December 2009, § 53.

3 Parliamentary Assembly of the Council of Europe, 'Opinion No. 216: Draft Protocol No. 12 to the European Convention on Human Rights', 2000.

4 Council of Europe, 'Protocol No. 12 to the Convention for the Protection of Human Rights and Fundamental Freedoms: Explanatory Report', Strasbourg: Council of Europe, 2000.

The Court's approach to discrimination

The Court has repeatedly stated that Article 14 is not an autonomous provision but has effect only in relation to other Convention rights. Although the Court has determined that the application of Article 14 does not presuppose a violation of another aspect of the Convention, there is no room for its use unless the facts of the complaint fall within the ambit of one or more of the other substantive provisions. The Court's approach to Article 14 has evolved over time: in earlier judgments relating to sexual orientation, the Court would not consider an Article 14 complaint once it had found a violation of another substantive provision. In *Smith and Grady v the United Kingdom*, for example, the Court found in favour of the applicants' Article 8 complaint but would not consider their Article 14 complaint because it 'amounts in effect to the same complaint, albeit seen from a different angle'.[5] More recently, however, the Court has issued judgments in respect of Article 14 complaints in addition to other aspects of the Convention. In *Alekseyev v Russia*, for example, the Court held that the refusal to grant the applicant a permit to assemble in public for the purpose of holding a 'gay pride' demonstration violated his Article 11 rights and his Article 14 rights taken in conjunction with Article 11. This is an important development since the Court now explicitly addresses the social discrimination that is the basis for interferences by public authorities with the Convention rights of homosexuals.

In its review of Article 14 complaints, the Court employs a four-stage analysis to determine whether any difference in treatment amounts to discrimination under the Convention. First, the Court examines whether the complaint falls within the ambit of one of the other substantive provisions of the Convention. The Court has stated that Article 14 is applicable if the 'subject-matter of the disadvantage [. . .] constitutes one of the modalities of the exercise of a right guaranteed',[6] or the interference in question is 'linked to the exercise of a right'.[7] For Article 14 to be applicable, therefore, it is enough for the facts of the case to fall within the ambit of one or more of the other provisions. Furthermore, if a state has gone beyond its contracted duties under the Convention and introduced further rights within its jurisdiction, then Article 14 prohibits discrimination in respect of those rights if they relate to a substantive provision of the Convention (and Protocol 12 extends this to any right set forth by law). As Baker notes, determining the scope of

5 *Smith and Grady v the United Kingdom*, nos. 33985/96 and 33986/96, 27 September 1999, ECHR 1999-VI, § 115. See also: *A.D.T. v the United Kingdom*, no. 35765/97, 31 July 2000, ECHR 2000-IX.

6 *National Union of Belgian Police v Belgium*, no. 4464/70, 27 October 1975, Series A no. 19, § 45.

7 *Schmidt and Dahlström v Sweden*, no. 5589/72, 6 February 1976, Series A no. 21, § 39.

Article 14 'calls for an open-textured consideration of whether the claimant's enjoyment of a Convention right or freedom on a basis of equality with other members of society has been impaired by a state measure or decision' and this presumes that 'the area of enjoyment of the right in question extends well beyond the protection of the specific Convention article involved'.[8] Wintemute argues that the scope of Article 14 is wide because the Court can use two routes to make it applicable: 'either the *opportunity* denied or the *ground* for the denial must fall "within the ambit" of the other Convention right'.[9]

If the Court determines that an Article 14 complaint falls within the ambit of another substantive provision, it proceeds to a second stage of analysis that involves considering whether the alleged reason for the discrimination is one of the grounds listed in Article 14. Since the Convention does not list sexual orientation as a ground, early complaints to Strasbourg relied upon 'sex'. However, in its review of a complaint brought about differences in the 'age of consent' for homosexual and heterosexual sexual acts in *Sutherland v the United Kingdom*, the Commission clarified that sexual orientation is a ground under Article 14:

> The different minimum ages for lawful sexual relations between homosexuals and heterosexuals are a difference based on sexual orientation. In terms of Article 14 [. . .], it is not clear whether this difference is a difference based on 'sex' or on 'other status'. The Commission for its part considers that it is not required to determine whether a difference based on sexual orientation is a matter which is properly to be considered as a difference on grounds of 'sex' or of 'other status'. In either event, it is a difference in respect of which the Commission is entitled to seek justification.[10]

The Court, accepting the Commission's interpretation, has consistently held that sexual orientation is a ground covered by Article 14 and this stage of analysis is now perfunctory.

The third stage of analysis concerns determining whether the complainant is in a relatively similar or analogous situation with another class of persons who are treated more favourably. The purpose of this comparison, as White and Ovey argue,

8 A. Baker, 'The Enjoyment of Rights and Freedoms: A New Conception of the "Ambit" under Article 14', *Modern Law Review* 65, 2006, 714–737 at 737.

9 R. Wintemute, ' "Within the Ambit": How Big is the "Gap" in Article 14 European Convention on Human Rights?', *European Human Rights Law Review* 4, 2004, 366–382 at 371.

10 *Sutherland v the United Kingdom*, no. 25186/94, Commission report, 1 July 1997, § 50–51.

> is to enable the Court to determine whether the less favourable treatment is attributable to one of the Article 14 prohibited grounds of discrimination, and not to other factors. For the test to function, the situation of the applicant and the comparator must be analogous in all material respects so that it can properly be concluded that the difference between them arises from an Article 14 ground.[11]

There are some general problems with this stage of analysis in the Court's case law given that it is often missing from published judgments and, where it does appear, its application is often inconsistent. As I discuss below, this stage continues to prove problematic in respect of complaints relating to sexual-orientation discrimination.

The final stage of an Article 14 review by the Court concerns an analysis of whether any difference in treatment by a public authority has a reasonable and objective justification. A recent formulation of the Court's approach at this stage in respect of sexual orientation is given in *Kozak v Poland*:

> it must be established that there is no objective and reasonable justification for the impugned distinction, which means that it does not pursue a 'legitimate aim' or that there is no 'reasonable proportionality between the means employed and the aim sought to be realised' [. . .] Furthermore, when the distinction in question operates in this intimate and vulnerable sphere of an individual's private life, particularly weighty reasons need to be advanced before the Court to justify the measure complained of. Where a difference of treatment is based on sex or sexual orientation the margin of appreciation afforded to the State is narrow and in such situations the principle of proportionality does not merely require that the measure chosen is in general suited for realising the aim sought but it must also be shown that it was necessary in the circumstances. Indeed, if the reasons advanced for a difference in treatment were based solely on the applicant's sexual orientation, this would amount to discrimination under the Convention.[12]

Although *Kozak* suggests that contracting states have little or no margin of appreciation in respect of differential treatment based on sexual orientation, this view is not reflected elsewhere in the Court's case law. For instance, in *Schalk and Kopf v Austria*, the Court held that, although same-sex and different-sex couples are in analogous situations in respect of their intimate relationships, the Austrian state had not exceeded its margin of appreciation in

11 R.C.A. White and C. Ovey, *The European Convention on Human Rights (5th Edition)*, Oxford: Oxford University Press, 2010, pp. 558–559.

12 *Kozak v Poland*, no. 13102/02, 2 March 2010, § 91–92.

differentiating between people on the grounds of sexual orientation when excluding same-sex couples from civil marriage. The Court stated that:

> the scope of the margin of appreciation will vary according to the circumstances, the subject matter and its background; in this respect, one of the relevant factors may be the existence or non-existence of common ground between the laws of the Contracting States.[13]

The judgments in *Kozak* and *Schalk and Kopf* are contradictory and, as I discuss below, they create considerable ambiguity in the Court's approach to discrimination on the grounds of sexual orientation.

The long road to Article 14

As I discussed in Chapter 1, Article 14 was invoked in the first application relating to homosexuality that was lodged with the Commission in 1955.[14] Since that time, applicants have regularly and consistently relied upon Article 14 in a wide range of complaints about sexual orientation discrimination. However, it was not until 1999 that the Court first found a violation of Article 14 in respect of a complaint about discrimination on the grounds of sexual orientation.[15] Until this time, the Court refused to consider Article 14 complaints brought in relation to homosexuality even when it found violations of rights under other articles of the Convention. For example, the applicant in *Dudgeon v the United Kingdom* claimed that the criminalization of male homosexuality created a difference in treatment based on sex, which violated his rights under Article 14 taken in conjunction with Article 8, but the Court, having upheld the applicant's Article 8 complaint, stated that the two complaints addressed the same issue and that there was no need to rule on the merits of the Article 14 complaint.[16] The majority's view in *Dudgeon*, 'that a clear inequality of treatment' was not 'a fundamental aspect of the case',[17] produced dissent from Judges Evrigenis and Garcia De Enterria who argued that the difference in treatment complained of 'ought to have been examined under Article 14' and to not do so deprived Article 14 'in great part of its substance and function in the system of substantive rules established under the Convention'.[18] However, recognition that differential treatment based on sexual orientation amounts to discrimination under Article 14 has been a slow

13 *Schalk and Kopf v Austria*, no. 30141/04, 24 June 2010, § 98.
14 *W.B. v Federal Republic of Germany*, no. 104/55, Commission decision, 17 December 1955.
15 *Salgueiro da Silva Mouta v Portugal*, no. 33290/96, 21 December 1999, ECHR 1999-IX.
16 *Dudgeon v the United Kingdom*, no. 7525/76, 22 October 1981, Series A no. 45.
17 Ibid., § 69.
18 Ibid., Dissenting opinion of Judges Evrigenis and Garcia De Enterria.

and recent development in the Court. I examine the evolution of Article 14 in respect of a number of issues below.

The 'age of consent'

One of the principal issues relating to sexual orientation that has been contested under Article 14 is the difference in treatment created by laws that maintain a higher minimum age for homosexual sexual acts in comparison to heterosexual acts. The Court's jurisprudence has been significant in encouraging the repeal of legislation in contracting states that have sought to maintain distinctions between ages of sexual consent based on sexual orientation. For example, when, in April 2011, the Supreme Court of Gibraltar held that differential minimum ages for heterosexual and homosexual activities maintained by the Criminal Offences Act 1960 violated rights guaranteed by the Gibraltar Constitution, it placed significant emphasis on Strasbourg jurisprudence in this area.[19] However, whilst all but one of the contracting states have now eliminated any differences in the minimum ages for sexual acts in respect of sexual orientation from their domestic law (Article 347 of the Criminal Code of Greece maintains a different minimum age for indecent acts between males for financial gain), the Court's role in encouraging this should not be overstated. Although the Court's recognition that this form of difference in treatment is in violation of Article 14 has been an important development, it came at the point when the vast majority of contracting states had already equalized the minimum ages for homosexual and heterosexual acts in their domestic laws.

The first complaint in respect of different minimum ages for homosexual and heterosexual acts was lodged in Strasbourg in 1975 and, in response, the Commission requested that the interested parties submit written considerations of whether the criminal law that maintained different ages contravened the applicant's rights under Article 14.[20] The government stated that the punishment of 'homosexual relationships with adolescents' did maintain a difference of treatment based on sex but that this was 'justified by the requirements of a policy of deterrence' designed to protect young men from the risks of homosexuality. The Commission declared the application inadmissible on the grounds that the 'necessity of social protection or the existence of a

19 '[. . .] this court is enjoined *inter alia* to take account of decisions of the European Commission of Human Rights and European Court of Human Rights when dealing with any question which has arisen in connection with the rights and freedoms protected by Chapter I of the Constitution'. *The Chief Minister of Gibraltar and Her Majesty's Attorney General for Gibraltar v Equality Group GGR and The Secretary of State for Foreign and Commonwealth Affairs*, Supreme Court of Gibraltar, 2009 C No. 272, Judgment of 8 April 2011.

20 *X. v Federal Republic of Germany*, no. 5935/72, Commission decision, 30 September 1975.

corresponding danger'[21] provided both reasonable and objective criteria to justify the difference in treatment and that, furthermore, the 'threat and employment of criminal sanctions constitute [. . .] means which are not disproportionate to the object pursued, i.e. that of protection'.[22] The Commission subsequently declared a similar facts complaint against the United Kingdom admissible but concluded in its report that maintaining a higher minimum age for male homosexual sex was a proportionate response to the aim of protecting young men.[23]

In *Dudgeon v the United Kingdom*, the Court gave significant weight to the Commission's previous interpretation of the Convention when it dismissed the applicant's Article 14 claim. In a dissenting opinion, Judge Matscher agreed that the facts of the case disclosed no violation of Article 14 but criticized the majority for not ruling on its merits:

> In my view, when the Court is called on to rule on a breach of the Convention which has been alleged by the applicant and contested by the respondent Government, it is the Court's duty, provided that the application is admissible, to decide the point by giving an answer on the merits of the issue that has been raised. The Court cannot escape this responsibility by employing formulas that are liable to limit excessively the scope of Article 14 [. . .] to the point of depriving it of all practical value.[24]

It was not until *Sutherland v the United Kingdom* that the Commission's interpretation of differential minimum ages of consent changed. In response to the two principal arguments advanced by the UK government to defend the higher age of consent for male homosexual sex – that 'young men between the ages of 16 and 18 do not have a settled sexual orientation and that the aim of the law is to protect such vulnerable young men' and 'that society is entitled to indicate its disapproval of homosexual conduct and its preference that children follow a heterosexual way of life'[25] – the Commission stated that neither argument offered a reasonable and objective justification for maintaining the difference in treatment. The Commission legitimized its departure from its previous decisions by invoking an ontological conception of homosexuality that, as I discussed in Chapter 2, challenged the idea that a homosexual orientation is the result of corruption. It stated that 'sexual

21 Ibid., p. 56.

22 Ibid.

23 *X. v the United Kingdom*, no. 7215/75, Commission decision, 7 July 1977; Commission report, 12 October 1978; Committee of Ministers, 12 June 1979.

24 *Dudgeon v the United Kingdom*, no. 7525/76, 22 October 1981, Series A no. 45, Dissenting opinion of Judge Matscher, § II.

25 *Sutherland v the United Kingdom*, no. 25186/94, Commission report, 1 July 1997, § 63.

orientation is fixed in both sexes by the age of 16 and that men aged 16–21 are not in need of special protection because of the risk of their being "recruited" into homosexuality'.[26] The Court did not consider the complaint because, in light of legislation introduced by the United Kingdom government to equalize the age of consent, it struck the case from its list.[27]

It was not until 2003, in *L. and V. v Austria*, that the Court found a violation of Article 14 in respect of an age of consent complaint.[28] The application was the latest in a series of complaints against section 209 of the Austrian Criminal Code – which maintained a higher minimum age for homosexual acts – that had all previously been declared inadmissible by the Commission.[29] In *L. and V.*, the Court reiterated the Commission's interpretation of Article 14 in *Sutherland* and held:

> To the extent that Article 209 of the Criminal Code embodied a predisposed bias on the part of a heterosexual majority against a homosexual minority, these negative attitudes cannot of themselves be considered by the Court to amount to sufficient justification for the differential treatment any more than similar negative attitudes towards those of a different race, origin or colour.[30]

Whilst the Court's judgment in respect of the actual complaint was hardly groundbreaking (since Austria's Constitutional Court had already invalidated Article 209[31]), its more general statement – that discrimination on the basis of sexual orientation is as unacceptable under Article 14 as discrimination based on race – has been of significant importance for the development of Convention rights for non-heterosexuals.

'Home' and 'family life'

In the 1980s and 1990s, the Commission declared inadmissible applications brought under Article 14 in respect of differences in treatment in housing provision on the grounds of sexual orientation.[32] In 2003, however, the Court

26 Ibid., § 64.

27 *Sutherland v the United Kingdom* (striking out) [GC], no. 25186/94, 27 March 2001. See also: *Small v the United Kingdom* (striking out), no. 7330/06, 2 June 2009.

28 *L. and V. v Austria*, nos. 39392/98 and 39829/98, 9 January 2003, ECHR 2003-I.

29 *Zukrigl v Austria*, no. 17279/90, Commission decision, 13 May 1992; *H.F. v Austria*, no. 22646/93, Commission decision, 26 June 1995.

30 *L. and V. v Austria*, nos. 39392/98 and 39829/98, 9 January 2003, ECHR 2003-I, § 52.

31 Upon the request for a constitutional review by the Innsbruck Regional Court, the Constitutional Court of Austria held on 21 June 2009 that Article 209 of the Criminal Code was unconstitutional.

32 *S. v the United Kingdom*, no. 11716/85, Commission decision, 14 May 1986; *Röösli v Federal Republic of Germany*, no. 28318/95, Commission decision, 15 May 1996.

upheld an Article 14 complaint in *Karner v Austria* regarding the difference in treatment experienced by a homosexual applicant when he was debarred from succeeding to his deceased partner's tenancy under Austrian law. As I discussed in the previous chapter, the Court focused on the 'home' limb of Article 8 when reviewing the difference in treatment under Article 14. A number of third-party interveners – ILGA-Europe, Liberty and Stonewall – explicitly invoked the existence of Protocol 12 of the Convention to support their argument that difference in treatment on the grounds of sexual orientation constitutes unjustifiable discrimination. The respondent government justified domestic legislation, which granted preferential tenancy rights to married couples, as a proportionate measure designed to protect the 'traditional family'. Whilst the Court accepted that the 'protection of the family in the traditional sense is, in principle, a weighty and legitimate reason which might justify a difference in treatment',[33] it went on to state that it 'is rather abstract and a broad variety of concrete measures may be used to implement it'.[34] Stating that a narrow margin of appreciation was available to contracting states in respect of differences in treatment based on sexual orientation, the Court held that the government had not provided convincing or weighty reasons to show that the difference in treatment was necessary to meet the aim of protecting the traditional family. The Court did not engage in any explicit analysis of the analogous situation of the applicant with married couples when reaching its decision that the domestic legislation created a violation of the applicant's Article 14 rights taken in conjunction with Article 8.

In *Kozak v Poland*, the Court strengthened its judgment in *Karner* by explicitly rejecting the government's argument that an assessment of the 'emotional, economic or other quality' of the applicant's homosexual relationship had not been the basis for excluding him from succession to his deceased partner's tenancy and held that the sole reason for his exclusion was his sexual orientation.[35] The Court rejected the government's claim that the differential treatment of homosexual and heterosexual couples, as a measure designed to protect the traditional family founded on a 'union of a man and a woman', was justifiable under the Convention:

> given that the Convention is a living instrument, to be interpreted in the light of present-day conditions [. . .], the State, in its choice of means designed to protect the family and secure, as required by Article 8, respect for family life must necessarily take into account developments in society

33 *Karner v Austria*, no. 40016/98, 24 July 2003, ECHR 2003-IX.
34 Ibid.
35 *Kozak v Poland*, no. 13102/02, 2 March 2010.

> and changes in the perception of social, civil-status and relational issues, including the fact that there is not just one way or one choice in the sphere of leading and living one's family or private life.[36]

The Court held that the blanket exclusion of persons living in a homosexual relationship from succession to a tenancy could not be deemed necessary since it did not show a reasonable relationship of proportionality between the aim sought and the means employed.

Parental rights/adoption of a child

The Court has considered a range of issues under Article 14 in respect of applications lodged by the biological and non-biological parents of children who have complained about inequalities in parental rights based on sexual orientation. In a number of judgments, the Court has developed important rights for gay and lesbian parents under the Convention. In *Salgueiro da Silva Mouta v Portugal*,[37] which concerned a complaint against the award of custody by the Lisbon Court of Appeal of the applicant's biological daughter to his ex-wife rather than to himself because of his sexual orientation, the Court considered whether differential treatment between homosexuals and heterosexuals in the sphere of parental custody was a violation of Article 14. In its review, the Court paid particular attention to the language used by the Lisbon Court, which had stated, *inter alia*, that homosexuality was 'an abnormality and children should not grow up in the shadow of abnormal situations'.[38] The government, in its defence, submitted that the Lisbon Court had not made the applicant's sexuality central to its decision but had 'merely touched' on it.[39] The Court did not accept this argument and stated that the applicant's homosexuality was a factor that was decisive in the Lisbon Court's final decision. As so often in the Court's case law on sexual orientation, the explicitness of the homophobic language used by the domestic authorities was decisive in persuading the Court to regard the difference in treatment as discriminatory under Article 14.[40]

In respect of non-biological parent–child relations, the Court has been less supportive of complaints brought by homosexuals. In *Craig v the United Kingdom*, the applicant complained that, because of an order from the High Court of England and Wales, which stated that the applicant's partner could

36 Ibid., § 98.
37 *Salgueiro da Silva Mouta v Portugal*, no. 33290/96, 21 December 1999, ECHR 1999-IX.
38 Ibid., § 14.
39 Ibid., § 32.
40 P. Johnson, 'Heteronormativity and the European Court of Human Rights', *Law and Critique*, 23(1), 2012, 43–66.

not permit her children to come into contact with or remain in the company of the applicant or of any other person known to be a lesbian, she suffered discrimination under Article 14. Curiously, the applicant advanced the claim that this treatment was discriminatory since it only applied to female, and not male, homosexuals. The Court deemed this complaint inadmissible, stating that:

> the applicant compares her position to that of all male homosexuals. Since [her partner] is a female homosexual and has a continuing relationship with the applicant, the Court does not find that the applicant and other female homosexuals can be compared and considered analogous to all male homosexuals in the particular context and, therefore, no question of a discriminatory difference in treatment within the meaning of Article 14 of the Convention arises.[41]

There is significant ambiguity in the Court's case law in respect of discrimination experienced by homosexuals seeking to adopt a child. With regard to the adoption of a non-biologically related child by a same-sex couple, no complaint has been lodged with the Court. This is essentially because of the difficulty in establishing a claim under Article 14 when the Convention does not contain any right to adoption. Although *Karner* and *Kozak* explicitly regard any differential treatment on the grounds of sexual orientation to be discriminatory under Article 14, it remains to be seen whether this holds in respect of adoption. In relation to the adoption of a child by an individual in a same-sex relationship with the child's biological parent, the Commission has previously deemed complaints inadmissible. In *Kerkhoven, Hinke and Hinke v Netherlands*, the Commission very tersely stated that 'as regards parental authority over a child, a homosexual couple cannot be equated to a man and a woman living together' for the purposes of Article 14.[42] However, the Court has recently declared *Gas and Dubois v France* admissible, which concerns an application by two women in a long-term relationship who, although both providing full-time care for the biological child of one of the applicants, complain about the refusal by French authorities to allow the non-biological parent to legally adopt the child.[43] The Court has declared that this complaint falls within the ambit of both the private life and family life limbs of Article 8. This reflects a growing acceptance by the Court of the approach to Article 14 argued for by Wintemute, whereby Article 14 is triggered because the grounds for differential treatment (rather than the opportunity itself) are

41 *Craig v the United Kingdom* (dec), no. 45396/99, 21 March 2000, § 1(d).
42 *Kerkhoven, Hinke and Hinke v Netherlands*, no. 15666/89, Commission decision, 19 May 1992.
43 *Gas and Dubois v France* (dec), no. 25951/07, 31 August 2010.

recognized to fall under another substantive provision.[44] In view of this, it seems certain that the Court will follow the same line of reasoning in another similar facts case that is pending against Austria.[45] Protocol 12 provides scope to develop future complaints against differential treatment based on sexual orientation in the sphere of adoption if applicants can argue that a right to be considered for adoption is defined by law in a contracting state and it is being applied in a discriminatory manner.

Whilst the Court has not provided any support to same-sex couples who experience discrimination in the adoption of children, it has significantly evolved Article 14 in respect of adoption by single homosexuals. In both *Fretté v France* and *E.B. v France*, the Court determined that complaints against French adoption authorities for operating a policy of excluding single homosexual applicants from gaining authorization to adopt a child were admissible under Article 14 because, concerning sexual orientation, they fell within the ambit of the private life limb of Article 8. The decisive factor in the Court's decision to deem the complaints admissible under Article 14 was the existence of Article 343-1 of the French Civil Code, which allows 'any person over twenty-eight years of age' to apply to adopt a child. There was considerable dissent in both cases regarding the majority's admissibility decision. In *Fretté*, in which the Court ultimately rejected the applicant's complaint, Judge Costa joined by Judges Jungwiert and Traja argued that the complaint was not admissible under Article 14 because it did not concern an aspect of private or family life protected by Article 8. Costa argued that the 'fundamental paradox of this judgment seems to me that it would have been easier to justify the rejection of the complaint on the legal basis of the inapplicability of Article 14 than to declare Article 14 applicable and then find no breach of it'.[46]

In *E.B. v France*, where the majority found that the complaint 'undoubtedly' fell within the scope of Article 8, a range of dissenting opinions were made. Judge Zupančič stated that, because the adoption of a child is a 'privilege' rather than a 'right', it was therefore 'inconsistent to consider that there has been any kind of violation' of Article 14.[47] Judge Loucaides, advancing a more blatantly homophobic form of reasoning, argued that homosexuals, as 'persons with some peculiarity', must 'accept that they may not qualify for certain activities which, by their nature and under certain

44 R. Wintemute, '"Within the Ambit": How Big is the "Gap" in Article 14 European Convention on Human Rights?'

45 *X. and Others v Austria*, No. 19010/07, Statement of facts, 2 February 2009.

46 *Fretté v France*, no. 36515/97, 26 February 2002, ECHR 2002-I, Partly concurring opinion of Judge Costa joined by Judges Jungwiert and Traja.

47 *E.B. v France* [GC], no. 43546/02, 22 January 2008, Dissenting opinion of Judge Zupančič.

circumstances, are incompatible with their lifestyle or peculiarity'.[48] Judge Mularoni offered a more careful consideration of the majority's admissibility decision:

> In my view, we should not be asking – and leaving unanswered – the wrong question, namely, whether the 'right' to adopt should or should not fall within the ambit of Article 8 of the Convention taken alone [. . .] No right to adoption is recognized by domestic legislation or by the relevant international instruments, and the parties do not dispute this. On the other hand, we should establish – and this absolutely must be done and done clearly – whether the possibility of adopting a child afforded by domestic legislation does or does not fall within the ambit of Article 8. If the answer remains that it does not, I find it incomprehensible, as I have said above, to conclude that the right to seek authorization 'undoubtedly' falls within the ambit of Article 8 and that, accordingly, Article 14 taken together with Article 8 is applicable. Frankly, I find this conclusion illogical.[49]

The majority in *E.B.* did not find it 'illogical' to state that Article 14 was applicable because, in making the applicant's sexual orientation the decisive factor on which her application to adopt was assessed, the French authorities had invoked a most intimate aspect of her private life as grounds for differential treatment. The judgment in *E.B.* is extremely important because it demonstrates that the Court is willing to engage a wider reading of the substantive provisions of the Convention when Article 14 is invoked. Whilst it does not suggest that the Court has wholly accepted Wintemute's argument that private life is relevant to every aspect of sexual orientation discrimination,[50] it does show that the Court will use private life as a basis for considering claims under Article 14 that would not fall within the ambit of Article 8 alone. However, it seems certain that, had it not been for the existence of Article 343-1 of the French Civil Code, which established a right for 'any person' to adopt, the Court would not have deemed *E.B.* admissible. The judgment does not, therefore, establish a right for single homosexuals to adopt, but it does, as Judge Costa stated, send a clear message that 'a person seeking to adopt cannot be prevented from doing so merely on the ground of his or her homosexuality'.[51]

48 Ibid., Dissenting opinion of Judge Loucaides.

49 Ibid., Dissenting opinion of Judge Mularoni.

50 R. Wintemute, ' "Within the Ambit": How Big is the "Gap" in Article 14 European Convention on Human Rights?'

51 *E.B. v France* [GC], no. 43546/02, 22 January 2008, Dissenting opinion of Judge Costa joined by Judges Türmen, Ugrekhelidze and Jočienė.

Freedom of assembly

In two recent cases, *Bączkowski and Others v Poland*[52] and *Alekseyev v Russia*,[53] the Court has evolved its Article 14 jurisprudence in respect of Article 11 by finding in favour of homosexual applicants who lodged complaints against refusals to grant permits to hold public demonstrations. *Alekseyev* is the more significant of the two cases, for reasons I will discuss in Chapter 7. The applicant complained that he had been treated in a discriminatory manner by the Moscow authorities that were responsible for processing his application for a permit to hold a gay pride event. The Court concluded in its consideration of the Article 11 claim that the main reason for imposing a ban on the event was the authorities' explicit disapproval of demonstrations that they considered promoted homosexuality. In this respect, the Court paid particular attention to the link between the strong personal opinions expressed by the mayor of Moscow (who was reported to have said, among other things, that homosexuality is 'unnatural' and that gay pride demonstrations 'stir up society, which is ill-disposed to such occurrences of life'[54]) and the refusal to grant a permit for the event. In light of the centrality of sexual orientation to the decision making of the public authorities, the Court found that the applicant had suffered discrimination on the grounds of his sexual orientation under Article 14 taken in conjunction with Article 11.

Four major gaps for homosexual rights under Article 14

In *Schalk and Kopf v Austria*, the Court made a clear statement on the limits of protection available to homosexuals under Article 14 when taken in conjunction with Article 8:

> On the one hand the Court has held repeatedly that, just like differences based on sex, differences based on sexual orientation require particularly serious reasons by way of justification [. . .] On the other hand, a wide margin is usually allowed to the State under the Convention when it comes to general measures of economic or social strategy.[55]

In juxtaposing these two issues in this way – sexual orientation on the one hand, economic and social strategy on the other – the Court reaffirmed a long-standing view that contracting states enjoy a wide margin of appreciation in respect of certain matters to differentiate between persons on the

52 *Bączkowski and Others v Poland*, no. 1543/06, 3 May 2007.
53 *Alekseyev v Russia*, nos. 4916/07, 25924/08 and 14599/09, 21 October 2010.
54 Ibid., § 8.
55 *Schalk and Kopf v Austria*, no. 30141/04, 24 June 2010, § 97.

enumerated grounds in Article 14. In other words, homosexuals cannot rely on 'automatic' protection under Article 14 because, even if their complaint is deemed to fall within the ambit of Article 8 (or another substantive provision of the Convention), states have discretion to pursue differential treatment based on sexual orientation in respect of economic or social strategy. As a result of this there are major gaps in the protection available to homosexuals under Article 14. I discuss four of these below.

Economic benefits

In *Mata Estevez v Spain*, the applicant complained that his inability to claim the pension rights of his deceased same-sex partner violated his rights under Articles 8 and 14 of the Convention.[56] The Court noted that the Convention does not guarantee any right to a pension and was equivocal about whether the complaint fell within the ambit of the private life limb of Article 8. It concluded that even if it did the interference did not violate the applicant's Article 8 rights because, in pursuing the legitimate aim of protecting the heterosexual family based on marriage, the difference in treatment fell within the state's margin of appreciation.[57] It is arguable that subsequent judgments by the Court in *Karner* and *Kozak* (which established that the protection of the 'traditional' family is not an objective or reasonable justification for the blanket exclusion of same-sex partners from benefits available to different-sex partners) and *Schalk and Kopf* (which established that a same-sex relationship is analogous to a different-sex relationship for the purposes of family life under Article 8) overturn the judgment in *Mata Estevez*. This is certainly supported by the judgment in *P.B. and J.S. v Austria*, in which the Court upheld the applicants' complaint that legislation affording accident and sickness insurance cover to the heterosexual partners of civil servants, but not to same-sex partners, was discriminatory under Article 14.[58] In this case, the Court confirmed that, in matters relating to sexual orientation, the state's margin of appreciation was narrow and found that the difference in treatment discriminated against the applicants in respect of their right to respect for their family life. However, elsewhere in its recent case law, the Court has not followed this line of reasoning in respect of economic benefits.

In *Manenc v France*,[59] the Court declared inadmissible an application from a man who, following the death of his male partner with whom he had

56 *Mata Estevez v Spain* (dec), no. 56501/00, 10 May 2001, ECHR 2001-VI.

57 Ibid. See also: *Stec and Others v the United Kingdom* ([GC], nos. 65731/01 and 65900/01, 12 April 2006, ECHR 2006-VI) in which the Court confirmed the wide margin of appreciation available to contracting states to differentiate on the grounds of sex in the arrangement of pension benefits.

58 *P.B. and J.S. v Austria*, no. 18984/02, 22 July 2010.

59 *Manenc v France* (dec), no. 66686/09, 21 September 2010.

cohabited for 26 years and entered into a pacte civil de solidarité (civil partnership), was refused access to a survivor's pension. The applicant claimed that the basis for the refusal was that he had not been married to his deceased partner and that this constituted discrimination of persons who had entered into a pacte civil de solidarité and, more generally, to same-sex couples. In light of recent developments in the Court, it may be reasonable to expect that this case would have been deemed admissible and decided in favour of the applicant. However, the Court advanced a two-pronged form of analysis that damaged the applicant's claim. First, the Court contested whether the applicant was in an analogous situation with that of a surviving married spouse. The Court found that, whilst a pacte civil de solidarité under French law entailed a degree of solemn commitment, it differed from marriage in terms of the conditions for contracting and terminating it, as well as in its scope (particularly in respect of joint financial responsibilities). In light of this, the Court concluded that the applicant was not in an analogous situation with married persons. In addition, the Court stated that there was nothing to indicate that the difference in treatment experienced by the applicant was based on his sexual orientation but, rather, was an outcome of the fact that he was not married. This is a particularly perverse form of reasoning because, given that French law does not permit same-sex marriage, it was solely the applicant's sexual orientation that prohibited him from contracting civil marriage with his partner. However, relying upon the judgment in *Mata Estevez*, the Court found that French legislation on survivors' benefits pursued a legitimate aim, which was the protection of the family based on the bonds of marriage, and that limiting the scope of these economic benefits to married couples fell within the broad margin of appreciation available to contracting states.

Manenc demonstrates that same-sex couples face two serious problems when attempting to challenge economic discrimination in the Court: the first is the Court's approach to the question of analogous situations, and the second is the wide margin of appreciation available to states in the sphere of economic policy. With regard to analogous situation, in *Burden v the United Kingdom* the Court clearly stated that same-sex couples who have contracted civil partnerships in the United Kingdom are in a similar situation to those who are married:

> As with marriage, the Grand Chamber considers that the legal consequences of civil partnership [. . .], which couples expressly and deliberately decide to incur, set these types of relationship apart from other forms of co-habitation. Rather than the length or the supportive nature of the relationship, what is determinative is the existence of a public undertaking, carrying with it a body of rights and obligations of a contractual nature [. . .] [T]here can be no analogy between married and Civil Partnership Act couples, on one hand, and heterosexual or

> homosexual couples who choose to live together but not to become husband and wife or civil partners, on the other hand.[60]

The judgment in *Burden* has been used to declare inadmissible *Courten v the United Kingdom*[61] and *M.W. v the United Kingdom*,[62] which concerned differential treatment in respect of taxation and social security benefits on the grounds of sexual orientation. In both cases, the Court found that the applicants were in 'informal personal relationships' with their same-sex partners and that this distinguished them from those in civil partnerships or marriage. However, in *M.W.* the Court again stated that those in United Kingdom civil partnerships are indistinguishable from heterosexual married couples:

> In its judgment [in *Burden*], the Grand Chamber identified the fundamental difference between personal relationships that are based on a legally binding agreement giving rise to certain rights and duties for the parties and those that are not [. . .] Because that judgment was delivered after the entry into force of the Civil Partnership Act, the status of couples who had availed of the possibility of entering into a civil partnership could likewise be distinguished from informal personal relationships, however permanent and supportive. The relationship the applicant had with his partner came within the latter category, and so his situation is to be distinguished from that of a surviving spouse.[63]

The explanation for the divergent approaches in *M.W.* and in *Manenc* is the difference between the domestic civil partnership legislation in the United Kingdom and France. The Court views the legal conditions of a United Kingdom civil partnership to be similar to a heterosexual marriage and, consequently, finds that the two groups are in an analogous situation. The Court's willingness to recognize same-sex couples and different-sex couples as comparable is dependent, therefore, upon the existence of domestic legislation that establishes their similarity. This means that, in respect of legal differences established between married heterosexual couples and same-sex couples in civil partnerships, the Court will maintain the margin of appreciation available to contracting states in the area of economic policy (something that the Court of Justice of the European Union was not prepared to do in respect of employment benefits in *Römer v City of Hamburg*).[64] *Courten*

60 *Burden v the United Kingdom* [GC], no. 13378/05, 29 April 2008, § 65.

61 *Courten v the United Kingdom* (dec), no. 4479/06, 4 November 2008.

62 *M.W. v the United Kingdom* (dec), no. 11313/02, 23 June 2009.

63 Ibid.

64 *Jürgen Römer v City of Hamburg*, Court of Justice of the European Union, 10 May 2011, C-147/08.

and *M.W.* also show that the Court is unwilling to recognize a distinction between unmarried same-sex partners and married couples as discriminatory in respect of economic matters. This is problematic since, in many contracting states, same-sex partners are unable to legally validate their relationships and gain recognition for their analogous situation with heterosexual married partners. In respect of distinctions between unmarried same-sex couples and unmarried heterosexual couples, the Court has made some progress. In *P.B. and J.S.*, the Court showed that it would recognize a distinction between unmarried homosexual couples and unmarried heterosexual couples as discriminatory under Article 14. However, the Court's case law demonstrates that, in the sphere of economic discrimination, homosexuals lack comprehensive protection.

Civil partnership/marriage

A further and related gap in protection from discrimination for homosexuals is created by the Court's unwillingness to recognize that the exclusion of same-sex partners from the rights associated with civil marriage (created by a legal prohibition on same-sex marriage or by the absence of an equivalent system of legal recognition) constitutes a violation of Article 14. In *Schalk and Kopf v Austria*, the Court held that although same-sex couples constitute a 'family' for the purposes of Article 8, are in a relatively similar situation to different-sex couples with regard to their need for legal recognition and protection of their relationships, and that particularly serious reasons are required to justify a difference in treatment, that the exclusion of a same-sex couple from marriage does not violate rights under Article 14 taken in conjunction with Article 8.[65] As I will discuss in Chapter 6, this interpretation of Article 14 was influenced by the Court's view that, because Article 12 did not impose an obligation on contracting states to grant same-sex couples access to marriage, 'Article 14 taken in conjunction with Article 8, a provision of more general purpose and scope, cannot be interpreted as imposing such an obligation either'.[66] In respect of the lack of opportunity for same-sex couples to enter into a legal partnership equivalent to marriage, the Court stated that, whilst it was not called upon to examine whether the absence of any mechanism for granting legal recognition would constitute a violation of Article 14 (because, in the time since *Schalk and Kopf* was lodged, Austrian law had made civil partnerships available to same-sex couples through the Registered Partnership Act), it would not reproach a contracting state for not having introduced civil partnership legislation earlier.

65 *Schalk and Kopf v Austria*, no. 30141/04, 24 June 2010.
66 Ibid., § 101.

The applicants in *Schalk and Kopf* claimed that, because the state had chosen to provide same-sex couples with an alternative means of recognition, it was therefore obliged to confer a status on those couples that corresponded to marriage in every respect. The Court was not convinced by this argument, arguing that contracting states 'enjoy a certain margin of appreciation as regards the exact status conferred by alternative means of recognition'.[67] The Court went on to state:

> the Registered Partnership Act gives the applicants a possibility to obtain a legal status equal or similar to marriage in many respects [. . .] While there are only slight differences in respect of material consequences, some substantial differences remain in respect of parental rights. However, this corresponds on the whole to the trend in other member States [. . .] Moreover, the Court is not called upon in the present case to examine each and every one of these differences in detail. [I]t would go beyond the scope of the present application to examine whether these differences are justified. On the whole, the Court does not see any indication that the respondent State exceeded its margin of appreciation in its choice of rights and obligations conferred by registered partnership.[68]

The Court's reliance on consensus analysis and, in light of it, its invocation of the margin of appreciation doctrine can be seen, as I argued in Chapter 3, as a device to legitimize its own moral view. Instead of engaging in an analysis of the proportionality of the difference in treatment created by the civil partnership legislation, and a consideration of the justification offered by the state, the Court defaulted to consensus analysis to confirm the state's margin. There was considerable dissent to this approach because of its failure to address the 'legal vacuum' in the period when the applicants' partnership had no legal recognition:

> Having identified a '*relevantly similar situation*' [. . .], and emphasised that '*differences based on sexual orientation require particularly serious reasons by way of justification*' [. . .], the Court should have found a violation of Article 14 taken in conjunction with Article 8 of the Convention because the respondent Government did not advance any argument to justify the difference of treatment, relying in this connection mainly on their margin of appreciation [. . .] However, in the absence of any cogent reasons offered by the respondent Government to justify the difference of treatment, there should be no room to apply the margin of appreciation. Consequently, the '*existence or non-existence of common ground between the laws*

67 Ibid., § 108.
68 Ibid., § 109.

> *of the Contracting States'* [. . .] is irrelevant as such considerations are only a *subordinate* basis for the application of the concept of the margin of appreciation. Indeed, it is only in the event that the national authorities offer grounds for justification that the Court can be satisfied, taking into account the presence or the absence of a common approach, that they are better placed than it is to deal effectively with the matter.
>
> Today it is widely recognized and also accepted by society that same-sex couples enter into stable relationships. Any absence of a legal framework offering them, at least to a certain extent, the same rights or benefits attached to marriage [. . .] would need robust justification, especially taking into account the growing trend in Europe to offer some means of qualifying for such rights or benefits.[69]

However, for the majority, no 'robust justification' was required to defend differential treatment in the legal recognition available to homosexual and heterosexual partners. Rather, the Court relied on the margin of appreciation to confirm the state's discretion in maintaining heteronormative priviledge in respect of the legal recognition of relationships.[70] This runs counter to Recommendation CM/Rec(2010)5 of the Committee of Ministers, which states that: 'Where national legislation recognizes registered same-sex partnerships, member states should seek to ensure that their legal status and their rights and obligations are equivalent to those of heterosexual couples in a comparable situation.'[71] The Court should have sought to determine whether there was a justification for the Austrian state not meeting this obligation under Article 14.

Immigration rights for same-sex couples

As I discussed in the previous chapter, there remains a significant gap in the Court's case law regarding discrimination experienced by sexual minorities in the sphere of immigration and asylum law. A significant absence is any interpretation of the Convention that offers protection to immigrant same-sex partners of European citizens from differential treatment based on sexual orientation. In the first immigration complaint related to sexual orientation that invoked Article 14, two male applicants argued that the refusal by immigration authorities to allow the first applicant to remain in the United Kingdom on the basis of his stable homosexual relationship with the second

69 Ibid., Joint dissenting opinion of Judges Rozakis, Spielmann and Jebens.

70 P. Johnson, 'Challenging the Heteronormativity of Marriage: The Role of Judicial Interpretation and Authority', *Social and Legal Studies* 20(3), 2011, 349–367.

71 Council of Europe, 'Recommendation CM/Rec(2010)5 of the Committee of Ministers to Member States on Measures to Combat Discrimination on Grounds of Sexual Orientation or Gender Identity', § 24.

applicant was, in the absence of any possible recognition of their relationship under the immigration rules in force at the time, a violation of their rights under Article 8 and (because they were treated differently to heterosexuals couples) Article 14.[72] The Commission rejected the Article 8 claim (in respect of both private and family life) and, in respect of the Article 14 complaint, found that there was no question of proportionality to answer since the applicants did not, as a homosexual couple, fall within immigration rules pertaining to families. In this and two further cases,[73] the Commission relied upon its decision in *S. v the United Kingdom* to deem the applications inadmissible under Article 14:

> The Commission accepts that the treatment accorded to the applicant (a recognized lesbian) was different from the treatment she would have received if the partners had been of different sexes.
>
> The Commission finds that the aim of the legislation in question was to protect the family, a goal similar to the protection of the right to respect for family life guaranteed by Article 8 [. . .] of the Convention. The aim itself is clearly legitimate. The question remains, however, as to whether it was justified to protect families but not to give similar protection to other stable relationships. The Commission considers that the family (to which the relationship of heterosexual unmarried couples living together as husband and wife can be assimilated) merits special protection in society and it sees no reason why a High Contracting Party should not afford particular assistance to families. The Commission therefore accepts that the difference in treatment between the applicant and somebody in the same position whose partner had been of the opposite sex can be objectively and reasonably justified.[74]

One might reasonably expect that the Court's judgment in *Schalk and Kopf* overturns this interpretation of the Convention, given that it establishes that same-sex relationships constitute a family under Article 8 and that same-sex partners are in need of the same legal protections as different-sex couples. However, in the absence of any case law, the situation remains unclear since the Court did not establish in *Schalk and Kopf* that distinctions between those in legally registered partnerships and married heterosexuals constitute a violation of Article 14. Furthermore, in *Karner*, the Court did not rule out the possibility that a policy designed to protect the 'traditional' family by excluding same-sex couples from certain rights may be proportionate. In

72 *W.J. and D.P. v the United Kingdom*, no. 12513/86, Commission decision, 13 July 1987.
73 *C. and L.M. v the United Kingdom*, no. 14753/89, Commission decision, 9 October 1989; *Z.B. v the United Kingdom*, no. 16106/90, Commission decision, 10 February 1990.
74 *S. v the United Kingdom*, no. 11716/85, Commission decision, 14 May 1986.

addition to this, the decision in *Manenc* regarding analogous situation signals that the Court has not fully accepted that same-sex families are truly equivalent to married, heterosexual families. Although the Parliamentary Assembly of the Council of Europe recommended that the Committee of Ministers urge member states to 'review their policies in the field of social rights and protection of migrants in order to ensure that homosexual partnership and families are treated on the same basis as heterosexual partnerships and families',[75] there is no explicit mention of immigration in Recommendation CM/Rec(2010)5 of the Committee of Ministers.[76] These combined elements demonstrate the absence of a clear commitment to equality in immigration rights for same-sex partners and provide obstacles to successful complaints under Article 14. In contracting states that do not offer legal recognition for same-sex partnerships, this leaves gay men and lesbians especially vulnerable.

Employment

To date, the Court has not issued a judgment in respect of an Article 14 complaint about discrimination in employment on the grounds of sexual orientation. Whilst the Court found, in several cases relating to the armed forces, that dismissal from employment on the grounds of sexual orientation, and intrusive investigations into sexual orientation, violated Article 8 rights, it did not consider the issue as discrimination under Article 14.[77] As such, there is a significant gap in the Court's case law in respect to both direct and indirect discrimination in employment on the ground of sexual orientation. One of the factors limiting the Convention's impact on employment law is its ineffectiveness at addressing discrimination by private employers. However, in respect of employment policies developed by the state, the Convention is relevant. Unusually in matters relating to sexual orientation, it is the Court of Justice of the European Union that has taken a lead on this issue. The Court of Justice in *Römer v City of Hamburg*,[78] reflecting the commitment to prohibiting sexual orientation discrimination in employment established by Council

75 Parliamentary Assembly of the Council of Europe Recommendation 1470 (2000) 'Situation of Gays and Lesbians and Their Partners in Respect of Asylum and Immigration in the Member States of the Council of Europe', § 7(ii)d.

76 Council of Europe, 'Recommendation CM/Rec(2010)5 of the Committee of Ministers to Member States on Measures to Combat Discrimination on Grounds of Sexual Orientation or Gender Identity'.

77 *Smith and Grady v the United Kingdom*, nos. 33985/96 and 33986/96, 27 September 1999, ECHR 1999-VI; *Lustig-Prean and Beckett v the United Kingdom*, nos. 31417/96 and 32377/96, 27 September 1999.

78 *Jürgen Römer v City of Hamburg*, Court of Justice of the European Union, 10 May 2011, C-147/08.

Directive 2000/78/EC,[79] as well as the more general commitments of the Treaty of Lisbon,[80] held that same-sex couples in civil partnerships must have access to all the employment benefits available to married couples. This strengthens the principle established by the Court of Justice in *Tadao Maruko v Versorgungsanstalt der deutschen Bühnen* that, where a state has enacted civil partnership legislation that places same-sex couples in an analogous position with heterosexual married couples, a difference in treatment between them in areas covered by European Union anti-discrimination law will amount to direct discrimination based on sexual orientation contrary to Council Directive 2000/78/EC.[81] It is likely that this will have an impact on the Strasbourg Court's interpretation of Article 14 in respect of sexual orientation discrimination.

Conclusion: is the future bright under Protocol 12?

At the time of writing, 18 contracting states have ratified Protocol 12 of the Convention and, as a result, have extended to their citizens protection against discrimination by any public authority in respect of any right established in law. As Wintemute argues, if every state ratified Protocol 12 then it would supersede Article 14 and the requirement that a complaint concerning discrimination must fall within the ambit of one of the other Convention provisions would cease to exist.[82] This would leave the Court free to examine any differential treatment by a public authority in respect of legal rights and decide if it had an objective and reasonable justification. This would provide some increased scope for gay and lesbian applicants to complain about discriminatory treatment across a wider range of issues. However, because the Court is already willing to engage in a wide reading of the other substantive provisions of the Convention and accept that discrimination on the grounds of sexual orientation falls within their ambit for the purposes of Article 14 (for example, in *E.B. v France*), Protocol 12 is important only insofar as it puts beyond any doubt the principle that sexual minorities must not be discriminated against in the enjoyment of any right set forth by law.

Is the potential for the increased ratification of Protocol 12 the basis for optimism for homosexuals? In light of the Court's case law, there are reasons

79 European Union Council Directive 2000/78/EC of 27 November 2000 establishing a general framework for equal treatment in employment and occupation.

80 Treaty of Lisbon amending the Treaty on European Union and the Treaty establishing the European Community, signed at Lisbon, 13 December 2007, *Official Journal of The European Union*, C306.

81 *Tadao Maruko v Versorgungsanstalt der deutschen Bühnen*, Court of Justice of the European Union, 1 April 2008, C-267/06.

82 R. Wintemute, 'Filling the Article 14 "Gap": Government Ratification and Judicial Control of Protocol No. 12 ECHR: Part 2', *European Human Rights Law Review* 5, 2004, 484–499.

to be both hopeful and cautious. The Court has made clear that it will interpret the concept of discrimination under Protocol 12 to mean 'treating differently, without an objective and reasonable justification, persons in similar situations'.[83] Given the Court's admissibility decision in *Manenc v France*, the issue of analogous situation is likely to continue to cause difficulties for those in same-sex partnerships who are not deemed comparable to heterosexual couples. Even though the applicants in *Manenc* had contracted a civil partnership, the judgment in *Schalk and Kopf v Austria* suggests that the Court is unwilling to recognize differential treatment between those in heterosexual marriage and those in homosexual civil partnerships as discriminatory. If a contracting state enacted legislation that made marriage available to 'everyone' and then subsequently discriminated against individuals on the grounds of sexual orientation, Protocol 12 would provide a means to complain. However, in states that continue to operate a 'separate but equal' system of partnership registration, or offer same-sex partners no legal registration at all, the Court's current jurisprudence in respect of Article 14 does not suggest that a complaint would be more successful under Protocol 12.

Of course, the question of whether claims based on Protocol 12 are more likely to succeed in the Court depends entirely on the Court's attitude towards the justifications offered by contracting states in respect of differential treatment based on sexual orientation. Although the Court has established that 'particularly weighty reasons need to be advanced before the Court to justify' differential treatment based on sexual orientation and that 'if the reasons advanced for a difference in treatment were based solely on the applicant's sexual orientation, this would amount to discrimination under the Convention',[84] it has confirmed in *Schalk and Kopf* (where the difference in treatment complained of *was* based solely on the applicants' sexual orientation) that it will afford a state a margin of appreciation to differentiate between individuals on the basis of sexual orientation. Whilst there is every reason to be sanguine about the Court's approach to the objective and reasonable test – because it has set a high threshold for contracting states to reach – there remain areas of policy and practice where a state's justification may be deemed to meet these criteria. There are, as I have shown, several areas in which the Court's case law fails to establish definitively that differential treatment on the grounds of sexual orientation constitutes discrimination under the Convention. As I explore in the next chapter, one of the most significant areas that will face increasing contestation concerns discrimination in respect of marriage.

83 *Sejdić and Finci v Bosnia and Herzegovina* [GC], nos. 27996/06 and 34836/06, 22 December 2009, § 55.

84 *Kozak v Poland*, no. 13102/02, 2 March 2010, § 92.

Chapter 6

A right to marriage?

Same-sex relationships and Article 12

In the previous chapter, I examined the use of Article 14 of the Convention to challenge forms of discrimination based on sexual orientation. In respect of various forms of unequal treatment that are created and sustained by the domestic law of contracting states, Article 14 has provided an important basis for evolving the Court's interpretation of the other substantive provisions of the Convention (most notably Article 8) to address the discrimination of homosexuals. With regard to discrimination in marriage law, the use of Article 14 in this way is made problematic by the existence of Article 12 of the Convention which, in providing a discrete right to marry, states that:

> Men and women of marriageable age have the right to marry and to found a family, according to the national laws governing the exercise of this right.

As the Court has recently acknowledged, the wording of Article 12 is distinctly different to that of the other substantive provisions of the Convention that grant rights to 'everyone' or specify that 'no one' must be subject to certain forms of treatment.[1] Like the domestic marriage laws of many contracting states, as well as other international human rights instruments such as the Universal Declaration of Human Rights,[2] Article 12 specifies that the right to marry is limited to 'men and women'. This textual construction has frequently been interpreted to mean that the right is delimited to biologically opposite persons and that, as a consequence, same-sex partners are excluded from it. Whilst this heteronormative interpretation of Article 12 is not inevitable – since 'men and women' could be understood to encompass

1 *Schalk and Kopf v Austria*, no. 30141/04, 24 June 2010, § 55.

2 Article 16(1) of the Universal Declaration of Human Rights states: 'Men and women of full age, without any limitation due to race, nationality or religion, have the right to marry and to found a family. They are entitled to equal rights as to marriage, during marriage and at its dissolution.'

same-sex relationships or Article 12 could be read in light of Article 1, which requires contracting states to 'secure to everyone' all of the rights and freedoms in the Convention – it is the interpretation most recently adopted by the Court in *Schalk and Kopf v Austria*:

> The Court observes that, looked at in isolation, the wording of Article 12 might be interpreted so as not to exclude the marriage between two men or two women. However, in contrast, all other substantive Articles of the Convention grant rights and freedoms to 'everyone' or state that 'no one' is to be subjected to certain types of prohibited treatment. The choice of wording in Article 12 must thus be regarded as deliberate. Moreover, regard must be had to the historical context in which the Convention was adopted. In the 1950s marriage was clearly understood in the traditional sense of being a union between partners of different sex.[3]

The Court's emphasis on the Convention's relationship to 'traditional' marriage is highly significant. Whilst contemporary debates about same-sex marriage comprise multi-faceted and complex social, cultural, political and ethical arguments that extend beyond issues of law and human rights, challenges to the legal construction of heteronormative marriage are fundamental to those who are excluded from this institution. Therefore, Article 12 of the Convention, and the Court's interpretation of it, should be seen as pivotal in the ongoing struggle to enable legal equality in marriage on the grounds of sexual orientation.

Same-sex marriage, heteronormativity and human rights

Same-sex couples seeking access to civil marriage have sought redress from their legislative exclusion to it through the courts of various jurisdictions both within and outside of Europe.[4] In doing so, they have claimed that laws prohibiting them from contracting marriage are a form of direct discrimination, which functions to deny them access to a fundamental social institution. For example, in *Minister of Home Affairs v Fourie & Lesbian and Gay Equality Project and Eighteen Others v Minister of Home Affairs*, heard by the Constitutional Court of South Africa, the applicants argued that in excluding same-sex couples from 'publicly celebrating their love and commitment to each other' the law (which defined marriage as 'a union of one man with one woman') 'shuts them out' from the wider 'public recognition' and 'rights and responsibilities' that flow

3 *Schalk and Kopf v Austria*, no. 30141/04, 24 June 2010, § 55.
4 See, for example: *Wilkinson v Kitzinger* (2006) EWHC 2022 (Fam).

from marriage.[5] The Constitutional Court of South Africa upheld the complaint, finding that the law represented a 'harsh if oblique statement [. . .] that same-sex couples are outsiders, and that their need for affirmation and protection of their intimate relations as human beings is somehow less than that of heterosexual couples'.[6] As I discussed in Chapter 2, the South African Court explicitly challenged the lack of value accorded to same-sex partnerships by a heteronormative system, which 'reinforces the wounding notion' that they 'do not fit into normal society' and signals that their 'capacity for love, commitment and accepting responsibility is by definition less worthy of regard than that of heterosexual couples'.[7] This argument resonates with the widespread (although contested)[8] belief that challenging the 'long-standing heteronormativity inscribed in laws that deny marriage to same-sex couples'[9] is the 'engine' to address and end all discrimination against non-heterosexuals and establish their formal legal equality with heterosexuals.[10]

Opponents of same-sex marriage often conceptualize marriage very differently, seeing its legal construction not as a mechanism through which non-heterosexuals are discriminated against but as the reflection of a traditional institution founded upon the central principle of sex difference. In this sense, protecting marriage is not, it is argued, concerned with a denial of legal and human rights to non-heterosexuals, but with the continuation of a socially important and distinctive way of life. As the defendants in *Perry v Schwarzenegger* argued, in a case heard by the United States District Court for the Northern District of California, when defending a voter-enacted amendment to the California Constitution that stated: 'Only marriage between a man and a woman is valid or recognized in California'[11]:

> preserving marriage [is] not an attack on the gay lifestyle [but] protects our children from being taught in public schools that 'same-sex marriage' is the same as traditional marriage [. . .] While death, divorce, or other circumstances may prevent the ideal, the best situation for a child is to be

5 *Minister of Home Affairs v Fourie (2005) & Lesbian and Gay Equality Project and Eighteen Others v Minister of Home Affairs (2005)*, 1 December 2005, ZACC 19, § 1–2.

6 Ibid., § 71.

7 Ibid.

8 For a critique of the view that gaining legal access to civil marriage will result in a transformation of heteronormative social relations or a weakening of social discrimination on the grounds of sexual orientation, see: R. Robson, *Sappho Goes to Law School: Fragments in Lesbian Legal Theory*, New York: Columbia University Press, 1998.

9 V. Taylor, K. Kimport, N. Van Dyke and E.A. Andersen, 'Culture and Mobilization: Tactical Repertoires, Same-Sex Weddings, and the Impact on Gay Activism', *American Sociological Review* 74, 2009, 865–890 at 865–866.

10 R. Harding, 'Dogs Are "Registered", People Shouldn't Be': Legal Consciousness and Lesbian and Gay Rights', *Social and Legal Studies* 15(4), 2006, 511–533.

11 Article I, section 7.5 of the Constitution of California.

> raised by a married mother and father. [W]hile gays have the right to their private lives, they do not have the right to redefine marriage for everyone else.[12]

The question of whether non-heterosexuals possess a 'right to redefine' existing laws that prohibit them from contracting civil marriage is fundamental to considerations of same-sex marriage and Article 12 of the Convention. Given the significant exclusion of same-sex partners from civil marriage in Europe (at the time of writing, only seven of the 47 contracting states allow same-sex marriage[13]), applicants to the Court have begun to invoke Article 12 to challenge hetero-normative marriage law. Although, as I examine in more detail below, the Court adopted a conservative interpretation of Article 12 in its first consideration of same-sex marriage in *Schalk and Kopf v Austria*,[14] the textual construction of the right to marry in the Convention should not be seen as forever precluding same-sex couples from the right that it grants. Courts around the world have examined similarly constructed marriage provisions in domestic law and found them to be in violation of constitutional and human rights.[15] There is no reason, therefore, why the Strasbourg Court could not adopt a similar position in the future.

However, Strasbourg jurisprudence in respect of same-sex marriage is particularly underdeveloped. Unlike in matters relating to the criminalization of private sexual acts, where the Court was a world leader in establishing that the sexual privacy of homosexual men was a human right, the Court's jurisprudence on same-sex marriage has shown little evolution. This reflects the general state of international law and its negligible impact on the legal organization of civil marriage in nation states.[16] The Council of Europe has shown little commitment to encouraging either the Court or contracting states to adopt an inclusive interpretation of marriage. For example, the Committee of Ministers, in its recommendation of measures to combat discrimination on the grounds of sexual orientation, only went so far as to state: 'Where national legislation recognizes registered same-sex partnerships, member states should seek to ensure that their legal status and their rights and obligations are equivalent to those of heterosexual couples in a comparable situation.'[17] The

12 *Perry v Schwarzenegger* (2010), In the United States District Court for the Northern District of California, No C 09-2292 VRW, § 6–7.

13 Same-sex civil marriage is legal in Belgium, Iceland, the Netherlands, Norway, Portugal, Spain and Sweden.

14 *Schalk and Kopf v Austria*, no. 30141/04, 24 June 2010.

15 P. Johnson, 'Challenging the Heteronormativity of Marriage: The Role of Judicial Interpretation and Authority', *Social and Legal Studies* 20(3), 2011, 349–367.

16 International Commission of Jurists, *Sexual Orientation, Gender Identity and Justice: A Comparative Law Casebook*, Geneva: ICJ, 2011.

17 Council of Europe, 'Recommendation CM/Rec(2010)5 of the Committee of Ministers to Member States on Measures to Combat Discrimination on Grounds of Sexual Orientation or Gender Identity', § 24.

Committee of Ministers also invited those contracting states that do not offer same-sex partners a form of legal registration 'to consider the possibility of providing, without discrimination of any kind, including against different-sex couples, same-sex couples with legal or other means to address the practical problems related to the social reality in which they live'.[18] Such an invitation hardly addresses the legal exclusion from marriage that same-sex couples experience in most contracting states. Nor does it offer any challenge to the introduction of separate civil partnership legislation that many argue creates an Apartheid-like policy of 'separate but equal' arrangements for homosexual and heterosexual couples. Similarly, whilst Article 9 of the Charter of Fundamental Rights of the European Union has deliberately omitted the reference to men and women, which suggests an inclusive approach to conceptualizing marriage as a human right, it maintains that any right to marriage is guaranteed in accordance with national law and that there is no requirement that nation states should facilitate same-sex marriage.[19]

The legal construction of marriage in nation states around the world remains trenchantly heteronormative. Whilst 10 states currently permit same-sex marriage and some have introduced civil-partnership legislation, others have enacted new legislation designed to explicitly exclude same-sex partners from contracting marriage.[20] In light of this it is legitimate to argue, as Morgan does, that:

> from a liberal, positivist point of view, we [gay men and lesbians] have had some success. We have made some gains in being included in the heteronormative system. But [. . .] we have not been very successful at breaking down that system. We have not managed [. . .] to challenge the heteronormative assumptions upon which the system is based.[21]

Morgan's observation echoes the more general complaint that, in terms of marriage, 'law supports the heteronormative discourses in our culture and our

18 Ibid., § 25.

19 The *Explanations Relating to the Charter of Fundamental Rights* (Official Journal of the European Union, 14 December 2007, 2007/C 303/02) state that Article 9 of the Charter of Fundamental Rights of the European Union 'neither prohibits nor imposes the granting of the status of marriage to unions between people of the same sex'.

20 For example, in Nigeria ('A Bill for An Act to Prohibit Marriage Between Persons of Same Gender, Solemnization of Same and for Other Matters Related Therewith', Parliament of Nigeria, SB.05/C895, 2011) and the United States of America (Defense of Marriage Act (Pub.L. 104–199, 110 Stat. 2419, enacted 21 September 1996, 1 U.S.C. § 7 and 28 U.S.C. § 1738C)).

21 W. Morgan, 'Queering International Human Rights Law', in C.F. Stychin, and D. Herman (eds.), *Law, Sexuality: The Global Arena*, Minneapolis: University of Minnesota Press, 2001, p. 211.

politics that elevate and protect heterosexual social arrangements even as they cause hardship to those living outside those boundaries'.[22] Given the level of exclusion from marriage that same-sex partners experience, the evolution of Strasbourg jurisprudence in respect of Article 12 is one of the most vital and pressing issues facing those who wish to develop this area of lesbian and gay human rights.

Strasbourg jurisprudence in respect of same-sex marriage and Article 12

Prior to the Court's first consideration of same-sex marriage in *Schalk and Kopf v Austria*, the Strasbourg organs had paid little attention to the rights of homosexual partners under Article 12.[23] The Commission issued only one decision in respect of an Article 12 complaint lodged by a same-sex couple prior to the Court's judgment in *Schalk and Kopf*. Whilst in part this is because of a lack of Article 12 complaints brought by applicants, it can also be seen as the outcome of the pervasive heteronormative understanding of marriage embedded in the Court's jurisprudence. The Court's strongly heteronormative conception of marriage is made clear in a number of judgments issued in respect of the rights of transsexuals to marry under Article 12. In *Rees v the United Kingdom*, the Court stated that 'the right to marry guaranteed by Article 12 refers to the traditional marriage between persons of opposite biological sex. This appears also from the wording of the Article which makes it clear that Article 12 is mainly concerned to protect marriage as the basis of the family'.[24] This understanding of marriage, in which biological sex, reproduction and the family are invoked as imperatives for excluding 'non-traditional' couples from the rights guaranteed by Article 12, has seen little evolution. In *Cossey v the United Kingdom*, the Court found that the 'attachment to the traditional concept of marriage [which underpins Article 12] provides sufficient reason for the continued adoption [. . .] of biological criteria for determining a person's sex for the purposes of marriage'.[25] In *Christine Goodwin v the United Kingdom*, the Court departed from this position and stated that the terms 'man' and 'woman' in Article 12 should no longer be understood to relate to 'purely biological criteria'.[26] The judgment in *Christine Goodwin*, which has been the basis for legislative changes in

22 S. Barclay, M. Bernstein and A-M. Marshall, *Queer Mobilizations: LGBT Activists Confront the Law*, New York: NYU Press, 2009, p. 14.

23 *Schalk and Kopf v Austria*, no. 30141/04, 24 June 2010.

24 *Rees v the United Kingdom*, no. 9532/81, 17 October 1986, Series A no. 106, § 49.

25 *Cossey v the United Kingdom*, no. 10843/84, 27 September 1990, Series A no. 184, § 46.

26 *Christine Goodwin v the United Kingdom* [GC], no. 28957/95, 11 July 2002, ECHR 2002-VI, § 100.

Europe that have afforded transsexuals legal recognition and rights in relation to their acquired sex (for example: The Gender Recognition Act 2004 in the United Kingdom), was initially viewed as providing a strong basis for advancing claims for same-sex marriage under Article 12.[27] However, in *Schalk and Kopf*, the Court stated that the principles established in *Christine Goodwin* did not impose any obligation on contracting states to grant same-sex couples access to marriage because *Christine Goodwin* was concerned with marriage of partners who are of different genders, even if gender is not defined by purely biological criteria. Whilst the Court's understanding of the relationship between biological sex and gender has therefore shown some evolution, its view that gender difference is a necessary precondition for exercising the right to marry under Article 12 has not.

Another factor influencing the Court's long-standing silence on same-sex relationships and Article 12 is, as I have argued in previous chapters, the general tendency of the Strasbourg organs to reduce all matters relating to homosexuality to sexual privacy. The issue of same-sex marriage extends beyond questions of 'sex rights' and encompasses a broader demand for the state legitimization of intimate and loving relationships and the social benefits that flow from these. Yet the Strasbourg organs have a long history of being unwilling to consider homosexual relationships in any terms other than those relating to sexual acts in private. Whilst, as I argued in Chapter 1, early petitions to the Commission complained about the impact of the criminalization of homosexual sexual acts on the love relationships of homosexual men, the Strasbourg organs have rarely acknowledged or considered homosexuality in this way. Article 12 complaints made by same-sex couples are a challenge to the Court's conceptualization of homosexuality because they focus attention not on *sex* but on long-term *love* relationships. In this sense, Article 12 complaints require the Court to pay attention to the 'personal, social and legal consequences'[28] of entering into a civil marriage that it has previously considered only in respect of 'traditional' (heterosexual) relationships.

Whilst considerations of same-sex marriage have generally been absent from Strasbourg jurisprudence, occasional references to homosexual relationships and Article 12 have been made. The first mention of homosexuality in respect of Article 12 was in the dissenting opinion of Mr. Schermers in *W. v the United Kingdom*.[29] This case concerned a complaint brought by a transsexual applicant about her inability to officially record her change of sex and, as a result of this, contract heterosexual civil marriage. In dissenting

27 R. Wintemute, 'From "Sex Rights" to "Love Rights": Partnership Rights as Human Rights', in N. Bamforth (ed.), *Sex Rights: The Oxford Amnesty Lectures 2002*, Oxford: Oxford University Press, 2005, p. 192.

28 *Schalk and Kopf v Austria*, no. 30141/04, 24 June 2010, § 49.

29 *W. v the United Kingdom*, no. 11095/84, Commission report, 7 March 1989.

from the majority opinion and arguing that transsexuals should be granted the right to marry under Article 12, Mr. Schermers went on to make a statement regarding homosexuality and marriage:

> The right to live in a family and – when of marriageable age – to found a family is of paramount importance for the individual. Denial of this right means condemnation to solitude and loneliness. There must be strong arguments to justify such a condemnation. In my opinion the fundamental human right underlying Article 12 should also be granted to homosexual and lesbian couples. They should not be denied the right to found a family without good reasons.[30]

Mr. Schermers' consideration of the impact of the exclusion from the rights guaranteed by Article 12 upon homosexuals is a rare moment in Strasbourg jurisprudence when the value of same-sex relationships is acknowledged. The claim that contracting states should provide strong arguments to justify prohibiting same-sex couples from marrying is founded on the view that the impact of such exclusion creates considerable emotional damage to individuals. Whilst Mr. Schermers' understanding of marriage and the family might be criticized for its normative assumptions about a universal need for individuals to enter into these institutions, his willingness to recognize the 'paramount importance' of marriage for homosexuals is atypical in Strasbourg jurisprudence. In light of Mr. Schermers' support for same-sex marriage, it is disappointing that he did not file a dissenting opinion in the decision given by the Commission just seven months later when, in *C. and L.M. v the United Kingdom*, it declared inadmissible the first Article 12 complaint by a same-sex couple.[31] In *C. and L.M.*, the Commission bluntly stated that, in light of the Court's case law on the rights available to transsexuals under the Convention, the applicant's 'relationship with her lesbian cohabitee does not give rise to a right to marry and found a family within the meaning of Article 12'.[32] The Commission did not take the view in *C. and L.M.*, therefore, that 'strong arguments' were necessary to justify the exclusion of same-sex partners from marriage. The Court retained this position, as I discuss below, in *Schalk and Kopf v Austria*, when it bypassed an analysis of the proportionality of excluding same-sex couples from marriage by granting contracting states a margin of appreciation to determine their own marriage arrangements in respect of sexual orientation.

Another significant consideration of same-sex partnerships can be found in *Burden v the United Kingdom* where, although the application did not involve a

30 Ibid., Partially dissenting opinion of Mr. Schermers.

31 *C. and L.M. v the United Kingdom*, no. 14753/89, Commission decision, 9 October 1989.

32 Ibid., § 3.

sexual orientation complaint or invoke Article 12, the Court made a number of statements about the nature of marriage.[33] In *Burden*, as I discussed in the previous chapter, the applicants, two co-habiting sisters, argued that denying them access to the same tax arrangements as homosexual couples who have contracted civil partnerships amounted to discrimination under Article 14. In dismissing the application on the grounds that the applicants were not in an analogous situation with those in a civil partnership, the Court indicated that it regarded homosexual civil partnerships as analogous to heterosexual marriage:

> Since the coming into force of the Civil Partnership Act in the United Kingdom, a homosexual couple now also has the choice to enter into a legal relationship designed by Parliament to correspond as far as possible to marriage [. . .] As with marriage, the Grand Chamber considers that the legal consequences of civil partnership under the 2004 Act, which couples expressly and deliberately decide to incur, set these types of relationship apart from other forms of co-habitation. Rather than the length or the supportive nature of the relationship, what is determinative is the existence of a public undertaking, carrying with it a body of rights and obligations of a contractual nature. Just as there can be no analogy between married and Civil Partnership Act couples, on one hand, and heterosexual or homosexual couples who choose to live together but not to become husband and wife or civil partners, on the other hand [. . .], the absence of such a legally binding agreement between the applicants renders their relationship of co-habitation, despite its long duration, fundamentally different to that of a married or civil partnership couple.[34]

However, in his concurring opinion in *Burden*, Judge Björgvinsson went to considerable length to express his heteronormative view of marriage and to give an assurance that, regardless of any changes introduced at a domestic level by contracting states, the Court had no role to play in requiring contracting states to make marriage available to same-sex couples:

> it should [. . .] be borne in mind that the institution of marriage is closely linked to the idea of the family, consisting of a man and a woman and their children, as one of the cornerstones of the social structure in the United Kingdom, as well as in the other Member States of the Council of Europe. On the basis of this assumption, a whole framework of legal rules, of both a private and public nature, has come into existence over a long period of time. These rules relate to the establishment of marriage

33 *Burden v the United Kingdom* [GC], no. 13378/05, 29 April 2008.
34 Ibid., § 65.

> and mutual rights and obligations between spouses in both personal and financial matters (including inheritance) and in relation to their children, if any, as well as with regard to taxes (including inheritance taxes), social security, and other matters. The applicability of such rules, or similar rules, in many of the Member States have gradually, step by step, and mostly upon the initiative of the legislature in the respective countries, been extended to cover relationships other than those traditionally falling under marriage in the formal legal sense, namely civil partnership couples (including individuals of the same sex), and thereby the legislator has responded to new social realities and changing moral and social values. However, it is important to have in mind that each and every step taken in this direction, positive as it may seem to be from the point of view of equal rights, potentially has important and far reaching consequences for the social structure of society, as well as legal consequences, *i.e.* for the social security and tax system in the respective countries. It is precisely for this reason that it is not the role of this Court to take the initiative in this matter and impose upon the Member States a duty further to extend the applicability of these rules with no clear view of the consequences that it may have in the different Member States. In my view it must fall within the margin of appreciation of the respondent State to decide when and to what extent this will be done.[35]

A similar view was adopted by the Court in its recent judgment in *Schalk and Kopf v Austria.*[36]

Schalk and Kopf v Austria

Schalk and Kopf v Austria was the first consideration by the Court of the rights available to same-sex couples under Article 12 of the Convention. *Schalk and Kopf* originated in 2002 when the Vienna Municipal Office refused a male couple the right to contract civil marriage under the Civil Code 1812, which states that marriage can only be contracted by persons of the opposite sex. The applicants lodged an unsuccessful appeal with the Vienna Regional Governor who informed them that Austrian law, and Article 12 of the Convention, guaranteed the right of marriage only to persons of the opposite sex. In a subsequent appeal in the Constitutional Court, the couple contended that marriage had evolved since the enactment of the Civil Code and that the law should be amended in light of present-day conditions. The Constitutional Court rejected this claim and cited Article 12 of the Convention to support its view that marriage was a right available only to men and women in

35 Ibid., Concurring opinion of Judge Björgvinsson.
36 *Schalk and Kopf v Austria*, no. 30141/04, 24 June 2010.

different-sex partnerships. The Constitutional Court's reading of Article 12 mirrors the interpretation of the High Court of England in Wales which, in *Wilkinson v Kitzinger*, stated that to accord 'a same-sex relationship the title and status of marriage would be to fly in the face of the Convention'.[37]

In their complaint to the Court, the applicants in *Schalk and Kopf* claimed that Article 12 should be read in light of present-day conditions[38] to acknowledge the existence and importance of same-sex partnerships. In addition, as I discussed in the previous chapter, the applicants argued that excluding same-sex couples from marriage constituted a form of discrimination contrary to Article 14 taken in conjunction with Article 8. By the time the Court heard the case, Austria had enacted the Registered Partnership Act, which, coming into force in January 2010, enables 'two persons of the same sex' to become 'registered partners' and 'thereby commit themselves to a lasting relationship with mutual rights and obligations'. There are a number of differences between marriage and registered partnership, with the most significant involving parental rights: registered partners, unlike married couples, cannot adopt a child, cannot adopt a stepchild and have no access to state-regulated assisted ('artificial') insemination. On the basis of these recognized differences, the Court refused an application from the Austrian government who argued that, in light of the enactment of the Registered Partners Act, the case should be struck from the Court's list.

The Court's response to the complaint in *Schalk and Kopf* was, unlike the highest courts in other jurisdictions (for example: Canada,[39] Mexico[40] and South Africa[41]), to adopt a conservative and heteronormative interpretation of marriage and to defer to the authority of contracting states. This is clear in the Court's rejection of the applicants' claim that, since the Convention is a living instrument, Article 12 should be read in light of the present-day existence of same-sex relationships. The Court's response to this was that, although 'the institution of marriage has undergone major social changes since the adoption of the Convention, [. . .] there is no European consensus regarding same-sex marriage'.[42] Relying upon consensus analysis in this way enabled the Court to bypass the need to engage in any consideration of proportionality and defer to the Austrian state's margin of appreciation. The Court's conservatism is also clearly demonstrated by its consideration of Article 9 of the Charter of

37 *Wilkinson v Kitzinger* (2006) EWHC 2022 (Fam), § 120.

38 See Chapter 3 for a discussion of this principle, which is derived from *Tyrer v the United Kingdom*, no. 5856/72, 25 April 1978, Series A no. 26, § 31.

39 *M. v H.* [1999] 2 SCR 3.

40 On 10 August 2010 the Supreme Court of Justice of the Nation of Mexico held that all states in Mexico were required to recognize same-sex marriages performed in other states.

41 *Minister of Home Affairs v Fourie (2005) & Lesbian and Gay Equality Project and Eighteen Others v Minister of Home Affairs (2005)*, 1 December 2005, ZACC 19.

42 *Schalk and Kopf v Austria*, no. 30141/04, 24 June 2010, § 58.

Fundamental Rights of the European Union which, as I noted above, has omitted any reference to gender in respect of the right to marry. In light of this, the Court stated that 'it would no longer consider that the right to marry enshrined in Article 12 must in all circumstances be limited to marriage between two persons of the opposite sex'.[43] Wintemute has interpreted this as an important change in the Court's interpretation of Article 12 and as a strong signal that it will evolve its jurisprudence to recognize a right to same-sex marriage in the future.[44] However, the Court also placed significant emphasis on the fact that Article 9 of the Charter, like Article 12 of the Convention, leaves the decision of whether to allow same-sex marriage to contracting states. In that respect, the Court stressed the importance of the 'deep-rooted social and cultural connotations' of marriage in Europe and stated that it 'must not rush to substitute' the legal provisions of 'national authorities, who are best placed to assess and respond to the needs of society'.[45] This privileging of 'traditional' heterosexual marriage can be seen as the defensive behaviour of the Court which, as Hodson observes, like a 'lurching ship entering choppy unchartered waters' sought the safe harbour of heteronormativity.[46]

Whilst the Court's interpretation of Article 12 in *Schalk and Kopf* can be seen to support a strongly heteronormative understanding of marriage, the concurring opinion offered by Judge Malinverni, joined by Judge Kovler, demonstrates an extreme nervousness at the slightest hint that same-sex relationships could fall within the scope of Article 12 in the future. Malinverni and Kovler felt 'unable to share the view that "looked at in isolation, the wording of Article 12 might be interpreted so as not to exclude the marriage between two men or two women" '[47] and went to significant lengths, via a description of the Vienna Convention on the Law Treaties, to state that there is 'no doubt in my mind that Article 12 of the Convention cannot be construed in any other way than as being applicable solely to persons of different sexes'.[48] Nor could Malinverni and Kovler accept the majority's view that, in light of Article 9 of the Charter of Fundamental Rights of the European Union, Article 12 must in all circumstances be limited to marriage between two persons of the opposite sex. These judges stated that 'Article 12 is inapplicable to persons of the same sex' and that 'Article 9 of the Charter

43 Ibid., § 61.

44 R. Wintemute, 'Equal Love, The Legal Case: Professor Robert Wintemute Explains the Legal Basis of the Application to the European Court of Human Rights', available HTTP: <http://equallove.org.uk/the-legal-case> (last accessed 20 February 2012).

45 *Schalk and Kopf v Austria*, no. 30141/04, 24 June 2010, § 62.

46 L. Hodson, *NGOs and the Struggle for Human Rights in Europe*, Oxford: Hart Publishing, 2011, p. 176.

47 *Schalk and Kopf v Austria*, no. 30141/04, 24 June 2010, Concurring opinion of Judge Malinverni joined by Judge Kovler, § 1.

48 Ibid.

should therefore have no bearing on the interpretation of Article 12 of the Convention as conferring a right to marry only on persons of different sexes'.[49]

The concurring opinion of Malinverni and Kovler may seem disproportionate in light of the majority judgment, which effectively foreclosed Article 12 rights to same-sex couples, but it is an example of the panicked response that is frequently produced when heteronormative social relations are challenged. It exemplifies the way in which heterosexual 'traditions' are reproduced and maintained by continuously shoring up their borders with those sexual and intimate relations that are imagined to be 'outside' and 'other' to heterosexuality.[50] Malinverni and Kovler's concurring opinion, and the judgment in *Schalk and Kopf* more generally, can be seen as an exercise in the reproduction of heteronormative privilege through the exclusion of homosexuals from the rights and benefits associated with marriage. The justifications given for such exclusion and segregation – the 'deep-rooted social and cultural connotations' of marriage – are similar to those once routinely advanced by liberal, democratic governments to legitimize distinctions based on ethnicity. As Justice Sachs of the Constitutional Court of South Africa has stated, in respect of same-sex marriage: 'proponents of segregation would vehemently deny any intention to cause insult' and 'justify the apartness as being a reflection of a natural or divinely ordained state of affairs', but such justifications serve as a 'threadbare cloak for covering distaste for or repudiation by those in power of the group subjected to segregation'.[51] Whilst, as I argued in Chapter 4, the judgment in *Schalk and Kopf* made the positive step of recognizing that same-sex relationships fall within the scope of the family life limb of Article 8, the Court's interpretation of Article 12 strongly endorses a heteronormative view of marriage. The judgment establishes that the Convention does not require contracting states to make marriage available to same-sex partners and, as I argued in the previous chapter, that a 'separate but equal' policy organized around civil partnerships does not contravene rights guaranteed by the Convention.

The future of same-sex marriage under Article 12

The Court's jurisprudence on marriage is trenchantly heteronormative. Although, as I argued above, the Court has progressively evolved its understanding of

49 Ibid.

50 See: J. Butler, *Gender Trouble: Feminism and the Subversion of Identity*, New York: Routledge, 1990; D. Fuss, 'Inside/Out', in D. Fuss (ed.), *Inside/Out: Lesbian Theories, Gay Theories*, New York: Routledge, 1991; D.M. Halperin, *Saint Foucault: Towards a Gay Hagiography*, New York: Oxford University Press, 1995; M. Warner, *Fear of a Queer Planet*, Minneapolis: University of Minnesota Press, 1993.

51 *Minister of Home Affairs v Fourie (2005) & Lesbian and Gay Equality Project and Eighteen Others v Minister of Home Affairs (2005)*, 1 December 2005, ZACC 19, § 150.

gender identity to acknowledge that gender is not determined by 'purely biological criteria' but also by 'the social role of the assigned gender',[52] it continues to regard gender difference as a prerequisite of the rights guaranteed by Article 12. Although, in *Schalk and Kopf*, the Court suggested that the organization of marriage in respect of gender difference is the result of 'social and cultural connotations', rather than an outcome of 'nature', it remains uncritical of this. The Court, therefore, offers no critique of how ideas of gender difference are used to justify the preservation of the heteronormative social construction of marriage. Other higher courts have argued that a failure to examine the presumption that gender difference is a requirement of civil marriage is akin to accepting marriage restrictions based on race. For example, the United States District Court for the Northern District of California held that to prohibit partners from marrying on the basis of their gender is analogous to the 'historical prevalence' of 'archaic, shameful or even bizarre' restrictions on marital partners in respect of race.[53] Yet the Court has shown little sign of engaging in a critical consideration of normative conceptions of marriage and, instead, has reiterated a heteronormative understanding of the wording of Article 12. In doing so, the Court has played a performative role in (re)constructing the heteronormative 'tradition' of marriage.

It is perhaps because of the Court's current interpretative position on Article 12 that a different strategy has been advanced in two recent applications, *Chapin and Charpentier v France*[54] and *Ferguson and Others v the United Kingdom*,[55] which both make complaints under Article 14 in conjunction with Article 12. In *Ferguson*, brought by eight couples in association with the 'Equal Love Campaign',[56] the complainants – four same-sex couples and four different-sex couples – argue that the United Kingdom's separate legal provisions for the registration of homosexual and heterosexual partners violate Article 14 of the Convention taken in conjunction with Article 12. The applicants argue that 'it is often better to examine cases of discrimination against minorities in Europe under Article 14, combined with another Convention right, rather than under the other Convention right taken alone'.[57] Combining Article 14 with Article 12 is a different approach to that taken in *Schalk and Kopf*, in which the applicants complained under Article 14 in conjunction with Article 8 and Article 12 alone. The complaint in *Ferguson* is designed to

52 *Christine Goodwin v the United Kingdom* [GC], no. 28957/95, 11 July 2002, ECHR 2002-VI, § 100.

53 *Perry v Schwarzenegger* (2010), In the United States District Court for the Northern District of California, No. C 09–2292 VRW, § 112.

54 *Chapin and Charpentier v France*, no. 40183/07, Statement of facts, lodged 6 September 2007.

55 *Ferguson and Others v the United Kingdom*, lodged with the Court on 2 February 2011.

56 Available HTTP: <http://equallove.org.uk/> (last accessed 20 February 2012).

57 *Ferguson and Others v the United Kingdom*, lodged with the Court on 2 February 2011, § 152.

encourage the Court to consider whether excluding same-sex couples from an opportunity that is provided to the majority under Article 12 amounts to discrimination under Article 14. The applicants hope that this strategy will require the United Kingdom to provide a justification for the difference in treatment that can satisfy the objective and reasonable test of the Court. They feel confident that 'the United Kingdom has no justification for maintaining the current system, other than tradition and a desire to avoid a confrontation with religious opponents of any form of legal marriage for same-sex couples'.[58]

The complaint in *Ferguson* is unusual in that the applicants explicitly state that they are not 'asking the Court to decide that all Council of Europe member states must permit same-sex couples to marry'.[59] Rather, the applicants request that the Court, in light of the judgment by the Court of Justice of the European Union in *Tadao Maruko v Versorgungsanstalt der deutschen Bühnen*[60] (which established that where a state has enacted civil-partnership legislation that places same-sex couples in an analogous position with heterosexual married couples, a difference in treatment between them, in areas covered by European Union anti-discrimination law, will amount to direct discrimination based on sexual orientation contrary to Council Directive 2000/78/EC[61] of the European Union), impose an 'obligation of consistency' on those European governments that have voluntarily created separate civil-partnership legislation for same-sex couples. Such an obligation would require those states to grant same-sex civil partners all of the rights of different-sex spouses, including the right to marry. If such a complaint were successful, it may risk discouraging those states that have not enacted legislation to recognize same-sex partnerships from doing so because it would trigger a further obligation to allow same-sex marriage. But the applicants in *Ferguson* argue that, having introduced civil-partnership legislation, the state should be required to recognize full equality between homosexual and heterosexual partners:

> The applicants respectfully urge the Court to impose an 'obligation of Consistency' on the United Kingdom, and require the United Kingdom to take the final, small step in the 150-year-long legal evolution of the treatment of same-sex couples, from 'criminals deserving the death penalty' to 'criminals' to 'pretended families' to 'civil partners', but not 'spouses', by finding that existing legislation on access to marriage and

58 Ibid., § 184.
59 Ibid., § 146.
60 *Tadao Maruko v Versorgungsanstalt der deutschen Bühnen*, Court of Justice of the European Union, 1 April 2008, C-267/06.
61 European Union Council Directive 2000/78/EC of 27 November 2000 establishing a general framework for equal treatment in employment and occupation.

> civil partnership discriminates on the ground of sexual orientation, and therefore violates Article 14 combined with Article 12 (right to marry) and Article 8 (respect for private life), or Articles 12 and 8 taken alone.[62]

If the complaint made under Article 14 taken in conjunction with Article 12 in *Ferguson* is deemed admissible, the applicants feel sure that any justification offered by the United Kingdom for the difference in treatment of same- and different-sex couples will fail to meet the objective and reasonable test of the Court. This view is given credence by the principle established in the Court's case law that any difference in treatment based on sexual orientation requires 'very weighty' and 'particularly serious reasons' to justify it[63] and that, furthermore, a difference of treatment based solely on the grounds of sexual orientation amounts to discrimination under the Convention.[64] Yet, despite the applicants' claim that 'tradition' or 'religious opposition' do not amount to an objective and reasonable justification, the significant weight placed by the Court on the 'deep-rooted social and cultural connotations' of marriage in *Schalk and Kopf* may suggest otherwise.

Conclusion

To give homosexual couples the full protection afforded to heterosexual couples by Article 12, the Court needs to use its living instrument doctrine to perform what Hodson aptly calls a 'dramatic resuscitation' on an aspect of the Convention that is becoming moribund in the social and legal context of contemporary Europe.[65] Maintaining a heteronormative understanding of Article 12 and deferring to the preferences of contracting states is unsustainable when the Council of Europe, as well as the European Union, are so firmly committed to ending discrimination on the grounds of sexual orientation. It is the European convergence in the commitment to end discrimination, rather than a consensus on same-sex marriage across contracting states, which should underwrite the Court's use of the living instrument doctrine. When present-day conditions consist of same-sex couples in every contracting state of the Council of Europe seeking access to civil marriage, the Court should declare that any state excluding homosexuals from this vital social institution restricts or reduces the right to marriage to the extent that the 'very essence of the right is impaired'.[66] This would bring the Court's interpretation of Article 12

62 *Ferguson and Others v the United Kingdom*, lodged with the Court on 2 February 2011, § 200.
63 *Karner v Austria*, no. 40016/98, 24 July 2003, ECHR 2003-IX, § 37.
64 *Kozak v Poland*, no. 13102/02, 2 March 2010, § 91–92.
65 L. Hodson, 'A Marriage By Any Other Name? Schalk and Kopf v Austria', *Human Rights Law Review* 11(1), 170–179 at 172.
66 *F. v Switzerland*, no. 11329/85, 18 December 1987, Series A no. 128, § 32.

into line with its evolved Article 14 jurisprudence which, as I discussed in the previous chapter, now stresses that differences in treatment based solely on sexual orientation are unacceptable under the Convention. The Court's focus should not be on its presumptive understanding of how the original drafters of the Convention conceived marriage, but on its long-standing commitment to a teleological evolution of the Convention so that it offers protection to individuals in the context of contemporary societies.

In order for the Court to evolve its Article 12 jurisprudence, it will need to engage in a critical assessment of the heteronormative assumptions that underpin its conception of marriage. It will need to examine marriage, like the United States District Court for the Northern District of California did, as an 'artefact' that is produced and sustained by broader ideological conceptions of how sex, gender and sexuality should be socially organized.[67] The Court should not passively reproduce the heteronormativity of marriage by uncritically accepting claims about its 'deep-rootedness' in European societies. Many forms of discrimination are long-standing but this does not mean that they do not violate fundamental human rights. The Court should examine the social normativity of excluding same-sex couples from marriage and question what justification can be offered for this. The Court should not hide, as it did in *Schalk and Kopf*, behind the idea that the issue of same-sex marriage is a 'sensitive area of social, political and religious controversy'.[68] Same-sex marriage is not a sensitive or controversial subject to those homosexual couples who wish to gain access to one of the most basic human rights currently guaranteed to heterosexuals by the Convention. Those who find the issue controversial and sensitive are those who fear a disturbance in the 'traditional' organization of heterosexual privilege and power. It is untenable for a human rights organization to shy away from the human rights demands of same-sex couples because it fears controversy. If the Court adopted that attitude consistently, it would fail to deliver the innovative interpretation of the Convention necessary to give the rights contained in it meaningful effect. This is not the position adopted by the Court, as I explore in the next chapter, in respect of Article 11 of the Convention where it has been critical of the exercise of heterosexual majoritarian power to violate the rights of homosexuals.

67 *Perry v Schwarzenegger* (2010), In the United States District Court for the Northern District of California, No. C 09–2292 VRW.

68 *Schalk and Kopf v Austria*, no. 30141/04, 24 June 2010, § 46.

Chapter 7

Expression, assembly and association

Articles 10 and 11

In this chapter, I consider how Strasbourg jurisprudence supports homosexuals in enjoying the full social and civil rights afforded by Articles 10 and 11 of the Convention. The rights guaranteed by Articles 10 and 11 – rights of expression, which include the freedom to hold opinions and to receive and impart information and ideas, and rights of peaceful assembly and association – are vitally important to gay men and lesbians in contemporary societies where they continue to experience discrimination. A recent report by the European Union Agency for Fundamental Rights recognized that public assembly and expression are critical means by which sexual minorities address and combat inequalities but that, when attempting to organize public assemblies, they continue to meet considerable opposition:

> In the past decade, bans or administrative obstacles have created problems for the organization of lawful and peaceful LGBT demonstrations in several EU Member States [. . .] [M]any incidences of hate speech and hate crime occur in the context of counter-demonstrations against LGBT people when exercising their freedom of expression and assembly through these events. In some Member States, public authorities have not been able or willing to ensure the safety of participants in LGBT demonstrations from attacks by counter-demonstrators.[1]

Yet, despite the importance of public expression and association for gay men and lesbians, and the recognized interference with these rights by public authorities in European states, the Court's case law in respect of Articles 10 and 11 is significantly underdeveloped in relation to sexual orientation. A key reason for this has been the Court's conception of homosexuality as an aspect of an individual's life that is related to the private, rather than the public,

1 European Union Agency for Fundamental Rights, *Homophobia, Transphobia and Discrimination on Grounds of Sexual Orientation and Gender Identity in the EU Member States: Summary of Findings, Trends, Challenges and Promising Practices*, Vienna: FRA, 2010, p. 17.

sphere. The Court's strong conception of homosexuality as an 'essentially private manifestation of the human personality',[2] which I explored in Chapter 4, has underpinned a reluctance to recognize the rights of gay men and lesbians to manifest this aspect of their 'human personality' in public. Recent judgments by the Court demonstrate, as I explore below, an evolution in its interpretation of Articles 10 and 11 in respect of sexual orientation discrimination. However, whilst some progress has been made, there remain significant gaps in the Court's jurisprudence that leave homosexuals vulnerable.

The Court's approach to Article 10

Article 10 of the Convention provides:

1 Everyone has the right to freedom of expression. This right shall include freedom to hold opinions and to receive and impart information and ideas without interference by public authority and regardless of frontiers. This Article shall not prevent States from requiring the licensing of broadcasting, television or cinema enterprises.
2 The exercise of these freedoms, since it carries with it duties and responsibilities, may be subject to such formalities, conditions, restrictions or penalties as are prescribed by law and are necessary in a democratic society, in the interests of national security, territorial integrity or public safety, for the prevention of disorder or crime, for the protection of health or morals, for the protection of the reputation or rights of others, for preventing the disclosure of information received in confidence, or for maintaining the authority and impartiality of the judiciary.

Like the other qualified rights of the Convention, Article 10 specifies that a public authority may only interfere with an individual's right to freedom of expression when it is prescribed by law, pursues one of a number of legitimate aims and is necessary in a democratic society. When reviewing Article 10 complaints, the Court considers whether any interference with freedom of expression addresses a pressing social need and, in doing so, strikes a proportionate balance between the means employed and the rights of the individual. Contracting states have a margin of appreciation available to them and the width of this will, in principle, be determined by an assessment of whether the reasons provided by a government for any interference are relevant and sufficient. However, the importance attached by the Court to Article 10 reflects the view expressed by the United Nations General Assembly at its first session in 1946 when it adopted Resolution 59(1): 'Freedom of

2 *Dudgeon v the United Kingdom*, no. 7525/76, 22 October 1981, Series A no. 45, § 60.

information is a fundamental human right and is the touchstone of all the freedoms to which the United Nations is consecrated.'[3] The Court has therefore consistently held that freedom of expression is a vital element of a democratic society and, as such, includes the right to convey ideas that may be unpopular and offensive to others:

> The Court's supervisory functions oblige it to pay the utmost attention to the principles characterizing a 'democratic society'. Freedom of expression constitutes one of the essential foundations of such a society, one of the basic conditions for its progress and for the development of every man. Subject to paragraph 2 of Article 10 [. . .], it is applicable not only to 'information' or 'ideas' that are favourably received or regarded as inoffensive or as a matter of indifference, but also to those that offend, shock or disturb the State or any sector of the population. Such are the demands of that pluralism, tolerance and broadmindedness without which there is no 'democratic society'. This means, amongst other things, that every 'formality', 'condition', 'restriction' or 'penalty' imposed in this sphere must be proportionate to the legitimate aim pursued.[4]

Given the emphasis the Court places on freedom of expression as an essential element of a democratic society, the approach of the Strasbourg organs to complaints relating to sexual orientation is, as I explore below, in need of significant evolution.

Freedom of expression and homosexuality

Freedom of expression has long been, and remains, foundational to the development of human rights for gay men and lesbians. The ability to express information and ideas about sexual orientation is vitally important for individuals who, by the very fact of their sexual identities and practices, are frequently marginalized in the social and civil spheres. Protecting the public voices of such individuals, whether expressed alone or collectively, is essential for improving both their social and private lives. For this reason, the Committee of Ministers of the Council of Europe have recognized that safeguarding freedom of expression is an essential element in ensuring the full human rights of sexual minorities and, in light of this, have stated that:

> Member states should take appropriate measures to ensure, in accordance with Article 10 of the Convention, that the right to freedom of expression

3 United Nations General Assembly, 'Resolution 59(1) Calling of an International Conference on Freedom of Information', Sixty-fifth plenary meeting, 14 December 1946.
4 *Handyside v the United Kingdom*, no. 5493/72, 7 December 1976, Series A no. 24, § 49.

> can be effectively enjoyed, without discrimination on grounds of sexual orientation or gender identity, including with respect to the freedom to receive and impart information on subjects dealing with sexual orientation or gender identity.[5]

In a recent report, the Council of Europe was optimistic about the progress that had been made in this area:

> Interference in the exercise of freedom of expression of LGBT persons is not frequent in Council of Europe member states. If it happens, it is usually directed at impeding expressions, opinions and information concerning sexual orientation or gender identity from being circulated because of possible negative reception by the majority population.[6]

It is certainly true that, in many contracting states, restrictions on the expression of ideas relating to homosexuality have receded. For example, the now infamous Section 28 of the Local Government Act 1988 of England and Wales – which stated that a local authority 'must not intentionally promote homosexuality or publish material with the intention of promoting homosexuality' or 'promote the teaching in any maintained school of the acceptability of homosexuality as a pretended family relationship' – was repealed by the Local Government Act 2003. However, whilst the Council of Europe is right to acknowledge that direct interference by public authorities with freedom of expression is infrequent, it fails to capture the subtle ways in which law continues to be used to suppress expression relating to homosexuality. For example, section 148 of the Learning and Skills Act 2000 of England and Wales continues to require that when children in state-maintained schools are given sex education they 'learn the nature of marriage and its importance for family life and the bringing up of children'. This legislation clearly privileges the expression of heteronormative ideas about the family and parenting since marriage is an exclusively heterosexual institution in the United Kingdom.

Heterosexist rhetoric on 'the family' has, in recent years, underpinned the introduction of bespoke legislation in a number of contracting states that is designed to curtail public expressions of homosexuality. For example, in July 2009, the Lithuanian Parliament amended the *Law on the Protection of Minors against the Detrimental Effect of Public Information* to prohibit any public

5 Council of Europe, 'Recommendation CM/Rec(2010)5 of the Committee of Ministers to Member States on Measures to Combat Discrimination on Grounds of Sexual Orientation or Gender Identity', § 13.

6 Council of Europe, *Discrimination on Grounds of Sexual Orientation and Gender Identity in Europe*, Strasbourg: Council of Europe Publishing, 2011, p. 76.

information 'whereby homosexual, bisexual or polygamous relations are promoted' (Article 4.14) and 'family relations are distorted, its values are scorned' (Article 4.15). The amendment was vetoed by the President and subject to further revision before its commencement. However, the most recent version of the law prohibits any public information 'which expresses contempt for family values, encourages the concept of entry into a marriage and creation of a family other than stipulated in the Constitution of the Republic of Lithuania and the Civil Code of the Republic of Lithuania' (Article 4.16).[7] The Civil Code of the Republic of Lithuania defines marriage as 'a voluntary agreement between a man and a woman' (Article 3.7).

Similar developments can be seen across the Russian Federation. For instance, in November 2011 the Legislative Assembly of St Petersburg overwhelmingly endorsed (by 37–1) a new bill that proposed to prohibit 'public actions aimed at propaganda of sodomy, lesbianism, bisexuality, and transgenderism among minors'.[8] At the second reading of the bill in February 2012, the Assembly showed similar support (by 31–6)[9] and, soon after, the bill was passed at a third reading (by 29–5).[10] The new law effectively bans any public expression of homosexuality and outlaws the public association and assembly of sexual minorities. Those found in breach of the law are subject to fines ranging from 3,000 to 50,000 rubles. The Ryazan Oblast passed similar legislation in 2006[11] and this has been followed more recently in the Arkhangelsk Oblast where, in November 2011, the Regional Assembly passed a law that prohibits the 'promotion of homosexuality among minors'.[12] Following the success of the legislation in the St Petersburg Assembly, the Moscow City Duma is reportedly planning to introduce comparable legislation.[13] The Ryazan Oblast law, which prohibits 'Public actions aimed at the promotion of homosexuality (sodomy and lesbianism) among minors', has been upheld by the Constitutional Court of the Russian Federation. In January 2010, the Constitutional Court dismissed a complaint that the law violated a number of provisions of the Russian Constitution, in particular Article 29 (right to freedom of thought and speech), Article 19 (ban on discrimination)

7 Seimas of the Republic of Lithuania, 'Law on the Protection of Minors Against the Detrimental Effect of Public Information', 10 September 2002 – No IX-1067, amended on 21 October 2011 – No. XI-1624.

8 Legislative Assembly of St Petersburg, 16 November 2011.

9 Ibid., 8 February 2012.

10 Ibid., 29 February 2012.

11 Ryazan Oblast, 'Law on the Protection of Morality and Health of Children in Ryazan Region (2006)', and 'Law of Ryazan Region on Administrative Offences (2008)'.

12 Regional Assembly of the Arkhangelsk Oblast, 17 November 2011.

13 UK Gay News, 'Moscow Authorities Now Propose Anti Gay Bill', 17 November 2011, available HTTP: <http://www.ukgaynews.org.uk/Archive/11/Nov/1701.htm> (last accessed 21 February 2012).

and Article 55 (allowance to limit citizens' constitutional rights only by federal law).[14] The Constitutional Court held that:

> the ban of such propaganda – as purposeful and uncontrolled activity connected to the dissemination of information which can harm the health, morals and spiritual development, including forming of distorted perceptions about social equivalence of traditional and nontraditional marriage relations, among persons, who are deprived, due to their age, of the ability to critically evaluate such information – can not be considered as breaching the constitutional rights of citizens.[15]

These recent developments, which demonstrate an increase in attempts by contracting states to legally curtail the freedom of expression of gay men and lesbians, demonstrate an urgent need for the Court to evolve its Article 10 jurisprudence in respect of sexual orientation.

The Court's Article 10 jurisprudence in respect of homosexuality

It is striking that the Court has never found in favour of a gay or lesbian applicant who has lodged an Article 10 complaint. Aside from two cases that involve discussions of homosexuality by journalists (which, as I examine below, concern public discussion of homosexuality in the press) and one case relating to the regulation of 'hate speech' (which did not involve a complaint brought by a homosexual applicant), there is no example in the Court's case law of an interference with the expression of sexual minorities being recognized as a violation of Article 10. Although applicants have invoked Article 10 in a range of complaints relating to various aspects of sexual orientation and expression, the Court has been unwilling to extend its protection to homosexuals.

Homosexuality as obscenity

Handyside v the United Kingdom remains one of the Court's most significant considerations of Article 10 and it was also the first case ever to reach the Court concerning issues relating to homosexuality.[16] The applicant in

14 Constitutional Court of the Russian Federation, Case No. 151-O-O/2010, 19 January 2010.

15 UK Gay News, 'Russian Court: Ban of "Gay Propaganda to Minors" is Constitutional', 31 March 2010, available HTTP: <http://www.ukgaynews.org.uk/Archive/10/Mar/3101.htm> (last accessed 21 February 2012).

16 *Handyside v the United Kingdom*, no. 5493/72, 7 December 1976, Series A no. 24.

Handyside was a publisher who intended to publish an English edition of 'The Little Red Schoolbook' – a Danish reference book for children originally published in Denmark in 1969, which contained a 25-page section entitled 'sex' that included a discussion of, among other things, homosexuality. Prior to the publication, the applicant was charged, prosecuted and convicted under the Obscene Publications Acts 1959 and 1964. On appeal, the Inner London Quarter Sessions upheld the applicant's conviction on the grounds that the book had the capacity to deprave and corrupt a substantial majority of children under 16 years of age. In respect of the content relating to homosexuality, the Quarter Sessions stated:

> the treatment of the subject of homosexuality [. . .] was a factual, very compassionate, understanding and valuable statement. But again, no matter how good one assessed the value of this section, it was hopelessly damning by its setting and context, and the fact that it only contained any suggestion of a stable relationship in relation to sex and that marriage received no such treatment at all. Moreover, there was a very real danger that this passage would create in the minds of children a conclusion that that kind of relationship was something permanent.[17]

When the applicant eventually published the book, he responded to the criticism that there was 'no mention in this section that boys who have such experiences grow out of it and have normal sexual relations including marriage' by amending it to include the line: 'many people go through a temporary homosexual phase at some stage in their life, usually when they are young'.[18]

In its review, the Commission decided unanimously that the punishment imposed upon the applicant constituted an interference with his Article 10 rights but did not find that it constituted a violation of the Convention. Regarding the interference as necessary in a democratic society, the Commission stated that in 'a pluralistic, open, tolerant society', which requires a 'delicate balance between the wishes of the individual and the utilitarian "greater good of the majority" ', restriction must be placed on 'obscene publication for the protection of morals of that society, particularly the morals of young people and children'.[19] There was considerable dissent in the Commission to the majority decision. Mr. Fawcett and Mr. Triantafyllides rejected the majority view that the interference was justified on the grounds of the 'protection of morals' and argued that, whilst the concept of morality

17 Ibid., § 34.

18 *Handyside v the United Kingdom*, no. 5493/72, Commission report, 30 September 1975, Dissenting opinion of Mr. Ermacora.

19 Ibid., § 146–149.

must include sex, 'the book cannot be fairly described as pornographic' and that 'there is, for various reasons, a measure of tolerance in the United Kingdom of publicity for sex, including homosexual activities, even when it is pornographic'.[20] Citing the publication of the book in other countries as evidence of a broader European consensus, Fawcett and Triantafyllides referred to the applicant's treatment as a purely 'symbolic prosecution'.[21] However, the Court accepted the majority view of the Commission and, finding that the prosecution of the applicant was necessary in a democratic society, stated:

> Basically the book contained purely factual information that was generally correct and often useful, as the Quarter Sessions recognised. However, it also included, above all in the section on sex and in the passage headed 'Be yourself' in the chapter on pupils [. . .], sentences or paragraphs that young people at a critical stage of their development could have interpreted as an encouragement to indulge in precocious activities harmful for them or even to commit certain criminal offences. In these circumstances, despite the variety and the constant evolution in the United Kingdom of views on ethics and education, the competent English judges were entitled, in the exercise of their discretion, to think at the relevant time that the Schoolbook would have pernicious effects on the morals of many of the children and adolescents who would read it.[22]

Handyside demonstrates that neither the Commission nor the Court regarded the prosecution of a purely factual discussion of homosexuality as a violation of the right to freedom of expression. Furthermore, it showed that the Strasbourg organs accepted and legitimized the view that public discussion of homosexuality has a 'pernicious' effect on individual and social morality. It is unsurprising, therefore, that the Commission deemed a series of subsequent applications, concerning the regulation of explicit homosexual sexual imagery, inadmissible under Article 10. For example, in *X. v the United Kingdom*, which concerned a complaint about the confiscation of two unsolicited packets sent though the post from Denmark containing pornographic magazines that depicted homosexual sex, the Commission stated that the interference was lawful and necessary for the protection of morals.[23] In *X. Ltd. and Y. v the United Kingdom*, the publisher and editor of a magazine complained about his

20 Ibid., Dissenting opinion of MM. Fawcett and Triantafyllides.

21 Ibid.

22 *Handyside v the United Kingdom*, no. 5493/72, 7 December 1976, § 52.

23 *X. v the United Kingdom*, no. 7308/75, Commission decision, 12 October 1978.

prosecution for publishing a poem, which described Jesus Christ engaged in homosexual sexual acts with the Apostles and other men, and a drawing that illustrated it.[24] The Commission deemed the application inadmissible, stating that if:

> it is accepted that the religious feelings of the citizen may deserve protection against indecent attacks on the matters held sacred by him, then it can also be considered as necessary in a democratic society to stipulate that such attacks, if they attain a certain level of severity, shall constitute a criminal offence triable at the request of the offended person.[25]

In *Scherer v Switzerland*, the Commission did uphold a complaint from the owner of 'a sex shop in Zurich for homosexual persons' who had been prosecuted for showing pornographic films to paying customers.[26] The Commission's willingness to find in favour of the applicant was, however, significantly influenced by the private nature of the activity involved:

> The Commission notes that the nature of the applicant's shop was not discernible from the street. Moreover, it was very unlikely that the projection room adjacent to the shop would be visited by persons who were unaware of the subject matter of the film. There was no danger of adults being confronted with the film against or without their intention to see it. It is furthermore undisputed that minors had no access to the film as there was a control in the shop ensuring that such persons had no access.[27]

The Commission concluded that the protection of morals did not form a legitimate aim that justified an interference with the applicant's rights because 'no adult was confronted unintentionally or against his will with the film'.[28] As such, the Commission stated that the applicant's conviction did not correspond to a pressing social need and that the interference with his right to freedom of expression was disproportionate to the aim pursued. A central factor in the Commission's reasoning was the measures taken by the applicant to maintain a strict separation between the homosexual imagery and 'the public' and, therefore, its decision cannot be seen to concern expression in the public sphere. Nevertheless, several members of the Commission dissented, arguing that 'one may be left to wonder in the particular circumstances of this

24 *X. Ltd and Y. v the United Kingdom*, no. 8710/79, Commission decision, 7 May 1982.
25 Ibid., § 12.
26 *Scherer v Switzerland*, no. 17116/90, Commission report, 14 January 1993, § 16.
27 Ibid., § 62.
28 Ibid., § 65.

case if a pornographic video film depicting homosexual acts for some one hundred and twenty minutes to the accompaniment of protracted moaning is indeed what the founding fathers of the Convention understood by freedom of expression'.[29] It is unfortunate that, in light of the applicant's death, the case was struck from the Court's list and no judgment was issued in respect of this important Article 10 complaint. However, the Commission's decision did establish that the display of homosexual sexual imagery in private constitutes a form of expression that falls within the scope of Article 10.

The expression of sexual orientation

In two complaints, both against the United Kingdom, applicants have invoked Article 10 to complain about the impact of law upon their ability to give expression to their sexual orientation. In *X. v the United Kingdom*, the applicant complained that, as a result of his imprisonment following a conviction for (now repealed) homosexual offences, his right to the free expression of his views was censored and, furthermore, he was denied his right to express feelings of love to other men.[30] The United Kingdom government stated that there had been no violation of Article 10 as the law complained of, which criminalized male homosexual sex between men over 21 years of age and those under 21,[31] did not infringe the applicant's freedom to express verbally, or in writing, his views on his own or others' homosexuality or prevent him from seeking a change in the law. The Commission rejected the applicant's claim regarding the interference with the expression of his views, but it did deem admissible his complaint regarding the impact of imprisonment on his ability to express feelings of love for other men. This afforded the potential for a creative interpretation of 'expression' to include the right to express sexual intimacy. However, in its subsequent report, the Commission stated that:

> the concept of 'expression' in Art. 10 concerns mainly the expression of the opinion and receiving and imparting information and ideas. This is clear from the second sentence of Art. 10. It does not encompass any notion of the physical expression of feelings in the sense submitted by the applicant.[32]

This is a problematic interpretation of Article 10 since it delimits the usefulness of the Convention in addressing the frequent regulation and suppression

29 Ibid., Dissenting opinion of Mr. E. Busuttil, joined by Mr. A. Weitzel and Mrs. J. Liddy as regards Article 10 of the Convention.

30 *X. v the United Kingdom*, no. 7215/75, Committee of Ministers, 12 June 1979.

31 Sexual Offences Act 1967.

32 *X. v the United Kingdom*, no. 7215/75, Commission report, 12 October 1978, § 173.

of expressions of intimacy experienced by homosexuals in the public sphere.[33] As a consequence, considerations of interferences with the expression of physical intimacy have remained consigned to the sphere of private life covered by Article 8.

In *Smith and Grady v the United Kingdom*, the Court refused to consider the applicants' complaint that a prohibition on homosexuality in the armed forces, and their subsequent discharge because of it, imposed limitations on their right to give expression to their sexual identity. The United Kingdom government stated that the applicants' discharges 'were not the result of any expression of information or ideas but rather a consequence of the fact of their homosexuality'.[34] This separation of 'expression' from 'fact' is problematic given that the 'facts' of the applicants' sexual orientation were only established by their expression – as I discussed in Chapter 4, it was the applicants' 'admission' of their homosexuality to the armed forces authorities that resulted in their dismissal from work. The applicants argued that:

> the right to give expression to one's sexuality encapsulated opinions, ideas and information essential to an individual and his or her identity. The policy of the Ministry of Defence forced them to live secret lives, denying them the simple opportunity to communicate openly and freely their own sexual identity which, in turn, had a chilling effect on them and was a powerful inhibiting factor in their right to express themselves.[35]

Whilst the Court found in favour of the applicants' Article 8 claim, it would not consider their Article 10 complaint. The Court stated that it:

> would not rule out that the silence imposed on the applicants as regards their sexual orientation, together with the consequent and constant need for vigilance, discretion and secrecy in that respect with colleagues, friends and acquaintances as a result of the chilling effect of the Ministry

33 There is now a diverse body of literature that examines how particular geographical spaces and landscapes are imprinted with cultural constructions of sexuality that, in turn, come to shape the experiences of those within them. See, for example: D. Bell and G. Valentine (eds.), *Mapping Desire: Geographies of Sexualities*, London: Routledge, 1995. One important element of this work has been the recognition that most 'everyday' public space is normalized as heterosexual and precludes non-heterosexual displays of desire. Hubbard's recent work argues that most public space is experienced by non-heterosexuals as 'aggressively heterosexual' and that the function of such space is to enforce conformity to a heteronormative construction of citizenship. See: P. Hubbard, 'Desire/Disgust: Mapping the Moral Contours of Heterosexuality', *Progress in Human Geography* 24, 2004, 191–217; P. Hubbard, 'Sex Zones: Intimacy, Citizenship and Public Space', *Sexualities* 4, 2001, 51–71.

34 *Smith and Grady v the United Kingdom*, nos. 33985/96 and 33986/96, 27 September 1999, ECHR 1999-VI, § 125.

35 Ibid., § 126.

> of Defence policy, could constitute an interference with their freedom of expression.[36]

However, the Court went on to state that the sole ground for the investigation and discharge of the applicants was their sexual orientation and, because homosexuality is 'an essentially private manifestation of human personality', the question of freedom of expression was subsidiary to the principal issue of private life.[37] The idea that the public expression of homosexuality is subsidiary to its private manifestation maintains a problematic conceptual separation between the private and public spheres that fails to address the ways in which the private sphere depends upon, and is produced because of, the social, cultural, civil, legal and political contexts in which it is situated. It also fails to grasp the ways in which public expression is often a vital mechanism through which citizens of a nation state protect their private freedoms. This is most obviously the case where public expression becomes imperative for contending and resisting attempts by a contracting state to discriminate against sexual minorities. This issue was central to *Morissens v Belgium* in which a teacher, who had taken part in a television broadcast in which she had discussed sexual orientation discrimination at work and, as a result of her appearance, had subsequently been suspended from her job, complained that prohibiting the discussion of her sexual orientation in the public sphere contravened her right to freedom of expression. The Commission declared the application inadmissible on the grounds that her dismissal from work was a proportionate reaction to the 'wide and immediate' accusations about her superiors on television and her lack of moderation as a civil servant.[38] The Court has, as I discuss below, evolved its Article 11 jurisprudence in respect of political demonstrations in public designed to contest sexual-orientation discrimination but, in relation to the expression of opinions, ideas and information about sexual identity, the Court's Article 10 jurisprudence remains underdeveloped.

Freedom of the press

The Court has considered two cases relating to the freedom of the press that have explicitly concerned sexual orientation. The Court generally regards the press as performing the function of a 'public watchdog' in democratic societies and sets a high value on its freedom of expression.[39] In *Kobenter and*

36 Ibid., § 127.

37 Ibid.

38 *Morissens v Belgium*, no. 11389/85, Commission decision, 3 May 1988.

39 *Goodwin v the United Kingdom* [GC], no. 17488/90, 27 March 1996, *Reports of Judgments and Decisions* 1996-II, § 39.

Standard Verlags GMBH v Austria, the Court considered a complaint by two applicants who had been prosecuted for the publication of an article in the newspaper *Der Standard* that criticized a decision in the Austrian courts and the presiding judge that made it.[40] The case originated in Linz Regional Court and concerned the publication of an article, in *The 13th – Newspaper of Catholics for Faith and Church*, which argued that 'homosexuals now crawl like rats out of their holes' and that 'nazi-methods should be applied to them'.[41] The Linz Regional Court found that certain passages of the article were insulting and ordered *The 13th* to pay compensation to four plaintiffs. However, the Regional Court acquitted the author of the article and included in its judgment a description of homosexuality that contained statements such as 'homosexuality includes also the lesbian world and, of course, that of animals'.[42] In response to this, the applicants in *Kobenter* published an article that criticized the judgment on the grounds that it lent 'support to a homophobe's venomous campaign with outrageous examples from the animal kingdom' and that the original trial was akin to 'the traditions of medieval witch trials'.[43] The presiding judge in the original case filed a private prosecution against the applicants and the St Pölten Regional Court, finding in his favour, convicted the applicants of defamation. In Strasbourg, the Court found in favour of the applicants' complaint that their conviction unnecessarily interfered with their rights to freedom of expression. It held 'that there is little scope under Article 10 § 2 of the Convention for restrictions on debate on questions of public interest'.[44] The judgment in *Kobenter* shows support for the protection of the public expression of ideas, opinions and information under Article 10 that challenge homophobic discourse.

In a subsequent case, the Court has considered the issue of newspapers exposing details about an individual's homosexual orientation. In *Porubova v Russia* the applicant, the editor of a Russian newspaper that had published a story alleging that two senior government officials were homosexual, complained about a conviction for criminal libel.[45] The applicant argued that during her trial it had not been established whether the information about the homosexual relationship between the officials had been false. The Court upheld her complaint, stating that the professional politicians 'inevitably and knowingly laid themselves open to close scrutiny of their every word and deed by both journalists and the public at large' and that 'the right of the public to be informed, which is an essential right in a democratic society, can even

40 *Kobenter and Standard Verlags GMBH v Austria*, no. 60899/00, 2 November 2006.
41 Ibid., § 9.
42 Ibid., § 11.
43 Ibid., § 13.
44 Ibid., § 32.
45 *Porubova v Russia*, no. 8237/03, 8 October 2009.

extend to aspects of the private life of public figures, particularly where politicians are concerned'.[46] The Court held that:

> Taking into account the role of journalists and the press in imparting information and ideas on matters of public concern, even those that may offend, shock or disturb, the Court holds that the applicant's conviction was not compatible with the principles embodied in Article 10 since the Russian courts did not identify a 'pressing social need' or adduce 'relevant and sufficient' reasons justifying the interference at issue. Therefore, the Court considers that the domestic courts overstepped the narrow margin of appreciation afforded to them where restrictions on debates of public interest are concerned, and that the interference was disproportionate to the aim pursued and not 'necessary in a democratic society'.[47]

The Court's interpretation of Article 10, to uphold the right of journalists to expose the sexual orientation of politicians, raises some important questions about the relevance of the Court's view on homosexual privacy rights under Article 8. Even though the Court singles out politicians as persons who have 'laid themselves open to close scrutiny', and will reject complaints under Article 10 where 'the sole purpose' of journalism is 'to satisfy the curiosity of a particular readership regarding the details of the applicant's private life',[48] its view that journalists can expose this 'essentially private manifestation of the human personality' is problematic. This is not least because such exposure, in homophobic societies, will often be designed to discredit individuals and encourage discrimination against them. Even where journalists uncover contradictions between the sexual practices of politicians and their public expressions on sexual orientation, the Court must balance the right to respect for private life with the right of the public to be informed of matters of political and social interest. Whilst this act of balancing is, as White and Ovey argue, 'a tricky one for all concerned',[49] no consideration has been given by the Court to either the ethics or political repercussions of 'outing'.

Protection from 'hate speech'

Gay men and lesbians are not only concerned to protect their own right to freedom of speech but also to be protected from the speech of others that is

46 Ibid., § 45.
47 Ibid., § 50.
48 *Von Hannover v Germany*, no. 59320/00, 24 June 2004, ECHR 2004-VI, § 65.
49 R.C.A. White and C. Ovey, *The European Convention on Human Rights (5th Edition)*, Oxford: Oxford University Press, 2010, p. 437.

designed to stir up hatred against them. Many states contracted to the Convention have introduced domestic legislation that criminalizes 'hate speech' directed at sexual minorities. For example, Part 3A of the Public Order Act 1986 of England and Wales criminalizes incitement to hatred on the grounds of sexual orientation.[50] The Council of Europe has confirmed that homophobic speech is covered by the term 'hate speech'[51] and the Court has stated in previous judgments that there can be no doubt that concrete expressions constituting hate speech, which may be insulting to particular individuals or groups, are not protected by Article 10 of the Convention.[52] The Court can deem applications inadmissible under Article 17 of the Convention if it considers that applicants seeking the protection of Article 10 have engaged in speech that is aimed at the destruction of the rights and freedoms of others.[53] However, the use of Article 17 in this way is uncommon and the Court tends to consider complaints under Article 10 in order to assess the proportionality of any interference. In doing so, it reviews the legality, legitimacy and necessity of any interference with freedom of expression. The Court has a long-standing commitment to protecting freedom of speech, particularly political speech, which it regards as an essential foundation for the existence and progress of a democratic society.[54] However, the Court has established that racist hate speech falls outside of the scope of protectable political speech. In *Féret v Belgium*, which concerned the dissemination of pamphlets that criticized immigrants living in Belgium, the Court stated that the intention of the speech was to incite hatred and that this created harm to immigrant groups, by insulting, ridiculing and defaming them, and represented a danger to the social peace and political stability of democratic states.[55] The Court has also, when reviewing particular forms of speech, attached particular importance to the truthfulness and factual basis of claims that are made.[56]

The Court's consideration of homophobic hate speech is in its infancy. In February 2012 the Court issued its first judgment, in *Vejdeland and Others v Sweden*, in response to a complaint about the regulation of speech concerning

50 R. Vanderbeck and P. Johnson, ' "If a Charge Was Brought Against a Saintly Religious Leader Whose Intention Was To Save Souls. . .": An Analysis of UK Parliamentary Debates Over Incitement To Hatred on the Grounds of Sexual Orientation', *Parliamentary Affairs* 64(4), 2011, 652–673.

51 A. Weber, *Manual on Hate Speech*, Strasbourg: Council of Europe Publishing, 2009.

52 *Jersild v Denmark*, no. 15890/89, 23 September 1994, Series A no. 298, § 35.

53 See, for example: *Norwood v the United Kingdom* (dec), no. 23131/03, 16 November 2004, ECHR 2004-XI.

54 *Sürek and Özdemir v. Turkey* [GC], nos. 23927/94 and 24277/94, 8 July 1999.

55 *Féret v Belgium,* no. 15615/07, 16 July 2009.

56 *Pedersen and Baadsgaard v Denmark* [GC], no. 49017/99, 17 December 2004, ECHR 2004-XI.

homosexuality.[57] The complaint was lodged by four applicants who were convicted of 'agitation against a national or ethnic group'[58] and, following several iterations of the case in the domestic Courts, were sentenced by the Supreme Court of Sweden, which imposed suspended sentences on three of the applicants and imposed a fine and a term of probation on the other. The applicants had been convicted for the distribution of leaflets in a secondary school that contained, *inter alia*, statements such as:

> Homosexual Propaganda (*Homosexpropaganda*)
>
> In the course of a few decades society has swung from rejection of homosexuality and other sexual deviances (*avarter*) to embracing this deviant sexual proclivity (*böjelse*). Your anti-Swedish teachers know very well that homosexuality has a morally destructive effect on the substance of society (*folkkroppen*) and will willingly try to put it forward as something normal and good.
>
> – Tell them that HIV and AIDS appeared early with the homosexuals and that their promiscuous lifestyle was one of the main reasons for this modern-day plague gaining a foothold.
> – Tell them that homosexual lobby organisations are also trying to play down (*avdramatisera*) paedophilia, and ask if this sexual deviation (*sexuella avart*) should be legalized.[59]

The applicants disputed that the leaflets expressed contempt for homosexuals and claimed that their intention was to 'start a debate about the lack of objectivity in the education dispensed in Swedish schools'.[60] The applicants further argued that 'the wording in the leaflets was not hateful and did not encourage anyone to commit hateful acts'.[61] They argued that their conviction constituted a violation of their Article 10 rights.

In its review, the Court accepted that the conviction of the applicants did constitute an interference with their Article 10 rights. Furthermore, the Court concluded that the interference was prescribed by law and pursued the legitimate aim of 'the protection of the reputation and rights of others' within the meaning of Article 10(2) of the Convention. In respect of whether the interference was necessary in a democratic society, the Court unanimously agreed that it was and, as such, did not amount to a violation of the Convention. The Court's judgment is highly significant since it establishes that the regulation of homophobic hate speech does not necessarily constitute a violation

57 *Vejdeland and Others v Sweden*, no. 1813/07, 9 February 2012.
58 Ibid., § 9.
59 Ibid., § 8.
60 Ibid., § 10.
61 Ibid., § 26.

of Article 10 rights. However, the judgment is less than satisfactory for three reasons. First, in examining the wording of the leaflets, the Court stated that 'although these statements did not directly recommend individuals to commit hateful acts, they are serious and prejudicial allegations'.[62] The Court's suggestion that the impugned speech did not constitute hate speech (but, rather, serious and prejudicial allegations) because it did not 'directly recommend' that individuals carry out 'hateful acts' is somewhat confusing given that the Court held that 'inciting to hatred does not necessarily entail a call for an act of violence, or other criminal acts'.[63] Although the Court operates a very broad definition of hate speech – which includes 'insulting, holding up to ridicule or slandering specific groups of the population'[64] – it failed to decisively include the speech in question within this category.

A second problematic aspect of the judgment is that it fails to engage in a considered analysis of the content of the speech in question. In the place of such an analysis, the Court relied upon its judgment in *Smith and Grady v the United Kingdom* to state that discrimination based on sexual orientation is as serious as discrimination based on race, origin or colour.[65] This reliance on *Smith and Grady* produced criticism in two of the three concurring opinions filed with the judgment. Judges Spielmann and Nussberger argued that establishing a link between hate speech and the speech in question 'by mere reference to the *Smith and Grady* precedent' was insufficient and that 'the offending statements should have been defined more precisely'.[66] By contrast, Judges Yudkivska and Villiger stated that the impugned speech was 'clearly' a form of hate speech and that the judgment had failed to 'consolidate an approach to hate speech' by not examining the speech.[67]

The third aspect of the judgment that is less than satisfactory is the importance it accords to the intended audience of the speech in question. The Court placed considerable emphasis on the fact that the applicants had deposited the leaflets 'in the lockers of young people who were at an impressionable and sensitive age and who had no possibility to decline to accept them'.[68] It is telling that the Court invoked *Handyside v the United Kingdom* to support its judgment that young people must be protected from exposure to homophobic propaganda since this shows a significant shift away from the support it gave

62 Ibid., § 54.
63 Ibid., § 55.
64 Ibid.
65 *Smith and Grady v the United Kingdom*, nos. 33985/96 and 33986/96, 27 September 1999, ECHR 1999-VI.
66 *Vejdeland and Others v Sweden*, no. 1813/07, 9 February 2012, Concurring opinion of Judge Spielmann joined by Judge Nussberger.
67 Ibid., Concurring opinion of Judge Yudkivska joined by Judge Villiger.
68 Ibid., § 56.

in *Handyside* to the regulation of 'homosexual propaganda'.[69] In two concurring opinions, in which judges expressed 'the greatest hesitation'[70] and 'some hesitation'[71] at agreeing with the majority, it was the fact that the speech in question had been directed at children in a school that was crucial to their decision to find no violation of Article 10. For instance, Judge Zupančič stated that he could agree with the judgment insofar as it was based predominantly on the fact that the target audience was in a school because schools 'are definitely a protected setting where only those authorized to distribute any kind of information may do so'.[72] Judges Spielmann and Nussberger stated that they 'agreed, albeit very reluctantly, to find no violation because the distribution of the leaflets took place at a school which none of the applicants attended and to which they did not have free access' and that, furthermore, there was 'a real problem of homophobic and transphobic bullying and discrimination in educational settings [that] may justify a restriction of freedom of expression'.[73] Spielmann and Nussberger stated that, 'against this background', they were satisfied that 'on balance' the applicants' convictions did not violate Article 10.

The recognition of a need to regulate speech to protect the 'impressionable' (presumably in order to prevent the cultivation of homophobic ideas) and of the links between such speech and the homophobic treatment of schoolchildren is certainly a welcome development. However, the considerable weight given to the school setting and the age of the audience as a justification to find the interference with the applicants' speech a 'balanced' response is problematic. It fails to make a decisive statement that *all* homophobic hate speech is beyond the protection of Article 10 because it represents a danger to the social peace and political stability of democratic societies.[74] Rather, the judgment suggests that the impugned speech may have been protected had it not been specifically addressed to a 'vulnerable group'. Judges Yudkivska and Villiger rejected outright this form of reasoning:

> cases like the present one should not be viewed merely as a balancing exercise between the applicants' freedom of speech and the targeted group's right to protect their reputation. Hate speech is destructive for democratic society as a whole, since 'prejudicial messages will gain some credence, with the attendant result of discrimination, and perhaps

69 *Handyside v the United Kingdom*, no. 5493/72, 7 December 1976, Series A no. 24.
70 *Vejdeland and Others v Sweden*, no. 1813/07, 9 February 2012, Concurring opinion of Judge Spielmann joined by Judge Nussberger.
71 Ibid., Concurring opinion of Judge Zupančič.
72 Ibid.
73 Ibid., Concurring opinion of Judge Spielmann joined by Judge Nussberger.
74 *Féret v Belgium*, no. 15615/07, 16 July 2009.

> even violence, against minority groups', and therefore it should not be protected.[75]

However, the judgment in *Vejdeland and Others* does not explicitly condemn the speech in question by placing it *in principle* outside of the protection of Article 10. Instead, it is equivocal about whether such speech constitutes hate speech. This is regrettable since the Committee of Ministers of the Council of Europe have provided a definition of hate speech that was easily applicable to the speech in question:

> the term 'hate speech' shall be understood as covering all forms of expression which spread, incite, promote or justify racial hatred, xenophobia, antisemitism or other forms of hatred based on intolerance, including: intolerance expressed by aggressive nationalism and ethnocentrism, discrimination and hostility against minorities, migrants and people of immigrant origin.[76]

It is unfortunate that the judgment suggests that describing homosexuality as a 'deviant sexual proclivity' that has 'a morally destructive effect on the substance of society'; as a form of sexual practice that leads to the 'modern-day plague' of AIDS; and as a 'lobby' for paedophilia, might not be regarded as promoting hatred, discrimination or hostility and, in some circumstances, may be protectable under Article 10.

The Court's approach to Article 11

Article 11 of the Convention provides:

1 Everyone has the right to freedom of peaceful assembly and to freedom of association with others, including the right to form and to join trade unions for the protection of his interests.
2 No restrictions shall be placed on the exercise of these rights other than such as are prescribed by law and are necessary in a democratic society in the interests of national security or public safety, for the prevention of disorder or crime, for the protection of health or morals or for the protection of the rights and freedoms of others. This Article shall not prevent the imposition of lawful restrictions on the exercise of these rights by members of the armed forces, of the police or of the administration of the State.

75 *Vejdeland and Others v Sweden*, no. 1813/07, 9 February 2012, Concurring opinion of Judge Yudkivska joined by Judge Villiger.
76 The Committee of Ministers of the Council of Europe, 'Recommendation No. R (97) 20'.

Article 11 establishes two sets of inter-related rights of association and assembly. Freedom of association, although most frequently discussed in the Court's case law in respect of the membership of political parties and trade unions, has been interpreted to provide a right for individuals to form collective groups with the aim of advancing common objectives that include the assertion of a 'minority consciousness':

> While in the context of Article 11 the Court has often referred to the essential role played by political parties in ensuring pluralism and democracy, associations formed for other purposes, including those protecting cultural or spiritual heritage, pursuing various socio-economic aims, proclaiming or teaching religion, seeking an ethnic identity or asserting a minority consciousness, are also important to the proper functioning of democracy. For pluralism is also built on the genuine recognition of, and respect for, diversity and the dynamics of cultural traditions, ethnic and cultural identities, religious beliefs, artistic, literary and socio-economic ideas and concepts. The harmonious interaction of persons and groups with varied identities is essential for achieving social cohesion. It is only natural that, where a civil society functions in a healthy manner, the participation of citizens in the democratic process is to a large extent achieved through belonging to associations in which they may integrate with each other and pursue common objectives collectively.[77]

The right to association is fundamentally linked to the right to assemble, in both public and private, for the purposes of holding meetings or demonstrations. The Court has made clear that the most important element of any assembly is not its political content but that its organization and execution is peaceful:

> A demonstration may annoy or give offence to persons opposed to the ideas or claims that it is seeking to promote. The participants must, however, be able to hold the demonstration without having to fear that they will be subjected to physical violence by their opponents; such a fear would be liable to deter associations or other groups supporting common ideas or interests from openly expressing their opinions on highly controversial issues affecting the community.

As with the other qualified rights in the Convention, interference with Article 11 rights by a public authority must be in accordance with the law, pursue a legitimate aim, and be necessary in a democratic society. In respect

77 *Gorzelik and Others v Poland* [GC], no. 44158/98, 17 February 2004, ECHR 2004-I, § 92.

of public demonstrations, where the expression of controversial views may create public disturbances, this raises important questions about the extent to which public authorities may justifiably interfere with assembly in the interests of national security or public safety, for the prevention of disorder or crime, for the protection of health or morals, or for the protection of the rights and freedoms of others.

Association, assembly and homosexuality

The right to association and assembly are of vital importance to sexual minorities. Association, both in the public and private spheres, has long been the foundation on which gay men and lesbians have cultivated and maintained both inter-personal and political relationships. Furthermore, assembling in public remains a vital element in campaigning for social and political change. Gay men and lesbians continue to suffer considerable interference with their right to association and assembly across a number of contracting states. By far the most consistently problematic aspect of this interference relates to 'gay pride' events. In a 2008 report, the International Lesbian and Gay Association (ILGA-Europe) outlined the difficulties encountered by lesbian and gay groups in various contracting states when attempting to gain permission for, and hold, gay pride events:

> The right of LGBT people to freedom of assembly has met with widespread opposition in many countries in Central, Eastern and South Eastern Europe in recent years. This opposition has manifested itself in a number of ways, particularly the banning of marches, the use of intolerant or derogatory language by leading politicians and faith representatives, violent attacks on demonstrators, and failure by the police to provide adequate protection.[78]

The situation in many contracting states is not improving. As I argued above, the development of new legislative measures in the Russian Federation designed to make gay pride events illegal shows an increase in intolerance for the public assembly of gay men and lesbians. In many other contracting states, public authorities use existing legal provisions, such as traffic legislation, to frustrate gay pride events and deny organizers permits to hold them. In response to one such refusal by the Budapest Police of Chief, who withheld a permit for a gay pride march in Budapest in 2011 on the grounds that the event would disrupt traffic, Amnesty International

78 ILGA-Europe, *Lesbian, Gay, Bisexual and Transgender Rights: Freedom of Assembly, Diary of Events by Country – August 2008*, ILGA-Europe, 2008.

stated that the decision was disproportionate and without reasonable justification.[79]

There are two principal issues raised under Article 11 in respect of gay pride demonstrations and these encompass both the negative and positive obligations of contracting states. First, there are the direct interferences by public authorities with demonstrations in the form of actions designed to disrupt them or prevent them from taking place. Second, where such events do take place, public authorities often fail to meet their positive obligations to ensure the protection of participants from counter-demonstrations. As the Council of Europe's Commissioner of Human Rights stated in June 2010:

> More than 20 gay pride events were organized in European cities during the month of May [2010]. In most cases there were no major problems reported. However, almost without exception, there were some incidents of disturbance or violence targeting these events – a fact which underlines the need for competent police protection.[80]

The Council of Europe has explicitly stated that contracting states must provide adequate protection to sexual minorities who participate in public demonstrations:

> Member states should ensure that law enforcement authorities take appropriate measures to protect participants in peaceful demonstrations in favour of the human rights of lesbian, gay, bisexual and transgender persons from any attempts to unlawfully disrupt or inhibit the effective enjoyment of their right to freedom of expression and peaceful assembly.[81]

Furthermore, the Council of Europe has urged contracting states to proactively denounce those who seek to disrupt the public assembly of sexual minorities:

> Public authorities at all levels should be encouraged to publicly condemn, notably in the media, any unlawful interferences with the right of individuals and groups of individuals to exercise their freedom of expression

79 Amnesty International, 'Hungary: Authorities Must Reverse Ban on Gay Pride March', 17 February 2011, available HTTP: <http://www.amnesty.org.uk/news_details.asp?NewsID=19260> (last accessed 21 February 2012).

80 T. Hammarberg, 'Pride Events Are Still Hindered – This Violates Freedom of Assembly', 2 June 2010, available HTTP: <http://commissioner.cws.coe.int/tiki-view_blog_post.php?postId=42> (last accessed 21 February 2012).

81 Council of Europe, 'Recommendation CM/Rec(2010)5 of the Committee of Ministers to Member States on Measures to Combat Discrimination on Grounds of Sexual Orientation or Gender Identity', § 15.

and peaceful assembly, notably when related to the human rights of lesbian, gay, bisexual and transgender persons.[82]

In contrast to its Article 10 jurisprudence, the Court has recently issued two judgments that significantly evolve its interpretation of Article 11 in respect of matters relating to sexual orientation. I examine these below to show that, whilst contracting states continue to attempt to frustrate the association and assembly of sexual minorities, the Court has clearly and decisively upheld the rights of gay men and lesbians to engage in peaceful public demonstrations.

The Court's Article 11 jurisprudence in respect of homosexuality

The first occasion Article 11 was considered in a complaint relating to sexual orientation was in *Dudgeon v the United Kingdom*.[83] Whilst the applicant did not invoke Article 11 himself, the Commission decided to examine, during the admissibility stage of the application, whether the criminalization of male homosexual sex interfered with either Article 10 or 11 rights:

> in view of the applicant's submissions concerning the scope of these offences, the Commission has considered ex officio whether this part of the application discloses any appearance of a violation of the applicant's right to freedom of expression, as guaranteed by Article 10, or of his right to freedom of association with others, as guaranteed by Article 11 [. . .] The Commission finds no indication whatsoever that the scope of these offences is such that they could render illegal advocacy of changes in homosexual laws and thus restrict the applicant's freedom of expression. Furthermore whilst the applicant suggests that 'explicit association' in groups, clubs or societies by homosexuals could be illegal and that counselling activities, befriending agencies and the like are of uncertain legal status, the Commission finds that the material submitted does not disclose that the scope of the offences is in fact such that their mere existence could restrict the exercise of the applicant's freedom of association in a manner contrary to Article 11.[84]

In a subsequent case, *Hauer and Guggenheim v Austria*, the Commission considered a complaint relating to a political demonstration in which the applicants, who had attended a memorial event in respect of war and fascism, unrolled a

82 Ibid., § 17.
83 *Dudgeon v the United Kingdom*, no. 7525/76, 22 October 1981, Series A no. 45.
84 *Dudgeon v the United Kingdom*, no. 7525/76, Commission decision, 3 March 1978, p. 131.

banner with the inscription 'Thousands of homosexual victims of concentration camps wait for their rehabilitation'.[85] Police officers confiscated the banner when the applicants refused to remove it. The applicants relied on Article 10, rather than Article 11, to argue that the actions of the police violated their right to freedom of expression. The Commission, noting that the 'applicants showed their banner on the occasion of a ceremony with a solemn character', found that the actions of the police were within the margin of appreciation afforded to the state.

Despite this inauspicious start to reviewing complaints relating to the assembly and association of sexual minorities, the Court has recently issued two judgments, in *Bączkowski and Others v Poland*[86] and *Alekseyev v Russia*,[87] which firmly establish the rights of gay men and lesbians to peaceful assembly and association for the purposes of political demonstration. In *Alekseyev*, the more significant of the two judgments, the Court considered a complaint about the repeated refusals by public authorities in Moscow to allow the applicant to hold a gay pride event. The Russian government argued that the public authorities had acted lawfully and within their margin of appreciation when refusing permission for the event. Furthermore, in light of statements made by several religious groups suggesting that the proposed assemblies would cause moral offence and raise significant safety issues, the government argued that the authorities were pursuing the legitimate aims of the protection of public safety and the prevention of disorder, the protection of morals, and the protection of the rights and freedoms of others. The government referred to a number of statements made by: The Union of Orthodox Citizens who advised the mayor of Moscow of their intention to conduct a mass protest in response to any pride march in Moscow; the objection of the Orthodox Church to a gay parade on the grounds that it was 'propaganda promoting sin'; the promise by the Supreme Mufti for Russia that Muslims and other 'normal people' in Russia would demonstrate against any pride march; and the head of the Muslim authority of Nizhniy Novgorod who argued that 'as a matter of necessity, homosexuals must be stoned to death'.[88] The Court upheld the applicant's complaints, finding a violation of Article 11 alone and Article 14 taken in conjunction with Article 11.

The most obvious and significant aspect of *Alekseyev* is the clear message that it sends to contracting states regarding the importance of respecting the freedom of assembly of homosexuals. The Court had taken a step towards this in its previous judgment in *Bączkowski and Others v Poland*, which concerned a complaint by the organization 'Foundation for Equality' against the Mayor

85 *Hauer and Guggenheim v Austria*, no. 18116/91, Commission decision, 13 October 1993.
86 *Bączkowski and Others v Poland*, no. 1543/06, 3 May 2007.
87 *Alekseyev v Russia*, nos. 4916/07, 25924/08 and 14599/09, 21 October 2010.
88 Ibid., § 62.

of Warsaw who had refused permission, using provisions in the Road Traffic Act 1997, for an assembly aimed at alerting the public on the issue of discrimination against sexual minorities.[89] In *Bączkowski and Others*, the Court followed its established process of review to consider whether the alleged breach of Article 11 was prescribed by law, pursued one or more legitimate aims, and was necessary in a democratic society. The Court gave significant consideration to the lawfulness of the ban and to the findings of the Polish Constitutional Tribunal who had also reviewed the legality of it. The Tribunal had judged that the use of the Road Traffic Act 1997 by public authorities to ban an assembly organized by homosexuals contravened rights guaranteed by the Polish Constitution and the Assemblies Act 1990. The Court reiterated the Tribunal's view of the unlawfulness of the ban and reached the judgment that the applicants had suffered a violation of their rights under Article 11. Because the Court accepted that the ban was unlawful, it did not feel it necessary to apply the legitimacy and necessity tests in its review. However, the Court stated that whilst it had often referred to the essential role of assemblies by political parties in ensuring the pluralism that is essential for democracy, it reiterated that it was also important to recognize the contribution of 'associations formed for other purposes' because:

> pluralism is also built on the genuine recognition of, and respect for, diversity and the dynamics of cultural traditions, ethnic and cultural identities, religious beliefs, artistic, literary and socio-economic ideas and concepts. The harmonious interaction of persons and groups with varied identities is essential for achieving social cohesion.[90]

This recognition of the importance of freedom of assembly on the grounds of 'cultural identity', and its centrality for achieving the 'harmonious interaction of persons', in respect of sexual orientation was an important first step in expanding the Court's Article 11 jurisprudence on homosexuality.

In *Alekseyev*, the Court significantly evolved its jurisprudence because, unlike in *Bączkowski and Others*, it did not focus on the issue of lawfulness. From the outset of its review, the Court dispensed with the parties' disputes regarding the legality and legitimacy of the ban. The Court stated that it could 'dispense with ruling on these points because, irrespective of the aim and the domestic lawfulness of the ban, it fell short of being necessary in a democratic society'.[91] The elevation of the necessity test in this way is extremely important because it decisively articulates the view that the existence of domestic law designed to curtail the public assembly of homosexuals

89 *Bączkowski and Others v Poland*, no. 1543/06, 3 May 2007.
90 Ibid., § 62.
91 *Alekseyev v Russia*, nos. 4916/07, 25924/08 and 14599/09, 21 October 2010, § 69.

does not in itself provide a justification for interference with the Article 11 rights of homosexuals. This should have far-reaching implications in those states that continue to enact legislation with the intention of restricting the freedom of expression and assembly of homosexuals because, while such restriction will be in accordance with the law, it will now be less likely to meet the necessity test of the Court. Nor will states now be able to assume that the legitimate aims prescribed by Article 11(2) provide a secure basis for justifying the restriction of the peaceful assembly of homosexuals. Whilst the Russian government argued that the interference of public authorities was justified because it pursued the legitimate aims of 'public safety' and 'the protection of health or morals or for the protection of the rights and freedoms of others', the Court stated that, although it would not consider the question of legitimacy, 'in any event the ban was disproportionate to either of the two alleged aims'.[92]

Alekseyev establishes that 'public safety' cannot provide an automatic justification to curtail assemblies based on sexual orientation. The Court rejected the Russian government's argument that, in light of the statements made by religious groups, it had not been possible for the public authorities to guarantee the safety of those taking part in the planned events. The Court stated that it could not accept the argument that 'the threat was so great as to require such a drastic measure as banning the event altogether, let alone doing so repeatedly over a period of three years'.[93] Furthermore, the Court stated that it was the duty of the state to take reasonable and appropriate measures to enable lawful demonstrations to proceed peacefully and that the public authorities had failed to do this by not undertaking an adequate assessment of the risks posed. This is significant because it places an important emphasis on the responsibility of public authorities to 'neutralize' the threat of violence towards homosexuals rather than to curtail their right to assembly in light of it. The Court stated that public authorities have a duty 'to address potential counter-protesters – whether by making a public statement or by replying to their petitions individually – in order to remind them to remain within the boundaries of the law when carrying out any protest actions'.[94] Giving considerable weight to the recommendation of the Council of Europe, the Court stated:

> As regards any statements calling for violence and inciting offences against the participants in a public event, such as those by a Muslim cleric from Nizhniy Novgorod, who reportedly said that homosexuals must be stoned to death [. . .] as well as any isolated incidents of threats

92 Ibid., § 79.
93 Ibid., § 77.
94 Ibid., § 75.

> of violence being put into practice, they could have adequately been dealt with through the prosecution of those responsible. However, it does not appear that the authorities in the present case reacted to the cleric's call for violence in any other way than banning the event he condemned. By relying on such blatantly unlawful calls as grounds for the ban, the authorities effectively endorsed the intentions of persons and organisations that clearly and deliberately intended to disrupt a peaceful demonstration in breach of the law and public order.[95]

The Court's view, that public authorities effectively endorse threats of anti-gay violence if they do not adequately respond to them, is in keeping with arguments in favour of the development and implementation of legislation designed to protect homosexuals from the effects of 'hate speech'. *Alekseyev* can be seen to validate measures that enhance the regulation of those that seek to incite hatred of, and violence towards, gay men and lesbians.

Alekseyev also repudiates the claim that the protection of morals provides a justification to limit the public assembly of homosexuals. Rejecting various claims by the Russian government that public discussion of homosexuality would adversely affect morals, particularly those of children and 'vulnerable adults', the Court endorsed assemblies designed 'to promote respect for human rights and freedoms and to call for tolerance towards sexual minorities'.[96] Whilst the Russian government argued that any discussion of homosexuality should take place in private or in designated meeting places with restricted access, the Court stated that there was no justification for such exclusion from the public sphere. On the contrary, the Court argued that it was the responsibility of public authorities to promote 'fair and public debate' that 'would benefit social cohesion by ensuring that representatives of all views are heard'.[97] The Court stated that this 'was exactly the kind of debate that the applicant in the present case attempted to launch, and it could not be replaced by the officials spontaneously expressing uninformed views which they considered popular'.[98]

The *Alekseyev* judgment also rejects the claim, widespread across contracting states, that protecting the rights and freedoms of religious believers provides an adequate justification for limiting the Article 11 rights of homosexuals.[99] The Russian government argued that the 'ideas of the event organisers were

95 Ibid., § 76.
96 Ibid., § 82.
97 Ibid., § 86.
98 Ibid., § 86.
99 R. Vanderbeck and P. Johnson, ' "If a Charge Was Brought Against a Saintly Religious Leader Whose Intention Was To Save Souls. . .": An Analysis of UK Parliamentary Debates Over Incitement to Hatred on the Grounds of Sexual Orientation.'

not neutral to the rest of society, but had actually encroached on the rights [and] lawful interests' of religious believers because 'the gay parades would be perceived by believers as an intentional insult to their religious feelings and a "terrible debasement of their human dignity"'.[100] It is significant that the Court gave no weight to these arguments. Whilst anti-gay individuals and organizations often seek to privilege their views on the basis that they are rooted in religious faith, the Court accorded religion no special status in the 'balance' of interests that characterize a democratic society. Relying on its judgment in *Bączkowski and Others,* the Court stated that 'democracy does not simply mean that the views of the majority must always prevail: a balance must be achieved which ensures the fair and proper treatment of minorities and avoids any abuse of a dominant position'.[101] The implication of this is that, no matter how dominant a religion is in a society, faith should not assume any special status in balancing the protection of the Article 11 rights of homosexuals with the rights and freedoms of others.

Alekseyev is important because it is the Court's strongest statement to date that the rights of homosexuals extend beyond the domestic sphere and that interference with the Article 11 rights of homosexuals requires particularly serious justification. This has significance for the Court's Article 10 jurisprudence, since the Court has recognized that, for the purposes of assembly designed as a means of peaceful protest, Article 11 is fundamentally related to Article 10. In *Ezelin v France*, the Court determined that Article 10 is to be regarded as a *lex generalis* in respect of Article 11, which is a *lex specalis*, and therefore the 'protection of personal opinions, secured by Article 10 [. . .], is one of the objectives of freedom of peaceful assembly as enshrined in Article 11'.[102] As I argued in Chapter 4, the judgment in *Alekseyev* implicitly reiterates the long-standing and problematic view that there are aspects of 'homosexual conduct' that must be separated from the public sphere in order to protect the 'morals' and 'views' of the heterosexual majority. However, the judgment provides a welcome platform from which to contest the continuing and increasing interference with the rights of gay men and lesbians to associate, assemble and speak freely in public about their sexual orientations and against political regimes that so often discriminate against them.

Conclusion

In May 2011, the Secretary General of the Council of Europe, Thorbjørn Jagland, issued a statement on the International Day against Homophobia and Transphobia in which he urged member states to 'start acting to end

100 *Alekseyev v Russia*, nos. 4916/07, 25924/08 and 14599/09, 21 October 2010, § 59–60.
101 Ibid., § 63.
102 *Ezelin v France*, no. 11800/85, 26 April 1991, Series A no. 202, § 37.

discrimination of Lesbian, Gay, Bisexual and Transgender people'.[103] Jagland paid particular attention to the fact that 'the rights to freedom of assembly and freedom of expression of these persons are violated in several European states'.[104] In the same month, and following the judgment in *Alekseyev v Russia*, the Mayor of Moscow refused permission for a gay pride event in Moscow for the sixth time and, when a small group of activists assembled in Moscow, *Gay Russia* reported that 18 were quickly arrested.[105] The events in Russia are an example of the discrimination of gay men and lesbians across many contracting states. The Court's judgment in *Alekseyev* is a vital development in attempting to tackle the problems sexual minorities face when they attempt to organize and enact gay pride events. The Committee of Ministers of the Council of Europe currently have the execution of *Alekseyev* under enhanced supervision and it is to be hoped that, given the ongoing blatant defiance of the judgment by the Russian authorities, it will exercise its maximum authority to compel the Russian Federation to remove anti-gay provisions that violate Article 11. The judgment in *Alekseyev* is unequivocal and the legislative and judicial hindrance of peaceful political demonstrations designed to promote equality on the grounds of sexual orientation is incompatible with it.

Whilst *Alekseyev* represents a considerable evolution in the Court's jurisprudence in respect of homosexuality, gay men and lesbians continue to experience a wide range of discriminatory treatment that falls within the ambit of Articles 10 and 11 but for which there has been no favourable judgment. It is vital that the Court evolves its Article 10 jurisprudence to better guarantee the freedom of expression of gay men and lesbians. This opportunity is available to the Court in a currently pending application, *Bayev v Russia*, which complains that the Ryazan Oblast law prohibiting 'Public actions aimed at the promotion of homosexuality (sodomy and lesbianism) among minors' violates Article 10.[106] In respect of Article 11, the Court needs to continue to find against states that attempt to frustrate the assembly and association of homosexual groups. One of the most effective ways in which the Court could raise the profile of its condemnation of interferences suffered by homosexuals in respect of expression, assembly and association would be, as I explore in the next chapter, to find in favour of a complaint brought under Article 3 of the Convention.

103 Council of Europe, 'International Day Against Homophobia and Transphobia: Statement of Secretary General Thorbjørn Jagland', Press release DC002(2011), 17 May 2011.

104 Ibid.

105 See report by Gay Russia, available HTTP: <http://www.gayrussia.eu/en/pride/moscow-pride/2011.php> (last accessed 21 February 2012).

106 *Bayev v Russia*, no. 67667/09, lodged 7 November 2009.

Chapter 8

Humiliation and debasement

Degrading treatment and Article 3

Article 3 of the Convention provides that:

> No one shall be subjected to torture or to inhuman or degrading treatment or punishment.

It is striking, given the wide spectrum of inhuman and degrading treatment and punishment to which homosexuals have been subjected since the Convention entered into force, that no Article 3 complaint relating to sexual orientation has been successful. Whilst, as I examine below, applicants have invoked Article 3 to complain about various forms of degrading treatment on the grounds of sexual orientation, the Court has been unwilling to recognize these. A result of the Court's reluctance to acknowledge that various forms of state-sanctioned discrimination of homosexuals violate Article 3 is that applicants have progressively come to rely upon it less over time. Although, as I discussed in Chapter 1, early applications to the Commission in the 1950s did invoke Article 3, the continuous failure of the Strasbourg organs to give sufficient credence to these complaints has meant that Article 3 has become rarely used in matters relating to sexual orientation. For example, although in *Dudgeon v the United Kingdom* the applicant had been subjected to insulting[1] and humiliating[2] remarks about his sexual orientation when questioned by the police, which had resulted in 'psychological injury and harm',[3] Article 3 was not invoked in the complaint. Similarly, although the applicant in *Alekseyev v Russia*[4] had been subjected to various forms of verbal abuse by public authorities (including the mayor of Moscow, who reportedly

1 *Dudgeon v the United Kingdom*, no. 7525/76, Commission report, 13 March 1980, § 44.
2 *Dudgeon v the United Kingdom*, no. 7525/76, Commission decision, 3 March 1978, p. 124.
3 Ibid., p. 120.
4 *Alekseyev v Russia*, nos. 4916/07, 25924/08 and 14599/09, 21 October 2010.

referred to homosexuality as 'satanic') and arrest,[5] no use was made of Article 3.[6] The lack of Article 3 complaints to the Court is startling in light of the persistent inhuman and degrading treatment of homosexuals throughout Europe.

In this chapter, I consider the Court's existing case law in respect of complaints relating to sexual orientation that have invoked Article 3. I argue that the systematic failure of the Court to recognize that homophobic treatment constitutes degradation contrary to Article 3 has produced a fundamental gap in the protection available to gay men and lesbians under the Convention. The consequence of the Court's aversion to recognizing that homophobic actions constitute a violation of Article 3 is that its jurisprudence fails to condemn various forms of hostility that are directed towards homosexuals in contemporary Europe. Because the Court has refused to recognize that forms of discrimination on the grounds of sexual orientation are often in violation of Article 3, it has failed to address such discrimination with one of the most powerful and weighty provisions of the Convention. I explore below why an evolution in the Court's approach to Article 3 is vital and how a shift in its interpretation of the Convention may be possible in the future.

Why Article 3 is important for homosexuals

Before I go on to examine the Court's general approach to Article 3, as well as its case law in respect of complaints relating to sexual orientation, I want to briefly consider why an evolution of the Court's interpretation of this aspect of the Convention is important for homosexuals. The primary reason why a development in the Court's jurisprudence is so badly needed is because Article 3 can address both the existence of homophobic social relations in contemporary societies and their impact upon individuals in a way that is distinctly different to the other substantive provisions of the Convention. The key difference of Article 3 is its capacity to condemn, in absolute and unqualified terms, discriminatory social practices directed at homosexuals. To demonstrate this, the recent complaint brought in *Wolfmeyer v Austria*, which did not invoke Article 3, is illustrative.[7]

The application in *Wolfmeyer* was lodged by a 37-year-old man who had been convicted, and then acquitted on appeal, of sexual offences under

5 BBC News, 'Moscow Bans "Satanic" Gay Parade', 29 January 2007, available HTTP: <http://news.bbc.co.uk/1/hi/world/europe/6310883.stm> (last accessed 21 February 2012).

6 The Court has a pending application filed by Mr. Alekseyev and others that complaining about homophobic statements made by the Governor of the Tambov Oblast, Oleg Betin, invokes Article 3. *Alekseyev, Bayev, Nepomnyaschiy v Russia*, no. 39954/09, lodged 22 September 2009.

7 *Wolfmeyer v Austria*, no. 5263/03, 26 May 2005.

Article 209 of the Austrian Criminal Code which, until its repeal subsequent to proceedings against the applicant, criminalized 'fornication' between a male over the age of 19 with another male aged between 14 and 18 (a framework that did not hold in respect of heterosexual sex). The applicant complained that as a result of proceedings against him, he had suffered 'humiliation' and 'public exposure' in the small provincial town where he resided and that, as a result, he had lost his employment.[8] In its review, the Court acknowledged that where details of applicants' 'most intimate private life' are 'laid open to the public', this must 'be considered as a profoundly destabilizing event' in their lives and, in light of this, upheld the complaint that the treatment of the applicant was in violation of Article 14 taken in conjunction with Article 8.[9] In one sense, the Court's willingness to acknowledge the 'destabilizing' effects of homophobic law shows a positive evolution of both its Article 8 and Article 14 jurisprudence because it recognizes the negative subjective results of discrimination. However, because the applicant relied on Articles 8 and 14, the Court's consideration of the 'profoundly destabilizing event' focused entirely on his 'private life'. The Court's judgment, which concentrates on the applicant's right to respect for his private life, is therefore problematic because it does not address the social conditions that created the destabilizing events. Rather than address the conditions that contributed to the applicant's sexual orientation being 'laid open', and the reactions that followed because of this, the judgment deals only with the applicant's right to maintain his sexual orientation 'in private'. By not dealing directly with the social hostility aimed at the applicant, the Court, as I discussed in Chapter 4, reiterated the social relations of the closet that encourage homosexuals to retreat to the private sphere. As I argue below, an evolution of the Court's interpretation of Article 3 is needed in order to directly address and condemn the social relations and practices in the public sphere that produce the profoundly destabilizing effects of homophobia experienced by gay men and lesbians.

The Court's approach to Article 3

The Court has stated that Article 3 is an absolute and unqualified right:

> The Convention prohibits in absolute terms torture and inhuman and degrading treatment or punishment, irrespective of the victim's conduct. Unlike most of the substantive clauses of the Convention and of Protocols Nos. 1 and 4, Article 3 makes no provision for exceptions and, under

8 Ibid., § 27.
9 Ibid., § 33.

> Article 15(2), there can be no derogation therefore even in the event of a public emergency threatening the life of the nation.[10]

However, as Addo and Grief argue, although conceived in absolute terms, Article 3 has not lent itself to precise definition or application by the Court:

> The case law gives an impression of shifting boundaries as regards the character and scope of the absolute nature of the prohibitions in Article 3. The Court is guided in its decision-making by such principles as 'effective protection' and 'margin of appreciation' through which relativity is injected into its thinking. Its practice under Article 3 is based not on objective criteria but on the effects of various subjective factors on the particular facts of each case, leading to decisions which can be hard to reconcile at least at first sight.[11]

In practice, therefore, the scope of Article 3 is relatively conceived and subjectively applied, depending on the context in which the actions complained of occur and the effects they produce upon the applicant. Nevertheless, in *The Greek Case*, the Commission attempted to define and delimit the textual meaning of Article 3:

> It is plain that there may be treatment to which all these descriptions apply, for all torture must be inhuman and degrading treatment, and inhuman treatment also degrading. The notion of inhuman treatment covers at least such treatment as deliberately causes severe suffering, mental or physical, which, in the particular situation, is unjustifiable.
>
> The word 'torture' is often used to describe inhuman treatment which has a purpose, such as the obtaining of information or confessions, or the infliction of punishment, and it is generally an aggravated form of inhuman treatment. Treatment or punishment of an individual may be said to be degrading if it grossly humiliates him before others or drives him to act against his will or conscience.[12]

However, the Commission also recognized that the 'borderline between harsh treatment on the one hand and a violation of Article 3 on the other is sometimes difficult to establish'.[13]

10 *Ireland v the United Kingdom*, no. 5310/71, 18 January 1978, Series A no. 25, § 163.

11 M.K. Addo and N. Grief, 'Does Article 3 of The European Convention on Human Rights Enshrine Absolute Rights?', *European Journal of International Law* 9, 1998, 510–524 at 514.

12 *The Greek Case*, nos. 3321/67, 3322/67, 3323/67 and 3344/67, Commission report, 5 November 1969, 12 (1969) YECHR, p. 186.

13 *McCallum v the United Kingdom*, no. 9511/81, Commission report, 4 May 1989, § 77.

One might expect that the spectrum of actions covered by Article 3, which range from the infliction of bodily harm to the gross humiliation of individuals, would have resulted in a successful complaint in the Court in relation to sexual orientation. Given that homosexuals have been imprisoned on the grounds of sexual orientation, physically abused whilst in confinement, and been subjected to forms of verbal abuse in various contexts, it is astonishing that such treatment has not been deemed to violate Article 3. One explanation of why no complaint has succeeded is the Court's stringent application of the principle that any treatment complained of must reach a minimum level of severity to trigger Article 3. The Court has attempted to maintain a high threshold for the minimum level of severity in order not to trivialize the substance of the provision or encourage rights inflation under it. However, the Court has recognized that determining the threshold 'depends on all the circumstances of the case, such as the duration of the treatment, its physical and mental effects and, in some cases, the sex, age and state of health of the victim'.[14] The Court has also recognized that the threshold for the minimum level of severity changes over time:

> The Court has previously examined cases in which it concluded that there had been treatment which could only be described as torture [. . .] However, having regard to the fact that the Convention is a 'living instrument which must be interpreted in the light of present-day conditions' [. . .], the Court considers that certain acts which were classified in the past as 'inhuman and degrading treatment' as opposed to 'torture' could be classified differently in future. It takes the view that the increasingly high standard being required in the area of the protection of human rights and fundamental liberties correspondingly and inevitably requires greater firmness in assessing breaches of the fundamental values of democratic societies.[15]

As a consequence of this, forms of treatment once regarded to fall outside of Article 3 can be re-categorized, in light of the changing standards of European societies, in order to address them with the 'firmness' required in contemporary democratic societies. The threshold for the minimum level of severity should, therefore, be no bar to bringing a successful complaint about sexual-orientation discrimination under Article 3.

The interpretative framework developed by the Court in respect of the different forms of treatment prohibited by Article 3 provides significant potential to bring complaints about sexual-orientation discrimination. The Court has defined inhuman treatment as that which can 'cause either actual

14 *Ireland v the United Kingdom*, no. 5310/71, 18 January 1978, Series A no. 25, § 162.
15 *Selmouni v France* [GC], no. 25803/94, 28 July 1999, ECHR 1999-V, § 101.

bodily harm or intense physical or mental suffering'.[16] In respect of the minimum level of severity, the Commission determined that any treatment must 'inflict severe mental or physical suffering on an individual'.[17] The Court has defined degrading treatment as treatment that 'is such to arouse in the victim feelings of fear, anguish and inferiority capable of humiliating and debasing them'.[18] This focus on actions that create feelings of fear, anguish and inferiority that humiliate and debase individuals provides scope to evolve the Court's interpretation of the Convention in respect of sexual orientation. The Court has already significantly developed this aspect of its jurisprudence in respect of race. In *Moldovan and Others v Romania*, in which a group of Roma applicants complained that after the destruction of their homes by police officers they were forced to live in very poor conditions, the Court paid particular attention to the 'general attitude of the authorities', which caused the applicants 'considerable mental suffering, thus diminishing their human dignity and arousing in them such feelings as to cause humiliation and debasement'.[19] In relation to the general attitudes of the authorities, the Court went on to state that:

> remarks concerning the applicants' honesty and way of life made by some authorities dealing with the applicants' grievances [. . .] appear to be, in the absence of any substantiation on behalf of those authorities, purely discriminatory. In this connection the Court reiterates that discrimination based on race can of itself amount to degrading treatment within the meaning of Article 3 of the Convention.[20]

The Court's view that forms of discrimination based on race can reach the minimum level of severity to be classified as degrading treatment contrary to Article 3 provides a foundation on which to make similar claims in respect of sexual orientation.

The Court's jurisprudence in respect of Article 3 complaints relating to homosexuality

Although the first Article 3 complaint relating to sexual orientation was lodged in 1959, Strasbourg jurisprudence has evolved very little since that time. Whilst, as I explore below, homosexual applicants have complained

16 *Kudła v Poland* [GC], no. 30210/96, 26 October 2000, ECHR 2000-XI, § 92.
17 *X. v Federal Republic of Germany*, no. 9191/80, unpublished.
18 *Kudła v Poland* [GC], no. 30210/96, 26 October 2000, ECHR 2000-XI, § 92.
19 *Moldovan and others v. Romania (no. 2)*, nos. 41138/98 and 64320/01, 12 July 2005, ECHR 2005-VII (extracts), § 110.
20 Ibid., § 111.

about a wide range of treatment, the Strasbourg organs have stubbornly refused to give them any credence.

Criminalization of homosexual sex

A German national, who claimed that the criminalization of male homosexual sex by paragraph 175 of the German Criminal Code constituted inhuman and degrading treatment, was the first applicant to lodge an Article 3 complaint relating to homosexuality.[21] As I discussed in Chapter 1, the Commission deemed all applications relating to paragraph 175 inadmissible but what is especially striking about *A.S. v Federal Republic of Germany* is the complete absence of any engagement by the Commission with the applicant's Article 3 claim. The Commission simply ignored the applicant's assertion that the criminalization of homosexual relationships constituted a form of human degradation. Although in subsequent complaints relating to paragraph 175 the Commission did engage with Article 3 claims, it never accorded them any serious consideration. For instance, in *H.S. v Federal Republic of Germany* the Commission bluntly stated that the applicant's complaint, that his conviction under paragraph 175 violated his Article 3 rights, did not 'disclose any apparent violation of the rights and freedoms set forth in the Convention'.[22] Similarly, in *G.W. v Federal Republic of Germany*, the Commission stated that the retention of photographs and fingerprints following convictions for paragraph 175 offences did not constitute a violation of Article 3.[23]

The Court has only considered one Article 3 complaint relating to the criminalization of male homosexual sex. In *Ladner v Austria*, the applicant complained about his conviction in 2002 by the Vienna Regional Criminal Court for sexual offences contrary to Article 209 of the Austrian Criminal Code, which, as I detailed in Chapter 5, maintained a higher 'age of consent' for male homosexual acts.[24] Following his conviction and the subsequent repeal of Article 209 from Austrian law, the applicant appealed against his conviction and this was dismissed on the grounds that the charges against the applicant had been served prior to the repeal of Article 209. A subsequent application to the Minister of Justice requesting a pardon also failed. In March 2003, the Minister of Justice replied to questions put by Parliament about the granting of pardons in cases of convictions under Article 209. During his answer, and using the file number and the date of the final decision by the Vienna Court of Appeal, the Minister referred to Mr. Ladner's case and stated

21 *A.S. v Federal Republic of Germany*, no. 530/59, Commission decision, 4 January 1960.
22 *H.S. v Federal Republic of Germany*, no. 704/60, Commission decision, 4 August 1960.
23 *G.W. v Federal Republic of Germany*, no. 1307/61, Commission decision, 4 October 1962.
24 *Ladner v Austria*, no. 18297/03, 3 February 2005.

that a pardon was not granted because his conduct was contrary to Article 207b of the Austrian Criminal Code (which criminalizes sexual acts in cases where an older person takes advantage of an adolescent's immaturity or of a predicament that has rendered them vulnerable). In particular, the Minister referred to the applicant as having 'taken advantage of [an] adolescent's predicament' who, 'following a conflict with his parents, temporarily lived in [the applicant's] apartment'.[25] The applicant complained that the Minister, by invoking Article 207b (of which he had not been convicted), described him in public as 'a sexual abuser who exploited his partners' and that this constituted a violation of his Article 3 rights. The applicant did not specify which aspect of Article 3 he relied upon and the Court similarly gave no consideration to this. The Court decided that in 'regard to the Minister's statement and, in particular, the fact that he did not mention the applicant's name', the treatment complained of did 'not reach the minimum level of severity required to fall within the scope of Article 3'.[26]

Three questions arise from the judgment in *Ladner*: first, would the use of Mr. Ladner's name by the Minister have constituted a form of treatment that was sufficient to reach the minimum level of severity required by Article 3? Given that the Court cites the absence of the applicant's name as particularly salient, it is reasonable to infer that had Mr. Ladner's name been mentioned, this would have placed the treatment within the ambit of Article 3. In light of this, a second question arises about the grounds on which the treatment might have been recognized as a violation of Article 3. Would it have been on the grounds that such treatment constitutes a form of degradation because it humiliates and debases the individual? If that is the case, it raises a third question about the relevance of the use of Mr. Ladner's name. Since the Minister's comments make a link between homosexual sexual activity and the sexual exploitation of children – a link that has long-standing and enduring social and cultural resonances across Europe – it is arguable that this in itself constitutes a form of degrading treatment of homosexual men. In other words, the Minister's actions arguably produce a humiliating and debasing effect not only upon the applicant but also upon an entire social group. Given that the applicant is regarded as belonging to the group in question, he can be seen to suffer from the net result of this degradation. The Court's focus in *Ladner*, on the absence of the use of the applicant's name, is problematic because it could be interpreted to mean that homosexuals do not suffer degradation when generic homophobic statements are made by public officials in contracting states and can only complain when such statements are directly addressed to them.

25 Ibid., § 12.
26 Ibid., § 28.

Treatment in detention

Several homosexual applicants have petitioned the Court to complain about treatment in detention subsequent to conviction for sexual and non-sexual offences. The Commission deemed several applications inadmissible and only one has reached the Court. In *X. v Germany*, the applicant made three complaints under Article 3 regarding the treatment he received during his trial, conviction and imprisonment for homosexual offences. First, the applicant claimed that:

> during his detention he was, on account of the nature of the charge against him, subject to ill treatment by the prison officials, in particular a guard by the name of Y. After his release he requested that criminal proceedings should be initiated against this guard but, on . . . 1960, the Public Prosecutor of E. upheld this decision on the grounds that the appeal was manifestly ill-founded and, in any event, not introduced by a lawyer.[27]

Second, the applicant claimed that he had been ordered to undergo a medical examination by the Regional court during his trial and that this 'is an example of degrading treatment'.[28] Third, the applicant made a more general complaint about the

> damages inherent in being officially classified as a homosexual, in view particularly of the fate meted out to homosexuals during the Nazi period when mass liquidation of such persons in concentration camps were an established feature and in view partly of the present German legislation on the matter.[29]

This application remains unusual in that the applicant did not invoke either Article 8 or Article 14 but relied solely on Articles 3, 5 and 6. The Commission decided, in respect of the first complaint about the ill-treatment suffered during detention, that 'it is to be pointed out that three judicial instances within the Federal Republic of Germany have refused to institute criminal proceedings against the person alleged to be responsible on the grounds that the Applicant's complaint was without foundation' and that 'the Applicant has not satisfied the Commission that these allegations are substantially true'.[30] The Commission therefore concluded that this part of the application

27 *X. v Federal Republic of Germany*, no. 986/61, Commission decision, 7 May 1962.
28 Ibid.
29 Ibid.
30 Ibid.

was manifestly ill-founded. However, it is highly unlikely, given the general approach of the Commission that I described in Chapter 1, that the existence of evidence sufficient to show the complaint was 'true' would have led to the application being deemed admissible under Article 3. With regard to the second complaint, the Commission stated that 'it is to be observed that medical examinations of accused persons constitute a normal and often desirable part of a thorough and conscientious investigation of a case'.[31] The Commission therefore deemed this part of the application manifestly ill-founded. And in respect of the claim that the criminalization of homosexuality produces 'inherent damage' in the individual, the Commission remained silent.

In *X. v Austria*, the applicant, who had been convicted of homosexual offences and sentenced to six years' imprisonment with the additional penalty of 'sleeping hard' and subsequently committed to a labour institution, complained that whilst in prison he was subjected to disciplinary measures in connection with his application to the Commission, that his living conditions in prison were inadequate, and that he suffered illness after being placed in solitary confinement for having violated prison rules.[32] The Austrian government submitted the following statement to the Commission in response to the applicant's allegations:

> It is untrue that the prisoner X was subjected to disciplinary measures in 1962 for lodging an application with the European Commission of Human Rights. Disciplinary action was taken against him because, over a period of time and in addition to the stationery issued to him, he unlawfully appropriated (stole) and hoarded specific types of stationery for other purposes. In the interests of the maintenance of prison order and discipline, such behaviour could clearly not be tolerated, the more so since prisoners who wish to lodge an application with the European Commission of Human Rights are immediately given the necessary stationery.
>
> It is true that, in January 1962, the prisoner was deprived of privileges for a month as a disciplinary measure for the insults levelled at Austrian justice in general and prison administrations in particular, in an application addressed to the Commission in which he used such expressions as: murderers of justice, murderers of the people, court terror, robbers of freedom, double-dealing, Nazi hierarchy, etc.
>
> It is obvious that such slander cannot be tolerated by the judicial authorities and calls for disciplinary measures.

31 Ibid.

32 *X. v Austria*, no. 1593/62, Commission decision, 4 July 1964.

> The Federal Ministry of Justice consequently considers that the Commission should declare this part of the Application inadmissible also.[33]

Although the Austrian government clearly confirmed that the applicant had been subject to punishment for verbalizing his protest against laws criminalizing homosexuality, the Commission deemed this part of the complaint inadmissible. The only aspect of the complaint that the Commission examined was whether the domestic authorities had hindered the applicant's right to effective individual petition. The Commission stated that, having carefully considered the impact of the punishment upon the applicant, his right of individual petition could have been seriously impaired if he was deterred from proceeding further with an application. However, the Commission also stated that 'it is no part of the effective exercise of the right of petition to make unnecessary or irrelevant offensive statements'.[34] As a result, the Commission found that the treatment of the applicant was reasonable in light of the comments that he had made about the Austrian authorities. What is striking about the Commission's review of this application is that it wholly failed to engage with the complaint about the degrading and inhuman treatment of the applicant on the grounds of his sexual orientation. A similar approach was taken in *S. v Germany*, in which the applicant, following his arrest and conviction for homosexual offences (and passport forgery) in Morocco, complained that the German diplomatic services did not intervene to protect him while he was in prison and thereby exposed him to the risk of torture and to inhuman conditions.[35] The Commission ignored the substance of the Article 3 complaint, stating that 'the subject of the applicant's complaint is not his treatment in a Moroccan prison' but 'the alleged failure of the German diplomatic authorities to take adequate action', and concluded that the Convention guaranteed no right to this form of diplomatic assistance.[36]

In October 2011 the Court issued its first judgment in respect of a complaint brought by a homosexual applicant about treatment in detention.[37] In *Stasi v France*, the applicant claimed that, subsequent to his conviction for embezzlement and fraud, he suffered a range of ill-treatment in detention from other inmates and that prison authorities had not taken the necessary measures to ensure his protection. For example, the applicant claimed that although he informed prison authorities that he had been the victim of rape during a previous period of detention, he was made to share a cell with another

33 Ibid.
34 Ibid.
35 *S. v Federal Republic of Germany*, no. 10686/83, Commission decision, 5 October 1984.
36 Ibid.
37 *Stasi v France*, no. 25001/07, 20 October 2011.

prisoner who ill-treated him because of his homosexuality. This treatment took the form of forcing him to wear a pink star, beating and burning him, depriving him of food and preventing him from leaving his cell to report his injuries. Medical certificates issued by the prison authorities testified to a range of physical injuries sustained by the applicant and the Court found that these established that the treatment complained of fell within the ambit of inhuman and degrading treatment contrary to Article 3. In reviewing the applicant's Article 3 complaint, the Court stated that insufficient proof was available to verify the allegations about the treatment by the fellow prisoner. With regard to the treatment of the applicant by the prison authorities, the Court found that in respect of every allegation made to the authorities, reasonable measures had been taken to protect the applicant from physical harm. For example, the Court noted that after the applicant had made his allegations of ill-treatment to the prison authorities, he had been transferred to another cell, allowed to shower alone and systematically accompanied when he moved around the prison. In respect of the applicant's claim that these measures did not adequately protect him (for instance, because he had been beaten in the shower block), the Court stated that in response to each allegation prison authorities had undertaken an investigation and no culprits could be identified. The Court also stated that the applicant had frequently failed to report incidents to the prison authorities and that they could not be held responsible for actions they were unaware of. In light of this, the Court found that the treatment of the applicant did not violate Article 3.

Judges Nussberger and Spielmann issued a strong joint dissenting opinion in *Stasi*, disagreeing with the majority's conclusion that prison authorities had taken all necessary measures to protect the applicant.[38] They argued that although the authorities had taken *some* measures to protect the applicant, these were insufficient to meet the positive obligations imposed by Article 3. Such obligations require prison authorities to undertake preventative measures to avoid the treatment suffered by the applicant. Nussberger and Spielmann argued that, because the applicant had revealed his vulnerability to ill-treatment on the grounds of his sexual orientation from the outset, the measures taken by prison authorities did not fulfil their positive obligation to protect him. They also argued that in the context of the prison environment, in which there is a 'law of silence', the authorities could not justify a lack of protection on the grounds that the applicant had not made complaints or provided documentation on each occasion he suffered ill-treatment. In the absence of special support and appropriate protection from the prison authorities, Nussberger and Spielmann argued that the treatment experienced by the applicant was in violation of Article 3.

38 Ibid., Joint dissenting opinion of Judges Nussberger and Spielmann.

That there has been no successful Article 3 complaint in respect of the treatment of homosexuals in detention is astonishing given the various forms of inhuman and degrading treatment that is the commonplace experience of gay men and lesbians across Europe. For example, Human Rights Watch and the International Gay and Lesbian Human Rights Commission have reported that, in Romania, homosexuals in detention are 'targeted by other inmates for sexual abuse, with the tolerance and even encouragement of guards'.[39] And the United Nations have recently reported that in Greece, 'detainees in a lesbian, gay and transgender section of a prison were reportedly denied access to an outside yard for two years, confined to their cells and a corridor at all times'.[40] Reports of gay men and lesbians being subjected to treatment contrary to Article 3 whilst in detention are frequently made in a number of contracting states. It is vital that the Court condemns such treatment and mandates the right of homosexuals to be free from all forms of degrading and inhuman practices. The Court has a number of applications pending that give it the opportunity to achieve this. For instance, in *X. v Turkey*, the homosexual applicant complains that, following his detention in custody for a number of offences, he was placed in a communal cell with heterosexual prisoners and, as a result of a request to be moved because of intimidation and harassment, prison officials referred to his sexual orientation as a disease and placed him in a single cell with an area of five square metres.[41] The applicant claims that this treatment is inhuman and constitutes unlawful and disproportionate interference with his right to physical and moral integrity. It is to be hoped that, in reviewing the merits of these and similar facts cases, the Court will evolve its jurisprudence to recognize that these forms of treatment are in violation of Article 3.

Treatment of service people in the armed forces

A number of applications have been lodged in Strasbourg by armed forces personnel who have complained that their treatment at work is in violation of Article 3. In *Fleming v the United Kingdom*, the applicant – a service woman in the Royal Air Force – complained that during an investigation into allegations that she was a homosexual, both she and her female partner had been interviewed by senior officers about the most intimate details of their private life. During these investigations, the applicants had been asked questions about their sexual practices, which included whether they had 'interfered

39 Human Rights Watch and the International Gay and Lesbian Human Rights Commission, *Public Scandals: Sexual Orientation and Criminal Law in Romania*, New York, 1998.

40 United Nations Human Rights Council, *Discriminatory Laws and Practices and Acts of Violence Against Individuals Based on their Sexual Orientation and Gender Identity: Report of the United Nations High Commissioner for Human Rights*, A/HRC/19/41, 17 November 2011, § 35.

41 *X. v Turkey*, no. 24626/09, Statement of facts, 9 September 2010.

sexually' with their 16–year-old foster daughter.[42] The Commission deemed the application inadmissible for being out of time and did not give any consideration as to whether this treatment was contrary to Article 3. However, in *Smith and Grady v the United Kingdom*, the applicants advanced a similar complaint about the treatment that they had been subjected to during investigations into their sexual orientation.[43] The applicants claimed that the investigations were 'based on crude stereotyping and prejudice [that] denied and caused affront to their individuality and dignity',[44] and argued that the questions put to them were 'hurtful and degrading' as well as 'prurient and offensive'.[45] Although the Court did not find in favour of the applicants, its judgment does show signs of evolution in its interpretation of Article 3 in respect of sexual orientation. The Court stated that, since treatment is degrading if it arouses in its victims 'feelings of fear, anguish and inferiority capable of humiliating and debasing them and possibly breaking their physical or moral resistance',[46] it would 'not exclude that treatment which is grounded upon a predisposed bias on the part of a heterosexual majority against a homosexual minority [. . .] could, in principle, fall within the scope of Article 3'.[47] The Court ultimately found that the investigation and discharge of the applicants from the armed forces, although 'undoubtedly distressing and humiliating',[48] did not reach the minimum level of severity to bring it within the ambit of Article 3. This is unfortunate since both applicants were subjected to protracted and invasive investigations into their sexual practices and intimate relationships that they experienced as both humiliating and debasing. Nevertheless, the Court's acknowledgement that treatment resulting from a predisposed bias against homosexuals can, in principle, reach the threshold of the minimum level of severity required by Article 3 offers potential for future complaints against discriminatory practices.[49] It is regrettable that this potential was not realized in *Stavros Marangos v Cyprus*, in which the applicant complained about the requirement to perform military service with the Cypriot National Guard because of his belief that, as a homosexual, he would be subjected to degrading treatment by other military personnel.[50] Because the complaint rested on an Article 6 claim that the Court

42 *Fleming v the United Kingdom*, no. 33987/96, Commission decision, 20 May 1997.
43 *Smith and Grady v the United Kingdom*, nos. 33985/96 and 33986/96, 27 September 1999, ECHR 1999-VI.
44 Ibid., § 119.
45 Ibid.
46 Ibid., § 120.
47 Ibid., § 121.
48 Ibid., § 122.
49 A similar facts case (*Goddard v the United Kingdom* (dec), no. 57821/00, 15 January 2002) was struck from the Court's list because a friendly settlement was reached by the parties.
50 *Stavros Marangos v Cyprus*, no. 12846/05, 4 December 2008.

rejected, no consideration was given to whether the prevalence of the institutional and systematic homophobia complained of by the applicant reached the minimum level of severity required by Article 3.

Deportation of asylum seekers

A number of complaints have been made against contracting states that have deported foreign nationals seeking asylum to a country where they claim to be at risk of treatment contrary to Article 3 because of their sexual orientation. For example, in *F. v the United Kingdom*, the applicant, an Iranian citizen living in the United Kingdom, complained that if deported to Iran he would face torture and ill-treatment and be at risk of extra-judicial killing contrary to Articles 2 and 3 of the Convention. An Immigration Appeal Tribunal in the United Kingdom had refused the applicant leave to remain because:

> though in theory homosexuality was punished harshly, in practice homosexuals were unlikely to encounter serious problems, in particular no person had been executed for homosexuality alone over the last 13 years. At the highest, the evidence produced by the applicant suggested that he might be at risk of ill-treatment if a future sexual partner decided to contact the courts and confess, implicating the applicant, which was implausible and the risk of this happening was too remote and speculative to give rise to substantial grounds for believing that the applicant would face a 'real risk' of Article 3 treatment.[51]

The applicant argued that, whilst there was under-reporting of executions and floggings for homosexual offences, there had been a series of documented cases where men had received sentences of capital (by beheading and hanging) and corporal punishment for engaging in homosexual acts. He further contended that, in detention, homosexuals were liable to be the subject of severe ill-treatment. Unlike Article 8, which I examined in Chapter 4, Article 3 places an obligation on a contracting state not to expel an individual to a country if he or she would be at risk of being subjected to torture or to inhuman or degrading treatment or punishment. In its review, the Court stated that the materials available to it did not 'disclose a situation of active prosecution by the authorities of adults involved in consensual and private homosexual relationships'[52] and that the applicant's claim formed a 'tenuous and hypothetical basis on which to assess the likelihood of Article 3 treatment occurring'.[53] The Court concluded that:

51 *F. v the United Kingdom* (dec), no. 17341/03, 22 June 2004.
52 Ibid.
53 Ibid.

> Although it is not disputed in theory [. . .] that very draconian punishment can be imposed on homosexual acts [and that] it must be acknowledged that the general situation in Iran does not foster the protection of human rights and that homosexuals may be vulnerable to abuse, the applicant has not established in his case that there are substantial grounds for believing that he will be exposed to a real risk of being subjected to treatment contrary to [Article 3].[54]

The Court reached the same judgment in *I.N.N. v the Netherlands*, a similar facts case in which the applicant complained that, if expelled to Iran, he would face the risk of treatment in breach of Article 3 on account of his homosexual orientation.[55] And in *Ayegh v Sweden*, in which the applicant claimed that her son had been raped and abused by his headmaster in Iran and that his return there would result in severe punishment for his involvement in homosexual acts, the Court entirely failed to address the question of homosexuality.[56]

The failure of the Court to uphold the Article 3 rights of homosexuals and protect them from being returned to contexts so obviously hostile to them is a major gap in contemporary gay and lesbian human rights. Even in the absence of systematic evidence regarding torture or inhuman practices, the Court should recognize that returning an individual to a country that operates a total legal prohibition on homosexual sex constitutes a form of degrading treatment contrary to Article 3. Repatriating individuals to such countries will inevitably create in them 'feelings of fear, anguish and inferiority capable of humiliating and debasing them and possibly breaking their physical or moral resistance'.[57] Because of this, the Court should not only regard the continuing criminalization of homosexuality in states around the world as a violation of Articles 8 and 14, but also as a breach of the most fundamental right to be free from degradation under Article 3. The Court currently has a case pending in which the applicant, an Iranian national who has been imprisoned twice in Iran for homosexual offences, complains that deportation from France to Iran will result in treatment contrary to Article 3.[58] It is to be hoped that the Court gives judicial effect to Recommendation CM/Rec(2010)5 of the Committee of Ministers, which states that contracting states 'should recognise that a well-founded fear of persecution based on sexual orientation or gender identity may be a valid ground for the granting of refugee status and asylum under national law' and 'ensure particularly that asylum seekers

54 Ibid.

55 *I.I.N. v the Netherlands* (dec), no. 2035/04, 9 December 2004.

56 *Ayegh v Sweden* (dec), no. 4701/05, 7 November 2006.

57 *Smith and Grady v the United Kingdom*, nos. 33985/96 and 33986/96, 27 September 1999, ECHR 1999-VI, § 120.

58 *K.N. v France*, no. 47129/09, Statement of facts, 10 May 2010.

are not sent to a country where their life or freedom would be threatened or they face the risk of torture, inhuman or degrading treatment or punishment, on grounds of sexual orientation or gender identity'.[59]

Conclusions: can Article 3 be evolved to better protect homosexuals?

Article 3 protects individuals from the most serious abuses of their physical, mental and moral integrity. In contemporary European societies, where homosexuals continue to be subjected to wide-ranging forms of discriminatory treatment, the absence of any successful Article 3 complaint constitutes a fundamental gap in the Court's jurisprudence. A contributing factor to the continuation of this gap is the distinct lack of complaints brought by gay men and lesbians under Article 3. Whilst the Court's existing jurisprudence does not encourage the view that Article 3 complaints will be successful, it is vital that individual applicants and non-governmental organizations bring these complaints more frequently. As with the development of Article 8 rights – which necessitated over 25 years of sustained petitioning to produce the first successful judgment in the Court – the evolution of Article 3 depends upon homosexuals consistently advancing complaints that press the Court to change its interpretive framework. But the evolution of the Court's interpretation of Article 3 also depends upon it relinquishing its own fixation on 'private life' when dealing with matters relating to sexual orientation. As I argued in Chapter 4, the siphoning of issues concerning homosexuality under the private life limb of Article 8 has led to a failure to guarantee sexual minorities the full protection of the Convention. For instance, in *Smith and Grady v the United Kingdom*, the Court comprehensibly failed to endorse the complaint that invasive investigations into an individual's homosexual orientation and practice and dismissal from employment constitutes a form of treatment that is degrading. The effects of such treatment upon the applicants in *Smith and Grady*, contrary to the Court's view, cannot be fully addressed through a consideration of private life. Rather, the Court should recognize that such treatment humiliates and debases individuals in such a way that it risks breaking their physical and moral resistance.

The United Nations have recently acknowledged that:

> members of sexual minorities are disproportionately subjected to torture and other forms of ill-treatment because they fail to conform to socially constructed gender expectations. Indeed, discrimination on grounds of

59 Council of Europe, 'Recommendation CM/Rec(2010)5 of the Committee of Ministers to Member States on Measures to Combat Discrimination on Grounds of Sexual Orientation or Gender Identity', § 42–43.

> sexual orientation or gender identity may often contribute to the process of the dehumanization of the victim, which is often a necessary condition for torture and ill-treatment to take place.[60]

This recognition that social discrimination creates the conditions for forms of ill-treatment and torture should be the foundation on which the Court evolves its Article 3 jurisprudence in respect of sexual orientation. The Court should adopt a more sociological approach to understanding how the social discrimination experienced by homosexuals constitutes degrading treatment and, left unaddressed, incubates the social conditions that can give rise to inhuman treatment and torture. It should recognize that every time a public official refers to homosexuality as a disease, claims that homosexuals are not fit to be parents or draws parallels between homosexuality and child sexual abuse, they degrade gay men and lesbians. It should recognize that every time homosexuals are denied access to goods and services on the basis of their sexual orientation, prevented from assembling and associating in public or dismissed from their jobs, they experience degradation. Such degradation cultivates and sustains the social stigma of homosexuality and produces detrimental physical and mental effects upon individuals. The key to evolving the Court's jurisprudence in this area depends, therefore, on the Court recognizing that the commonplace homophobia endemic in many contracting states routinely violates the right to be free from degrading treatment guaranteed by Article 3. Whilst the Court may be resistant to granting such recognition, and commentators will claim that it would lower the minimum level of severity under Article 3 and produce rights inflation, homosexual men and woman must continue to claim that discrimination on the grounds of sexual orientation debases, humiliates and degrades them and that, furthermore, failure to address such degradation sustains and encourages discrimination and ill-treatment.

60 United Nations Human Rights Council, *Discriminatory Laws and Practices and Acts of Violence Against Individuals Based on their Sexual Orientation and Gender Identity: Report of the United Nations High Commissioner for Human Rights*, § 34.

Conclusions

The Strasbourg organs have been issuing decisions and judgments in respect of a wide range of complaints relating to sexual orientation discrimination since 1955. Strasbourg case law on homosexuality is, as this book demonstrates, both wide and deep. However, because the former Commission and the Court have often been reluctant to uphold sexual orientation complaints, gay and lesbian human rights under the Convention have developed slowly. Although the Court's 1981 judgment in *Dudgeon v the United Kingdom*[1] marked a watershed in its jurisprudence, as well as in international law, it was followed by a long period in which the Strasbourg organs continued to deem inadmissible any complaints about sexual orientation discrimination except those relating to the criminalization of private sexual acts. It was not until the Commission deemed *Sutherland v the United Kingdom* admissible in 1996,[2] and delivered its favourable report in 1997,[3] that the Strasbourg organs began to recognize that a broader range of discrimination experienced by homosexuals violated the Convention. Since 1999, the Court has delivered a series of judgments establishing the rights of homosexuals to be free from discrimination when serving in the armed forces,[4] in the legal arrangement of the custody of a child,[5] in the provision of housing,[6] when applying to adopt a child[7] and when assembling in public.[8] However, in the same period, the Court has also rejected complaints about discrimination on the grounds of sexual orientation

1 *Dudgeon v the United Kingdom*, no. 7525/76, 22 October 1981, Series A no. 45.
2 *Sutherland v the United Kingdom*, no. 25186/94, Commission decision, 21 May 1996.
3 *Sutherland v the United Kingdom*, no. 25186/94, Commission report, 1 July 1997.
4 *Smith and Grady v the United Kingdom*, nos. 33985/96 and 33986/96, 27 September 1999, ECHR 1999-VI.
5 *Salgueiro da Silva Mouta v Portugal*, no. 33290/96, 21 December 1999, ECHR 1999-IX.
6 *Karner v Austria*, no. 40016/98, 24 July 2003, ECHR 2003-IX.
7 *E.B. v France* [GC], no. 43546/02, 22 January 2008.
8 *Alekseyev v Russia*, nos. 4916/07, 25924/08 and 14599/09, 21 October 2010.

in respect of marriage law,[9] economic benefits available to partners,[10] treatment in detention[11] and immigration and asylum law.[12] The realization of universal Convention rights for gay men and lesbians is far from complete and achieving it will require a considerable change in the Court's jurisprudence.

What sort of change is required to persuade the Court to interpret all forms of state-sanctioned discrimination based on sexual orientation to be in violation of the substantive rights of the Convention? Some argue that such a change would result from modifications in the 'legal culture'[13] or 'legal ideology'[14] of the Court. For this reason, scholars have sought to examine the values and beliefs of the Court's individual judges in order to assess how they influence the overall direction of judicial policy.[15] Whilst judicial temperament no doubt influences the outcome of individual complaints – as demonstrated by the large number of dissenting and concurring opinions examined throughout this book – its importance should not be overstated. As I have argued elsewhere, although the Court's judgments show that the standpoints of individual judges are important, judicial standpoints are produced by, operate in relation to and rely upon the broader sexual politics of contemporary societies.[16] For this reason, some commentators argue that the Court's judgments depend upon the 'mood' of Europe and see wider social change as essential to reshaping the Court's judicial policy 'in the light of present-day conditions'.[17] There are those who see the Court's judgments as essentially a reflection of the policy commitments of the Council of Europe and, because of this, seek to influence the Parliamentary Assembly, the Committee of Ministers and other decision-making bodies.[18] As I have argued throughout the book, the Court's jurisprudence is significantly influenced by the various recommendations issued by the organs and departments of the Council of Europe, but it certainly does not slavishly follow them. Some argue that the development of human rights depends upon ensuring the successful

9 *Schalk and Kopf v Austria*, no. 30141/04, 24 June 2010.
10 *Manenc v France* (dec), no. 66686/09, 21 September 2010.
11 *Stasi v France*, no. 25001/07, 20 October 2011.
12 *F. v the United Kingdom* (dec), no. 17341/03, 22 June 2004.
13 L. M. Friedman, 'Is There a Modern Legal Culture?', *Ratio Juris* 7, 1994, 117–131.
14 R. Cotterrell, 'The Concept of Legal Culture', in D. Nelken (ed.), *Comparing Legal Cultures*, Aldershot: Dartmouth, 1997, 13–29.
15 N-L. Arold, *The Legal Culture of the European Court of Human Rights*, Boston: Brill Academic Publishers, 2007.
16 P. Johnson, 'Challenging the Heteronormativity of Marriage: The Role of Judicial Interpretation and Authority', *Social and Legal Studies* 20(3), 2011, 349–367.
17 R. Wintemute, 'Consensus is the Right Approach for the European Court of Human Rights', *The Guardian*, Thursday 12 August 2010.
18 For example, NGOs such as ILGA-Europe.

implementation of the Court's judgments,[19] which in turn depends upon sustaining the willingness of member states to abide by the Court's decisions. Given the limited powers of enforcement at the Court's disposal and the criticism it now regularly receives for 'meddling' in the legal arrangements of contracting states, the evolution of Strasbourg jurisprudence is inevitably bound up with the Court's confidence to hold powerful contracting states to account.

There is, therefore, no 'silver bullet' that will result in the Court recognizing all forms of discrimination against gay men and lesbians as violating the Convention. However, if universal Convention rights for homosexuals are to be realized, it is essential that the Court changes its conceptualization of homosexuality. The Court's long-standing understanding of homosexuality as 'an essentially private manifestation of the human personality'[20] continues to underpin its interpretation of the Convention and this prevents it from recognizing the full range of civil rights to which gay men and lesbians seek access. As I have argued throughout the book, the Court's fixation on syphoning every issue relating to homosexuality into a consideration of 'privacy' often precludes it from addressing the wide range of social and public discrimination experienced by gay men and lesbians. The recent judgment in *Alekseyev v Russia* shows a positive development in recognizing that gay and lesbian rights must extend beyond private dwellings and encompass civil and social participation.[21] However, the Court still consistently relies upon a public/private binary when interpreting the Convention in respect of sexual orientation complaints, and has a tendency to reinforce the social relations of the closet. In doing so, the Court frequently leaves unaddressed a range of discrimination experienced in the public sphere.

There are many reasons to be optimistic about the potential to develop the Court's jurisprudence and expand the protection available to gay men and lesbians under the Convention. The Court was a world leader in accepting that sexual orientation is an immutable characteristic protectable as a human right and, whatever the limitations that essentialist understandings of sexuality impose (and they certainly do limit the re-imagination of human rights in respect of sexual identity as a chosen or fluid aspect of individuality), this provides a solid foundation on which to evolve the Court's jurisprudence. Just as the Court came to recognize that the immutable status of being 'a homosexual person'[22] made an individual a victim in respect of laws

19 B. Çali and N. Bruch, *Monitoring the Implementation of Judgments of the European Court of Human Rights: A Handbook for Non-Governmental Organizations*, London: University College London, 2011.

20 *Dudgeon v the United Kingdom*, no. 7525/76, 22 October 1981, Series A no. 45, § 60.

21 *Alekseyev v Russia*, nos. 4916/07, 25924/08 and 14599/09, 21 October 2010.

22 *Dudgeon v the United Kingdom*, no. 7525/76, Commission decision, 3 March 1978, p.118.

criminalizing homosexual sexual acts, so too can the Court recognize that the existence of other forms of discriminatory treatment on the grounds of sexual orientation victimizes lesbians and gay men. Considering sexual orientation to be an inherent and innate aspect of individuality that is equivalent to 'race, origin or colour'[23] has led the Court to make the recent statement that 'if the reasons advanced for a difference in treatment were based solely on the applicant's sexual orientation, this would amount to discrimination under the Convention'.[24] As I have argued, the Court's jurisprudence already shows a high degree of inconsistency in the application of this principle. However, the existence of the principle shows signs of significant development.

Bringing about change in the Court's interpretation of the Convention requires complaints to be made to Strasbourg. Although the Court certainly does not lack volume in the applications it receives, complaints need to be brought using a wider range of Convention articles than those most frequently relied upon. For instance, as I have argued, the development of the Court's Article 3 jurisprudence in respect of sexual orientation is vital. So too is an evolution of Articles 10, 11 and 12. Complaints need to be lodged with the Court in respect of these and other articles to force a consistent reconsideration of judicial policy and encourage recognition of the full range of rights available to gay men and lesbians. When making complaints, applicants need to innovate in the construction of their applications. The 'Equal Love' complaint that I examined in Chapter 6 – which was recently prepared by Wintemute and lodged with the Court – is an example of the now established practice of individual applicants collaborating with a campaign group or NGO to use the application process as a vehicle for influencing public opinion and exerting pressure on a contracting state.[25] This complaint can be seen to follow the long-standing strategy of lodging complaints in Strasbourg with a view to procuring a friendly settlement with a contracting state before a judgment by the Court. However, the 'Equal Love' application also engages a creative form of legal reasoning (in respect of Article 12) and an imaginative argument in respect of judicial method in an attempt to compel the Court to reflect on the moral principles underlying discrimination in marriage. This form of specialist and innovative expertise is often absent in complaints to the Court because applicants across contracting states lack access to the necessary economic and legal resources.

Given that throughout this book I have frequently complained that the Court fails to interpret the Convention in ways that guarantee the human rights of lesbians and gay men, it would be reasonable to conclude by asking if the Court's jurisprudence is important in the landscape of contemporary

23 *L. and V. v Austria*, nos. 39392/98 and 39829/98, 9 January 2003, ECHR 2003-I, § 52.
24 *Kozak v Poland*, no. 13102/02, 2 March 2010, § 92.
25 L. Hodson, *NGOs and the Struggle for Human Rights in Europe*, Oxford: Hart Publishing, 2011.

sexual politics. Whilst there are those who would argue that both the Convention and the Court are intrinsically conservative and of limited practical use, my own view is that the Court's jurisprudence on sexual orientation is of considerable importance. As I have argued, the Court's case law has an 'extra legal' influence that, although unquantifiable within the positivistic parameters often established by scholars to measure the effects of judgments, should not be underestimated. The Court has been instrumental in making sexual orientation a matter of human rights and establishing the homosexual as a subject of rights. In doing so, it has lent the symbolic authority of international law to those who struggle against homophobic discrimination. The Court has given 'psychological encouragement' to gay and lesbian activists throughout Europe,[26] as well as raising legal consciousness about rights among homosexuals more generally.[27] The Court's jurisprudence provides a discursive resource that allows individuals to speak against the wide range of heteronormative and heterosexist practices that underpin discrimination in contemporary European societies.[28] By incorporating homosexuality into the field of human rights the Court has humanized homosexuals and, in doing so, legitimized resistance by gay men and lesbians to the social, legal and political forces that continue to dehumanize us.

26 M.R. McLoughlin, 'Crystal or Glass?: A Review of Dudgeon v United Kingdom on the Fifteenth Anniversary of the Decision', *Murdoch University Electronic Journal of Law* 3(4), 1996, § 133.

27 R. Harding, *Regulating Sexuality: Legal Consciousness in Lesbian and Gay Lives*, London: Routledge, 2011.

28 For example, as I have argued elsewhere, the judgment in *E.B. v France* is an innovative and atypical legal consideration of, and challenge to, the heteronormative social relations of contemporary European societies. P. Johnson, 'Heteronormativity and the European Court of Human Rights', *Law and Critique*, 23(1), 2012, 43–66.

Bibliography

Addo, M.K. and Grief, N., 'Does Article 3 of The European Convention on Human Rights Enshrine Absolute Rights?', *European Journal of International Law* 9, 1998, 510–524.

American Psychiatric Association, *Diagnostic and Statistical Manual of Mental Disorders (DSM I)*, Arlington: American Psychiatric Association, 1952.

Amnesty International, 'Hungary: Authorities Must Reverse Ban on Gay Pride March', 17 February 2011, available HTTP: <http://www.amnesty.org.uk/news_details.asp?NewsID=19260> (last accessed 21 February 2012).

Anagnostou, D., 'Does European Human Rights Law Matter? Implementation and Domestic Impact of Strasbourg Court Judgments on Minority-Related Policies', *The International Journal of Human Rights* 14(5), 2010, 721–743.

Arai-Takahashi, Y., *The Margin of Appreciation Doctrine and the Principle of Proportionality in the Jurisprudence of the ECHR*, Oxford: Hart Publishing, 2001.

Arold, N-L., *The Legal Culture of the European Court of Human Rights*, Boston: Brill Academic Publishers, 2007.

Baker, A., 'The Enjoyment of Rights and Freedoms: A New Conception of the "Ambit" under Article 14', *Modern Law Review* 65, 2006, 714–737.

Baldwin, C., 'The European Court's Hidden But Hopeful Message on Same-Sex Marriage', *The Guardian*, 29 June 2010.

Ball, C.A., *The Morality of Gay Rights: An Exploration in Political Philosophy*, New York: Routledge, 2003.

Bamforth, N., 'Sexual Orientation Discrimination after *Grant v South-West Trains*', *Modern Law Review* 63, 2000, 694–720.

Bamforth, N., 'Families But Not (Yet) Marriages? Same-Sex Partners and the Developing European Convention "Margin of Appreciation" ', *Child and Family Law Quarterly* 23(1), 2011, 128–143.

Barclay, S., Bernstein, M. and Marshall, A.M., *Queer Mobilizations: LGBT Activists Confront the Law*, New York: NYU Press, 2009.

Bates, E., *The Evolution of the European Convention on Human Rights. From its Inception to the Creation of a Permanent Court of Human Rights*, Oxford: Oxford University Press, 2010.

Baxi, U., *The Future of Human Rights*, Oxford: Oxford University Press, 2002.

Bell, D. and Binnie, J., *The Sexual Citizen: Queer Politics and Beyond*, Cambridge: Polity Press, 2000.

Bell, D. and Valentine, G. (eds.), *Mapping Desire: Geographies of Sexualities*, London: Routledge, 1995.

Berlant, L. and Warner, M., 'Sex in Public', *Critical Inquiry* 24(2), 1998, 547–566.

Bernstein, M., 'Celebration and Suppression: The Strategic Uses of Identity by the Lesbian and Gay Community', *American Journal of Sociology* 103(3), 1997, 531–565.

Bingham, T., 'The Judges: Active or Passive?', *British Academy Maccabean Lecture*, Cardiff, 27 October 2005.

Bourdieu, P., *Pascalian Meditations*, Cambridge: Polity Press, 2000.

Bourdieu, P. and Wacquant, L.J.D., *An Invitation to Reflexive Sociology*, Cambridge: Polity Press, 1992.

Bratza, N., 'The Relationship Between the UK Courts and Strasbourg', *European Human Rights Law Review* 5, 2011, 505–512.

Butler, J., *Gender Trouble: Feminism and the Subversion of Identity*, New York: Routledge, 1990.

Butler, J., *Bodies that Matter: On the Discursive Limits of Sex*, London: Routledge, 1993.

Butler, J., *Excitable Speech: A Politics of the Performative*, New York: Routledge, 1997.

Butler, J., *Precarious Life: The Powers of Mourning and Violence*, London: Verso, 2004.

Butler, J., *Undoing Gender*, New York: Routledge, 2004.

Çali, B. and Bruch, N., *Monitoring the Implementation of Judgments of the European Court of Human Rights: A Handbook for Non-Governmental Organizations*, London: University College London, 2011.

Checkel, J.T., 'International Institutions and Socialization in Europe: Introduction and Framework', *International Organization* 59, 2005, 801–826.

Clinton, H.R., 'Remarks in Recognition of International Human Rights Day', Geneva: Palais des Nations, 6 December 2011, available HTTP: <http://www.state.gov/secretary/rm/2011/12/178368.htm> (accessed 17 February 2012).

Cohen-Jonathan, G., 'Respect for Private and Family Life', in R. St. J. Macdonald, F. Matscher and H. Petzold (eds.), *The European System for the Protection of Rights*, Alphen aan den Rijn: Kluwer, 1993.

Coleman, J., *The Conscience of Europe*, Strasbourg: Council of Europe, 1999.

Costa, J-P., 'On The Legitimacy of the European Court of Human Rights' Judgments', *European Constitutional Law Review* 7, 2011, 173–182.

Cotterrell, R., 'The Concept of Legal Culture', in D. Nelken (ed.), *Comparing Legal Cultures*, Aldershot: Dartmouth, 1997, 13–29.

Council of Europe, *Asylum and the European Convention on Human Rights*, Strasbourg: Council of Europe Publishing, 2010.

Council of Europe, *Discrimination on Grounds of Sexual Orientation and Gender Identity in Europe*, Strasbourg: Council of Europe Publishing, 2011.

Council of Europe, 'International Day Against Homophobia and Transphobia: Statement of Secretary General Thorbjørn Jagland', Press release DC002(2011), 17 May 2011.

de Beco, G. (ed.), *Human Rights Monitoring Mechanisms of the Council of Europe*, Abingdon: Routledge, 2011.

Devlin, P., *The Enforcement of Morals*, Oxford: Oxford University Press, 1965.

Douzinas, C., *Human Rights and Empire: The Political Philosophy of Cosmopolitanism*, London: Routledge, 2007.

Durkheim, E., *The Division of Labour in Society*, London: Macmillan, 1893/1998.

Dzehtsiarou, K., 'European Consensus and the Evolutive Interpretation of the European Convention on Human Rights', *German Law Journal* 12(10), 2011, 1730–1745.
European Commission of Human Rights, *Documents and Decisions*, The Hague: Martinus Nijhoff, 1959.
European Court of Human Rights, *Analysis of Statistics 2011*, Strasbourg: European Court of Human Rights, 2011.
European Court of Human Rights, *Annual Report 2011*, Strasbourg: Registry of the European Court of Human Rights, 2012.
European Union Agency for Fundamental Rights, *Homophobia, Transphobia and Discrimination on Grounds of Sexual Orientation and Gender Identity in the EU Member States: Summary of Findings, Trends, Challenges and Promising Practices*, Vienna: FRA, 2010.
Evans, D.T., *Sexual Citizenship: The Material Construction of Sexualities*, London: Routledge, 1993.
Fairfield, P., *Public/Private*, Lanham: Rowman and Littlefield, 2005.
Federal Constitutional Court (Entscheidungen des Bundesverfassungsgerichts), *The Constitutionality of Penal Regulation Against Male Homosexuality (vol.6)*, Tübingen: J.C.B. Mohr Verlag, 1957.
Fielding, N., 'Judges and Their Work', *Social and Legal Studies* 20(4), 2011, 97–115.
Foucault, M., *Discipline and Punish: The Birth of the Prison*, Harmondsworth: Penguin, 1977.
Foucault, M., *The History of Sexuality: Volume 1*, London: Penguin, 1979.
Foucault, M., 'Politics and the Study of Discourse', in G. Burchell, C. Gordon and P. Miller (eds.), *The Foucault Effect: Studies in Governmentality with Two Lectures by and an Interview with Michel Foucault*, Chicago: Chicago University Press, 1991.
Friedman, L.M., 'Is There a Modern Legal Culture?', *Ratio Juris* 7, 1994, 117–131.
Frowein, J., 'European Integration through Fundamental Rights', *Michigan Journal of Law Reform* 18, 1984, 5–28.
Fuss, D., *Identification Papers*, New York: Routledge, 1995.
Fuss, D., 'Inside/Out', in D. Fuss (ed.), *Inside/Out: Lesbian Theories, Gay Theories*, New York: Routledge, 1991.
Giddens, A., *The Transformation of Intimacy: Sexuality, Love and Eroticism in Modern Societies*, Cambridge: Polity Press, 1992.
Gilbert, G.N. and Mulkay, M.J., *Opening Pandora's Box: A Sociological Analysis of Scientists' Discourse*, Cambridge: Cambridge University Press, 1984.
Golder, B., 'Foucault's Critical (Yet Ambivalent) Affirmation: Three Figures of Rights', *Social and Legal Studies* 20(3), 283–312.
Golder, B. and Fitzpatrick, P., *Foucault's Law*, Abingdon: Routledge-Cavendish, 2009.
Goodman, R. and Junks, D., 'How to Influence States: Socialization and International Human Rights Law', *Duke Law Journal*, 2004, 621–703.
Grau, G., *Hidden Holocaust? Gay and Lesbian Persecution in Germany 1933–45*, London: Cassell, 1995.
Graupner, H., 'Austria', in D.J. West and R. Green (eds.), *Sociolegal Control of Homosexuality: A Multi-Nation Comparison*, New York: Kluwer, 1997, 269–287.
Grigolo, M., 'Sexualities and the ECHR: Introducing the Universal Sexual Legal Subject', *European Journal of International Law* 14, 2003, 1023–1044.
Hacking, I., 'Making Up People', in T.C. Heller, M. Sosna and D.W. Wellbery (eds.), *Reconstructing Individualism: Autonomy, Individuality, and the Self in Western Thought*, Palo Alto: Stanford University Press, 1986.

Hale of Richmond, Baroness, 'Beanstalk or Living Instrument? How Tall Can the ECHR Grow?', Bernard's Inn Reading 2011, available HTTP: <http://www.supremecourt.gov.uk/docs/speech_110616.pdf> (last accessed 18 February 2012).

Halperin, D.M., *Saint Foucault: Towards a Gay Hagiography*, New York: Oxford University Press, 1995.

Hammarberg, T., 'Pride Events Are Still Hindered – This Violates Freedom of Assembly', 2 June 2010, available HTTP: <http://commissioner.cws.coe.int/tiki-view_blog_post.php?postId=42> (last accessed 21 February 2012).

Harding, R., *Regulating Sexuality: Legal Consciousness in Lesbian and Gay Lives*, London: Routledge, 2011.

Harding, R., 'Dogs Are "Registered", People Shouldn't Be': Legal Consciousness and Lesbian and Gay Rights', *Social and Legal Studies* 15(4), 2006, 511–533.

Harding, S., 'Is There a Feminist Method?', in N. Tuana (ed.), *Feminism and Science*, Bloomington: Indiana University Press, 1989.

Harding, S., 'Whose Standpoint Needs the Regimes of Truth and Reality? Comment on Hekman's "Truth and Method: Feminist Standpoint Theory Revisited" ', *Signs: Journal of Women in Culture and Society* 22(2), 1997, 382–391.

Harris, D.J., O'Boyle, M., Bates, E.P. and Buckley, C.M., *Law of the European Convention on Human Rights*, Oxford: Oxford University Press, 2009.

Hart, H.L.A., *The Concept of Law*, Oxford: Oxford University Press, 1961.

Hart, H.L.A., *Law, Liberty and Morality*, Oxford: Oxford University Press, 1963.

Hart, L., 'Individual Adoption by Non-Heterosexuals and the Order of Family Life in the European Court of Human Rights', *Journal of Law and Society*, 36(4), 2009, 536–557.

Heger, H., *The Men with the Pink Triangle*, London: GMP, 1972.

Heinze, E., *Sexual Orientation: A Human Right, An Essay on International Human Rights Law*, Dordrecht: Martinus Nijhoff Publishers, 1995.

Heinze, E., 'Sexual Orientation and International Law: A Study in the Manufacture of Cross-Cultural "Sensitivity" ', *Michigan Journal of International Law* 22, 2001, 283–309.

Helfer, L.R., 'Finding a Consensus on Equality: The Homosexual Age of Consent and The European Convention on Human Rights', *New York University Law Review* 65, 1990, 1044–1100.

Helfer, L.R., 'Lesbian and Gay Rights as Human Rights: Strategies for a United Europe', *Virginia Journal of International Law* 32, 1991, 157–212.

Helfer, L.R. and Voeten, E., 'Do European Court of Human Rights Judgments Promote Legal and Policy Change?', unpublished paper, available HTTP: <http://scholarship.law.duke.edu/cgi/viewcontent.cgi?article=3025&context=faculty_scholarship> (last accessed 17 February 2012).

Hodson, L., *NGOs and the Struggle for Human Rights in Europe*, Oxford: Hart Publishing, 2011.

Hodson, L., 'A Marriage By Any Other Name? Schalk and Kopf v Austria', *Human Rights Law Review* 11(1), 2011, 170–179.

Hodson, L., 'Ties That Bind: Towards a Child-Centred Approach to Lesbian, Gay, Bi-Sexual and Transgender Families under the ECHR', *International Journal of Children's Rights* (in press), 2012.

Hoffman, R., Hutter, J. and Lautmann, R., 'Germany', in D.J. West and R. Green (eds.), *Sociolegal Control of Homosexuality: A Multi-Nation Comparison*, New York: Kluwer, 1997, 255–268.

Hoffmann, Lord, 'The Universality of Human Rights', *Law Quarterly Review* 125, 2009, 416–432.

Home Office, *Report of the Committee on Homosexual Offences and Prostitution* (Cmnd. 247), London: Home Office, 1957.

Hubbard, P., 'Sex Zones: Intimacy, Citizenship and Public Space', *Sexualities* 4, 2001, 51–71.

Hubbard, P., 'Desire/Disgust: Mapping the Moral Contours of Heterosexuality', *Progress in Human Geography* 24, 2004, 191–217.

Human Rights Information Bulletin, *The European Convention on Human Rights at 50*, Strasbourg: Council of Europe, 2000.

Human Rights Watch and the International Gay and Lesbian Human Rights Commission, *Public Scandals: Sexual Orientation and Criminal Law in Romania*, New York, 1998.

Hunt, A. and Wickham, G., *Foucault and Law: Towards a Sociology of Law as Governance*, London: Pluto Press, 1994.

Hyde, M., *The Other Love: An Historical and Contemporary Survey of Homosexuality in Britain*, London: Heinemann, 1970.

ILGA-Europe, *Lesbian, Gay, Bisexual and Transgender Rights: Freedom of Assembly, Diary of Events by Country – August 2008*, ILGA-Europe, 2008.

Ingraham, C., 'The Heterosexual Imaginary: Feminist Sociology and Theories of Gender', in S. Seidman (ed.), *Queer Theory/Sociology*, Oxford: Blackwell, 1996.

International Commission of Jurists, *Sexual Orientation, Gender Identity and Justice: A Comparative Law Casebook*, Geneva: ICJ, 2011.

Jackson, S., 'Gender, Sexuality and Heterosexuality: The Complexity (and Limits) of Heteronormativity', *Feminist Theory* 7(1), 2006, 105–121.

Johnson, P., *Love, Heterosexuality and Society*, London: Routledge, 2005.

Johnson, P., 'Challenging the Heteronormativity of Marriage: The Role of Judicial Interpretation and Authority', *Social and Legal Studies* 20(3), 2011, 349–367.

Johnson, P., 'Homosexuality, Freedom of Assembly and the Margin of Appreciation Doctrine of the European Court of Human Rights: *Alekseyev v Russia*', *Human Rights Law Review* 11(3), 2011, 578–593.

Johnson, P., 'Heteronormativity and the European Court of Human Rights', *Law and Critique*, 23(1), 2012, 43–66.

Kane, D.J., 'Homosexuality and the European Convention on Human Rights: What Rights?', *Hastings International and Comparative Law Review* 11, 1998, 447–486.

Kirby, M., *Judicial Activism: Authority, Principle and Policy in the Judicial Mind*, London: Sweet and Maxwell, 2004.

Kirby, M., 'Human Rights Insights: Homosexuality and Love', *The National Legal Eagle* 17(1), 2011, 3–7.

Kratochvíl, J., 'The Inflation of the Margin of Appreciation by the European Court of Human Rights', *Netherlands Quarterly of Human Rights* 29(3), 2011, 324–357.

Krickler, K., 'Homosexuals in Austria: Nazi Persecution and the Long Struggle for Rehabilitation', *Working Paper Series No.12 of the Canadian Centre for German and European Studies*, Toronto: Canada, 2008.

Krüger, H.C., 'European Convention on Human Rights: 50 Years of Growth', in Human Rights Information Bulletin, *The European Convention on Human Rights at 50*, Strasbourg: Council of Europe, 2000.

Latour, B., *The Making of Law: An Ethnography of the Conseil d'Etat*, Cambridge: Polity Press, 2010.

Leach, P., Paraskeva, C. and Uzelac, G., *International Human Rights and Fact-Finding: An Analysis of the Fact-Finding Missions Conducted by the European Commission and Court of Human Rights*, London: Human Right and Social Justice Research Institute at London Metropolitan University, 2009.

Lester of Herne Hill, Lord, 'Universality Versus Subsidiarity: A Reply', *European Human Rights Law Review* 1, 1998, 73–81.

Letsas, G., *A Theory of Interpretation of the European Convention on Human Rights*, Oxford: Oxford University Press, 2007.

Leznoff, M. and Westley, W.A., 'The Homosexual Community', in P.N. Nardi and B.E. Schneider (eds.), *Social Perspectives in Lesbian and Gay Studies: A Reader*, New York: Routledge, 1998.

Linhart, K., 'Decriminalization of Homosexuality and Its Effects on Family Rights: A German-US-American Comparison', *German Law Journal* 6, 2005, 943–966.

Loukaidēs, L.G., *Essays on the Developing Law of Human Rights*, Leiden: Martinus Nijhoff Publishers, 1995.

McCormick, I., *Secret Sexualities: A Sourcebook of 17th and 18th Century Writing*, London: Routledge, 1997.

McGhee, D., *Heterosexuality, Law and Resistance*, London: Routledge, 2001.

McGhee, D., 'Beyond Toleration: Privacy, Citizenship and Sexual Minorities in England and Wales', *The British Journal of Sociology* 55:3, 2004, 357–375.

McIntosh, M., 'The Homosexual Role', *Social Problems* 16, 1968, 182–192.

McLoughlin, M.R., 'Crystal or Glass?: A Review of Dudgeon v. United Kingdom on the Fifteenth Anniversary of the Decision', *Murdoch University Electronic Journal of Law* 3(4), 1996, § 133.

Macdonald, R., 'The Margin of Appreciation', in R.St.J. Macdonald, F. Matscher and H. Petzold (eds.), *The European System for the Protection of Rights*, Alphen aan den Rijn: Kluwer, 1993.

MacDougall, B., *Queer Judgments: Homosexuality, Expression, and the Courts in Canada*, Toronto: University of Toronto Press, 2000, p. 44.

Mahoney, P., 'Judicial Activism and Judicial Self-Restraint in the European Court of Human Rights: Two Sides of the Same Coin', *Human Rights Law Journal* 11, 1990, 57–88.

Massad, J.A., 'Re-Orienting Desire: The Gay International and the Arab World', *Public Culture* 14(2), 2002, 361–385.

Moeller, R.G., 'The Homosexual Man Is a "Man", the Homosexual Woman Is a "Woman": Sex, Society, and the Law in Postwar West Germany', *Journal of the History of Sexuality* 4(3), 1994, 395–429.

Moran, L.J., *The Homosexual(ity) of Law*, London: Routledge, 1996.

Moran, L.J., '*Laskey v the United Kingdom*: Learning the Limits of Privacy', *Modern Law Review* 61(1), 1998, 77–84.

Moreham, N.A., 'The Right to Respect for Private Life in the European Convention on Human Rights: a Re-examination', *European Human Right Law Review* 1, 2008, 44–79.

Morgan, W., 'Queering International Human Rights Law', in C.F. Stychin and D. Herman (eds.), *Law, Sexuality: The Global Arena*, Minneapolis: University of Minnesota Press, 2001.

Mowbray, A., 'The Creativity of the European Court of Human Rights', *Human Rights Law Review* 5(1), 2005, 57–79.

Myers, D.P., 'The European Commission on Human Rights', *The American Journal of International Law* 50(4), 1956, 949–951.

Nash, K., 'Between Citizenship and Human Rights', *Sociology* 43(6), 2009, 1067–1083.

Orakhelashvili, A., 'Restrictive Interpretation of Human Rights Treaties in the Recent Jurisprudence of the European Court of Human Rights', *European Journal of International Law* 14(3), 2002, 529–568.

Patterson, D., *Law and Truth*, New York: Oxford University Press, 1996.

Pettman, R., 'A Phenomenology of Human Rights', *Human Rights Research Journal* 2, 2004, 1–10.

Plummer, K., *The Making of the Modern Homosexual*, London: Hutchinson, 1981.

Pound, R., 'Mechanical Jurisprudence', *Columbia Law Review* 8(8), 1908, 605–623.

Rich, A., *Blood, Bread and Poetry: Selected Prose 1979–1985*, London: Virago Press, 1986.

Robson, R., *Sappho Goes to Law School: Fragments in Lesbian Legal Theory*, New York: Columbia University Press, 1998.

Roseneil, S., 'The Heterosexual/Homosexual Binary: Past, Present and Future', in D. Richardson and S. Seidman (eds.), *Handbook of Lesbian and Gay Studies*, London: Sage, 2002, 27–44.

Sachs, A., *The Strange Alchemy of Life and Law*, Oxford: Oxford University Press, 2009.

Saiz, I., 'Bracketing Sexuality: Human Rights and Sexual Orientation: A Decade of Development and Denial at the UN', *Health and Human Rights* 7(2), 2004, 48–80.

Schultz, C., *Paragraph 175*, Hamburg: MännerschwarmSkript Verlag, 1994.

Sedgwick, E., *Epistemology of the Closet*, Harmondsworth: Penguin, 1990.

Seel, P., *I, Pierre Seel, Deported Homosexual: A Memoir of Nazi Terror*, New York: Basic Books, 1995.

Singh, R., 'Is There a Role for the "Margin of Appreciation" in National Law After the Human Rights Act?', *European Human Rights Law Review* 1(4), 1999, 15–22.

Smart, C., *Feminism and the Power of Law*, London: Routledge, 1989.

Smart, C., 'Collusion, Collaboration and Confession: On Moving Beyond the Heterosexuality Debate', in D. Richardson (ed.), *Theorising Heterosexuality*, Buckingham: Open University Press, 1996.

Spackman, P.L., 'Grant v. South-West Trains: Equality for Same-Sex Partners in the European Community', *American University Journal of International Law and Policy* 12, 1997, 1063–1120.

Stammers, N., 'Social Movements and the Social Construction of Human Rights', *Human Rights Quarterly* 21(4), 980–1008.

Stone Sweet, A., 'A Cosmopolitan Legal Order: Constitutional Pluralism and Rights Adjudication in Europe', *Journal of Global Constitutionalism* (forthcoming), 2012, available HTTP: <http://works.bepress.com/cgi/viewcontent.cgi?article=1043&context=alec_stone_sweet> (last accessed 17 February 2012).

Stychin, C.F., *Law's Desire: Sexuality and the Limits of Justice*, London: Routledge, 1995.

Stychin, C.F., *Governing Sexuality: The Changing Politics of Citizenship and Law Reform*, Oxford: Hart, 2003.

Stychin, C.F., 'Same-Sex Sexualities and the Globalization of Human Rights Discourse', *McGill Law Journal* 49, 2004, 951–968.

Taylor, V., Kimport, K., Van Dyke, N. and Andersen, E.A., 'Culture and Mobilization: Tactical Repertoires, Same-Sex Weddings, and the Impact on Gay Activism', *American Sociological Review* 74, 2009, 865–890.

Turner, B., *Regulating Bodies: Essays in Medical Sociology*, London: Routledge, 1992.

UK Gay News, 'Russian Court: Ban of "Gay Propaganda to Minors" is Constitutional', 31 March 2010, available HTTP: <http://www.ukgaynews.org.uk/Archive/10/Mar/3101.htm> (last accessed 21 February 2012).

UK Gay News, 'Moscow Authorities Now Propose Anti Gay Bill', 17 November 2011, available HTTP: <http://www.ukgaynews.org.uk/Archive/11/Nov/1701.htm> (last accessed 21 February 2012).

United Nations Human Rights Council, *Discriminatory Laws and Practices and Acts of Violence Against Individuals Based On Their Sexual Orientation and Gender Identity: Report of the United Nations High Commissioner for Human Rights*, A/HRC/19/41, 17 November 2011.

Vanderbeck, R. and Johnson, P., ' "If a Charge Was Brought Against a Saintly Religious Leader Whose Intention Was To Save Souls . . .": An Analysis of UK Parliamentary Debates Over Incitement to Hatred on the Grounds of Sexual Orientation', *Parliamentary Affairs* 64(4), 2011, 652–673.

Vike-Freiberga, V., 'Statement By the President of Latvia Regarding Her Decision To Sign a Constitutional Amendment Defining Marriage as a Union of a Man and a Woman', 21 December 2005, available HTTP: <http://www.ilga-europe.org/europe/guide/country_by_country/latvia/latvian_president_signs_homophobic_constitutional_amendment> (last accessed 20 February 2012).

Volokh, A., 'Choosing Interpretative Methods: A Positive Theory of Judges and Everyone Else', *New York University Law Review* 83, 2008, 769–846.

Waaldijk, K. and Clapham, A., *Homosexuality: A European Community Issue*, Dordrecht: Martinus Nijhoff Publishers, 1993.

Warbick, C., 'The Structure of Article 8', *European Human Rights Law Review* 1, 1998, 32–44.

Warner, M., *Fear of a Queer Planet*, Minneapolis: University of Minnesota Press, 1993.

Weber, A., *Manual on Hate Speech*, Strasbourg: Council of Europe Publishing, 2009.

Weeks, J., Heaphy, B. and Donovan, C., *Same Sex Intimacies: Families of Choice and Other Life Experiments*, London: Routledge, 2001.

Weeks, J., 'Sexual Citizenship', *Theory, Culture and Society*, 15(3–4), 1999, 35–52.

Weil, G.L., 'Decisions on Inadmissible Applications by the European Commission of Human Rights', *The American Journal of International Law* 54(4), 1960: 874–881.

Weston, K., *Families We Choose: Lesbians, Gays, Kinship*, Irvington, NY: Columbia University Press, 1998.

White, R.C.A. and Ovey, C., *The European Convention on Human Rights (5th Edition)*, Oxford: Oxford University Press, 2010.

White, R.C.A. and Boussiako, I., 'Separate Opinions in the European Court of Human Rights', *Human Rights Law Review* 9(1), 2009, 37–60.

Wintemute, R., *Sexual Orientation and Human Rights: The United States Constitution, the European Convention, and the Canadian Charter*, Oxford: Clarendon Press, 1995.

Wintemute, R., '"Within the Ambit": How Big is the "Gap" in Article 14 European Convention on Human Rights?', *European Human Rights Law Review* 4, 2004, 366–382.

Wintemute, R., 'Filling the Article 14 "Gap": Government Ratification and Judicial Control of Protocol No. 12 ECHR: Part 2', *European Human Rights Law Review* 5, 2004, 484–499.

Wintemute, R., 'From "Sex Rights" to "Love Rights": Partnership Rights as Human Rights', in N. Bamforth (ed.), *Sex Rights: The Oxford Amnesty Lectures 2002*, Oxford: Oxford University Press, 2005.

Wintemute, R., 'Consensus Is the Right Approach for the European Court of Human Rights', *The Guardian*, Thursday 12 August 2010.

Wintemute, R., 'Equal Love, The Legal Case: Professor Robert Wintemute Explains the Legal Basis of the Application to the European Court of Human Rights', available HTTP: <http://equallove.org.uk/the-legal-case> (last accessed 20 February 2012).

Appendix 1

European Convention on Human Rights (truncated)

Convention for the Protection of Human Rights and Fundamental Freedoms

This is a truncated version of the text of the Convention that, amended by the provisions of Protocol No. 14, entered into force on 1 June 2010.

Article 1 – Obligation to respect human rights

The High Contracting Parties shall secure to everyone within their jurisdiction the rights and freedoms defined in Section I of this Convention.

Section I – Rights and freedoms

Article 2 – Right to life

1 Everyone's right to life shall be protected by law. No one shall be deprived of his life intentionally, save in the execution of a sentence of a court following his conviction of a crime for which this penalty is provided by law.

2 Deprivation of life shall not be regarded as inflicted in contravention of this article when it results from the use of force, which is no more than absolutely necessary:

  a in defence of any person from unlawful violence;
  b in order to effect a lawful arrest or to prevent the escape of a person lawfully detained;
  c in action lawfully taken for the purpose of quelling a riot or insurrection.

Article 3 – Prohibition of torture

No one shall be subjected to torture or to inhuman or degrading treatment or punishment.

Article 4 – Prohibition of slavery and forced labour

1 No one shall be held in slavery or servitude.
2 No one shall be required to perform forced or compulsory labour.
3 For the purpose of this article, the term "forced or compulsory labour" shall not include:

 a any work required to be done in the ordinary course of detention imposed according to the provisions of Article 5 of this Convention or during conditional release from such detention;
 b any service of a military character or, in case of conscientious objectors in countries where they are recognised, service exacted instead of compulsory military service;
 c any service exacted in case of an emergency or calamity threatening the life or well-being of the community;
 d any work or service which forms part of normal civic obligations.

Article 5 – Right to liberty and security

1 Everyone has the right to liberty and security of person. No one shall be deprived of his liberty, save in the following cases and in accordance with a procedure prescribed by law:

 a the lawful detention of a person after conviction by a competent court;
 b the lawful arrest or detention of a person for non-compliance with the lawful order of a court or in order to secure the fulfilment of any obligation prescribed by law;
 c the lawful arrest or detention of a person effected for the purpose of bringing him before the competent legal authority on reasonable suspicion of having committed an offence or when it is reasonably considered necessary to prevent his committing an offence or fleeing after having done so;
 d the detention of a minor by lawful order for the purpose of educational supervision or his lawful detention for the purpose of bringing him before the competent legal authority;
 e the lawful detention of persons for the prevention of the spreading of infectious diseases, of persons of unsound mind, alcoholics or drug addicts or vagrants;
 f the lawful arrest or detention of a person to prevent his effecting an unauthorised entry into the country or of a person against whom action is being taken with a view to deportation or extradition.

2 Everyone who is arrested shall be informed promptly, in a language which he understands, of the reasons for his arrest and of any charge against him.

3 Everyone arrested or detained in accordance with the provisions of paragraph 1.c of this article shall be brought promptly before a judge or other officer authorised by law to exercise judicial power and shall be entitled to trial within a reasonable time or to release pending trial. Release may be conditioned by guarantees to appear for trial.

4 Everyone who is deprived of his liberty by arrest or detention shall be entitled to take proceedings by which the lawfulness of his detention shall be decided speedily by a court and his release ordered if the detention is not lawful.

5 Everyone who has been the victim of arrest or detention in contravention of the provisions of this article shall have an enforceable right to compensation.

Article 6 – Right to a fair trial

1 In the determination of his civil rights and obligations or of any criminal charge against him, everyone is entitled to a fair and public hearing within a reasonable time by an independent and impartial tribunal established by law. Judgment shall be pronounced publicly but the press and public may be excluded from all or part of the trial in the interests of morals, public order or national security in a democratic society, where the interests of juveniles or the protection of the private life of the parties so require, or to the extent strictly necessary in the opinion of the court in special circumstances where publicity would prejudice the interests of justice.

2 Everyone charged with a criminal offence shall be presumed innocent until proved guilty according to law.

3 Everyone charged with a criminal offence has the following minimum rights:

  a to be informed promptly, in a language which he understands and in detail, of the nature and cause of the accusation against him;

  b to have adequate time and facilities for the preparation of his defence;

  c to defend himself in person or through legal assistance of his own choosing or, if he has not sufficient means to pay for legal assistance, to be given it free when the interests of justice so require;

  d to examine or have examined witnesses against him and to obtain the attendance and examination of witnesses on his behalf under the same conditions as witnesses against him;

  e to have the free assistance of an interpreter if he cannot understand or speak the language used in court.

Article 7 – No punishment without law

1 No one shall be held guilty of any criminal offence on account of any act or omission which did not constitute a criminal offence under national or

international law at the time when it was committed. Nor shall a heavier penalty be imposed than the one that was applicable at the time the criminal offence was committed.

2 This article shall not prejudice the trial and punishment of any person for any act or omission which, at the time when it was committed, was criminal according to the general principles of law recognised by civilised nations.

Article 8 – Right to respect for private and family life

1 Everyone has the right to respect for his private and family life, his home and his correspondence.

2 There shall be no interference by a public authority with the exercise of this right except such as is in accordance with the law and is necessary in a democratic society in the interests of national security, public safety or the economic well-being of the country, for the prevention of disorder or crime, for the protection of health or morals, or for the protection of the rights and freedoms of others.

Article 9 – Freedom of thought, conscience and religion

1 Everyone has the right to freedom of thought, conscience and religion; this right includes freedom to change his religion or belief and freedom, either alone or in community with others and in public or private, to manifest his religion or belief, in worship, teaching, practice and observance.

2 Freedom to manifest one's religion or beliefs shall be subject only to such limitations as are prescribed by law and are necessary in a democratic society in the interests of public safety, for the protection of public order, health or morals, or for the protection of the rights and freedoms of others.

Article 10 – Freedom of expression

1 Everyone has the right to freedom of expression. This right shall include freedom to hold opinions and to receive and impart information and ideas without interference by public authority and regardless of frontiers. This article shall not prevent States from requiring the licensing of broadcasting, television or cinema enterprises.

2 The exercise of these freedoms, since it carries with it duties and responsibilities, may be subject to such formalities, conditions, restrictions or penalties as are prescribed by law and are necessary in a democratic society, in the interests of national security, territorial integrity or public safety, for the prevention of disorder or crime, for the protection of health or morals, for the protection of the reputation or rights of others, for

preventing the disclosure of information received in confidence, or for maintaining the authority and impartiality of the judiciary.

Article 11 – Freedom of assembly and association

1 Everyone has the right to freedom of peaceful assembly and to freedom of association with others, including the right to form and to join trade unions for the protection of his interests.
2 No restrictions shall be placed on the exercise of these rights other than such as are prescribed by law and are necessary in a democratic society in the interests of national security or public safety, for the prevention of disorder or crime, for the protection of health or morals or for the protection of the rights and freedoms of others. This article shall not prevent the imposition of lawful restrictions on the exercise of these rights by members of the armed forces, of the police or of the administration of the State.

Article 12 – Right to marry

Men and women of marriageable age have the right to marry and to found a family, according to the national laws governing the exercise of this right.

Article 13 – Right to an effective remedy

Everyone whose rights and freedoms as set forth in this Convention are violated shall have an effective remedy before a national authority, notwithstanding that the violation has been committed by persons acting in an official capacity.

Article 14 – Prohibition of discrimination

The enjoyment of the rights and freedoms set forth in this Convention shall be secured without discrimination on any ground such as sex, race, colour, language, religion, political or other opinion, national or social origin, association with a national minority, property, birth or other status.

Article 17 – Prohibition of abuse of rights

Nothing in this Convention may be interpreted as implying for any State, group or person any right to engage in any activity or perform any act aimed at the destruction of any of the rights and freedoms set forth herein or at their limitation to a greater extent than is provided for in the Convention.

Article 18 – Limitation on use of restrictions on rights

The restrictions permitted under this Convention to the said rights and freedoms shall not be applied for any purpose other than those for which they have been prescribed.

Section II – European Court of Human Rights

Article 34 – Individual applications

The Court may receive applications from any person, non-governmental organisation or group of individuals claiming to be the victim of a violation by one of the High Contracting Parties of the rights set forth in the Convention or the protocols thereto. The High Contracting Parties undertake not to hinder in any way the effective exercise of this right.

Article 35 – Admissibility criteria

1 The Court may only deal with the matter after all domestic remedies have been exhausted, according to the generally recognised rules of international law, and within a period of six months from the date on which the final decision was taken.

2 The Court shall not deal with any application submitted under Article 34 that:

   a is anonymous; or

   b is substantially the same as a matter that has already been examined by the Court or has already been submitted to another procedure of international investigation or settlement and contains no relevant new information.

3 The Court shall declare inadmissible any individual application submitted under Article 34 if it considers that:

   a the application is incompatible with the provisions of the Convention or the Protocols thereto, manifestly ill-founded, or an abuse of the right of individual application; or

   b the applicant has not suffered a significant disadvantage, unless respect for human rights as defined in the Convention and the Protocols thereto requires an examination of the application on the merits and provided that no case may be rejected on this ground which has not been duly considered by a domestic tribunal.

4 The Court shall reject any application which it considers inadmissible under this Article. It may do so at any stage of the proceedings.

Protocol No. 12 to the Convention for the Protection of Human Rights and Fundamental Freedoms

Article 1 – General prohibition of discrimination

1 The enjoyment of any right set forth by law shall be secured without discrimination on any ground such as sex, race, colour, language, religion, political or other opinion, national or social origin, association with a national minority, property, birth or other status.

2 No one shall be discriminated against by any public authority on any ground such as those mentioned in paragraph 1.

Appendix 2

Chronological list of decisions and judgments of the Strasbourg organs in respect of homosexuality

Date	*Name*	*App. no.*	*Articles of the Convention invoked in complaint*								*Key issue*	*Significance*	*Decision/ Judgment*
			2	*3*	*8*	*10*	*11*	*12*	*14*	*Other*			
17/12/55	W.B. *v Germany*	104/55	X		X				X	17, 18	Criminalization of private sexual activity	First petition relating to homosexuality	Inadmissible
31/05/56	*E.G. v Germany*	135/55								6	Criminalization of private sexual activity		Inadmissible
28/09/56	K.H.W. *v Germany*	167/56			X				X		Criminalization of private sexual activity		Inadmissible
16/12/57	*X. v Germany*	261/57			X					6	Criminalization of private sexual activity		Inadmissible
04/01/60	*A.S. v Germany*	530/59		X	X						Criminalization of private sexual activity	First Article 3 complaint	Inadmissible
02/04/60	*H.K. v Germany*	600/59			X				X		Criminalization of private sexual activity	First complaint about the existence of criminal law rather than a conviction because of it	Inadmissible
04/08/60	*H.S. v Germany*	704/60		X					X	5, 6	Criminalization of private sexual activity	First explicit rejection of an Article 3 complaint	Inadmissible

Date	Name	App. no.	Articles of the Convention invoked in complaint								Key issue	Significance	Decision/ Judgment
			2	3	8	10	11	12	14	Other			
05/03/62	*X. v Austria*	1237/61								6	Criminalization of private sexual activity		Inadmissible
07/05/62	*X. v Germany*	986/61		X						5, 6	Criminalization of private sexual activity		Inadmissible
04/10/62	*G.W. v Germany*	1307/61		X	X				X	6	Criminalization of private sexual activity		Inadmissible
18/06/63	*W.R. v Austria*	1138/61								6	Criminalization of private sexual activity		Inadmissible
04/07/64	*X. v Austria*	1593/62	X	X	X				X	1, 5, 6, 7	Criminalization of private sexual activity		No further action taken
06/02/67	*X. v Germany*	2566/65							X	1, 5, 6, 9	Criminalization of private sexual activity	First Article 9 complaint	Inadmissible
21/07/70	*X. v Germany*	4119/69								6	Criminalization of private sexual activity		Inadmissible

(Continued overleaf)

Date	Name	App. no.	*Articles of the Convention invoked in complaint*								Key issue	Significance	Decision/ Judgment
			2	*3*	*8*	*10*	*11*	*12*	*14*	*Other*			
30/09/75	*X. v Germany*	5935/72			X				X	6	Minimum age of sexual consent	First 'age of consent' complaint	Inadmissible
04/04/74 30/09/75 07/12/76	*Handyside v UK*	5493/72				X			X	1, 7, 9, 13, 1 of P1	Freedom of expression (obscenity)	First case transmitted to the Court involving an issue relating to homosexuality; First Article 10 complaint	No violation
21/03/75 07/12/76	*Kjeldsen, Busk Madsen and Pedersen v Denmark*	5095/71 5920/72 5926/72			X				X	9, 2 of P1	Religious belief		No violation
12/10/78	*X. v UK*	7308/75			X	X				13	Freedom of expression (obscenity)		Inadmissible
07/07/77 12/10/78 12/06/79	*X. v UK*	7215/75			X	X			X		Minimum age of sexual consent	First complaint deemed admissible by the Commission	No violation

Date	Name	App. no.	Articles of the Convention invoked in complaint								Key issue	Significance	Decision/ Judgment
			2	3	8	10	11	12	14	Other			
03/03/78 13/03/80 22/10/81	*Dudgeon v UK*	7525/76			X	(X)	(X)		X		Criminalization of private sexual activity	First successful complaint relating to homosexuality in the Court; First consideration of Article 11 by the Commission	Violation Article 8, No violation of Article 14, Articles 10 and 11 inadmissible
07/05/82	*X. Ltd and Y. v UK*	8710/79				X			X	7, 9	Freedom of expression		Inadmissible
03/05/83	*X. and Y. v UK*	9369/81			X						Discrimination in immigration law	First 'family life' case	Inadmissible
12/10/83	*B. v UK*	9237/81			X				X		Criminalization of private sexual activity	First armed forces case	Inadmissible
07/05/84	*Desmond v UK*	9721/82			X				X		Minimum age of sexual consent		Inadmissible
05/10/84	*S. v Germany*	10686/83		X						5, 6	Treatment in detention		Inadmissible
17/07/86	*Johnson v UK*	10389/83			X				X		Criminalization of private sexual activity	First 'group sex' case	Inadmissible

(Continued overleaf)

Date	Name	App. no.	Articles of the Convention invoked in complaint								Key issue	Significance	Decision/ Judgment
			2	*3*	*8*	*10*	*11*	*12*	*14*	*Other*			
14/05/86	*S. v UK*	11716/85			X				X	13, 1 of P1	Discrimination in housing provision	First housing case	Inadmissible
13/07/87	*W.J. and D.P. v UK*	12513/86			X				X	1	Discrimination in immigration law	First immigration complaint under Article 14	Inadmissible
03/05/88	*Morissens v Belgium*	11389/85				X					Discrimination in employment	First employment case, under Article 10	Inadmissible
10/03/88	*X. v Switzerland*	11680/85			X						Criminalization of prostitution		Inadmissible
16/05/85 12/03/87 26/10/88	*Norris v Ireland*	10581/83			X					1, 13	Criminalization of private sexual activity		Violation of Article 8
09/10/89	*C. and L.M. v UK*	14753/89			X			X	X		Discrimination in immigration law	First Article 12 complaint	Inadmissible
10/02/90	*Z.B. v UK*	16106/90			X				X	13	Discrimination in immigration law		Inadmissible

Date	*Name*	*App. no.*	*Articles of the Convention invoked in complaint*								*Key issue*	*Significance*	*Decision/ Judgment*
			2	*3*	*8*	*10*	*11*	*12*	*14*	*Other*			
13/05/92	*Zukrigl v Austria*	17279/90			X				X		Minimum age of sexual consent		Inadmissible
19/05/92	*Kerkhoven, Hinke and Hinke v Netherlands*	15666/89			X				X		Discrimination in parental rights	First adoption case	Inadmissible
13/10/93	*Hauer and Guggenheim v Austria*	18116/91				X					Freedom of expression		Inadmissible
06/12/90 03/12/91 22/04/93	*Modinos v Cyprus*	15070/89			X						Criminalization of private sexual activity		Violation Article 8
11/05/92 14/01/93 25/03/94	*Scherer v Switzerland*	17116/90			X	X				6	Freedom of expression (obscenity)	First obscenity case deemed admissible, and violation of Article 10 recognized by the Commission	Struck off list
19/01/95	*Wilde, Greenhalgh and Parry v UK*	22382/93			X				X		Minimum age of sexual consent		Struck off list

(Continued overleaf)

Date	Name	App. no.	Articles of the Convention invoked in complaint								Key issue	Significance	Decision/ Judgment
			2	3	8	10	11	12	14	Other			
26/06/95	*H.F. v Austria*	22646/93			X				X	6	Minimum age of sexual consent		Inadmissible
06/09/95	*Reiss v Austria*	23953/94			X					6	Obscenity		Inadmissible
18/01/95	*V., W., X., Y. and Z. v UK*	22170/93			X				X		Criminalization of private sexual activity (sadomasochism)		Inadmissible
15/05/96	*Röösli v Germany*	28318/95			X				X		Discrimination in housing provision		Inadmissible
08/03/94 10/01/95 25/11/96	*Wingrove v UK*	17419/90				X					Censorship of homoerotic imagery on grounds of blasphemy		No violation
20/05/97	*Fleming v UK*	33987/96		X	X				X	13	Discrimination in employment		Inadmissible
18/01/95 26/10/95 19/02/97	*Laskey, Jaggard and Brown v UK*	21627/93 21826/93 21974/93			X				X	7	Criminalization of private sexual activity (sadomasochism)		No violation
10/07/98	*Sobhani v Sweden*	32999/96	X	X	X						Deportation of asylum seeker	First asylum case	Struck off list

Date	Name	App. no.	Articles of the Convention invoked in complaint								Key issue	Significance	Decision/ Judgment
			2	*3*	*8*	*10*	*11*	*12*	*14*	*Other*			
20/05/97 03/12/97 07/08/98	*Marangos v Cyrus*	31106/96		X	X				X	17, 3 of P4	Criminalization of private sexual activity		Not considered by Court
23/02/99 27/09/99	*Smith and Grady v UK*	33985/96 33986/96		X	X	X			X	5, 13	Prohibition on homosexuality in armed forces	Resulted in several other applications being struck off the Court's list in light of offer of friendly settlement from UK government	Violation of Article 8
23/02/99 27/09/99	*Lustig-Prean and Beckett v United Kingdom*	31417/96 32377/96			X				X		Prohibition on homosexuality in armed forces		Violation of Article 8
21/12/99	*Salgueiro da Silva Mouta v Portugal*	33290/96			X				X		Discrimination in parental rights	First successful parental rights case	Violation of Article 8 in conjunction with Article 14
21/03/00	*Craig v UK*	45396/99			X				X	6, 13	Discrimination in parental rights		Inadmissible
16/03/99 31/07/00	*A.D.T. v UK*	35765/97			X				X		Criminalization of private sexual activity	First successful 'group sex' case	Violation of Article 8

(Continued overleaf)

Date	Name	App. no.	Articles of the Convention invoked in complaint								Key issue	Significance	Decision/ Judgment
			2	*3*	*8*	*10*	*11*	*12*	*14*	*Other*			
05/09/00	*Cardoso and Johansen v UK*	47061/99		X	X						Discrimination in immigration law		Struck off list
21/05/96 01/07/97 27/03/01	*Sutherland v UK*	25186/94			X				X		Minimum age of sexual consent	Commission finds different 'age of consent' for homosexuals to be discriminatory under Article 8 in conjunction with 14	Struck off list
10/05/01	*Mata Estevez v Spain*	56501/00			X				X		Discrimination in pension benefits		Inadmissible
27/11/01	*Morris v UK*	31701/96			X				X		Minimum age of sexual consent		Struck off list
08/01/02	*Connell and Others v UK*	43495/98			X				X		Criminalization of private sexual activity		Struck off list
15/01/02	*Goddard v UK*	57821/00		X	X	X			X	13	Prohibition on homosexuality in armed forces		Struck off list

Date	*Name*	*App. no.*	*Articles of the Convention invoked in complaint*								*Key issue*	*Significance*	*Decision/ Judgment*
			2	*3*	*8*	*10*	*11*	*12*	*14*	*Other*			
26/02/02	*Fretté v France*	36515/97			X				X	6	Discrimination in adoption of a child		No violation (in respect of sexual orientation discrimination)
15/10/02	*Tosto v Italy*	49821/99			X				X		Discrimination in blood donation	First complaint about ban on blood donations from MSMs	Struck off list
05/09/00 22/10/02	*Beck, Copp and Bazeley v UK*	48535/99 48536/99 48537/99		X	X	X			X	13	Prohibition on homosexuality in armed forces		Violation of Article 8, Violation of Article 13
05/09/00 22/10/02	*Perkins and R v UK*	43208/98 44875/98			X				X		Prohibition on homosexuality in armed forces		Violation of Article 8
10/12/02	*Waite v UK*	53236/99							X	5	Minimum age of sexual consent		No violation (in respect of sexual orientation discrimination)

(*Continued overleaf*)

Date	*Name*	*App. no.*	*Articles of the Convention invoked in complaint*								*Key issue*	*Significance*	*Decision/ Judgment*
			2	*3*	*8*	*10*	*11*	*12*	*14*	*Other*			
22/11/01 09/01/03	*L. and V. v Austria*	39392/98 39829/98			X				X		Minimum age of sexual consent		Violation of Article 14 in conjunction with Article 8
22/11/01 09/01/03	*S.L. v Austria*	45330/99			X				X		Minimum age of sexual consent		Violation of Article 14 in conjunction with Article 8
11/09/01 24/07/03	*Karner v Austria*	40016/98			X				X		Discrimination in housing provision		Violation of Article 14 in conjunction with Article 8
27/05/03 10/02/04	*B.B. v UK*	53760/00			X				X		Minimum age of sexual consent		Violation of Article 14 in conjunction with Article 8
22/06/04	*F. v UK*	17341/03	X	X	X					5, 6	Deportation of asylum seeker		Inadmissible

Date	Name	App. no.	Articles of the Convention invoked in complaint								Key issue	Significance	Decision/ Judgment
			2	3	8	10	11	12	14	Other			
21/10/04	*Woditschka and Wilfling v Austria*	69756/01 6306/02			X				X		Minimum age of sexual consent		Violation of Article 14 in conjunction with Article 8
09/12/04	*I.N.N. v The Netherlands*	2035/04		X							Deportation of asylum seeker		Inadmissible
10/12/02 25/01/05	*Enhorn v Sweden*	56529/00								5	Deprivation of liberty	HIV/AIDS case	Violation of Article 5
03/02/05	*Ladner v Austria*	18297/03		X	X				X		Minimum age of sexual consent		Violation of Article 14 in conjunction with Article 8
08/03/05	*Fairfield and Others v UK*	24790/04				X				9	Freedom of expression	Contests the right to express public condemnation of homosexuality	Inadmissible
26/05/05	*Wolfmeyer v Austria*	5263/03			X				X		Minimum age of sexual consent		Violation of Article 14 in conjunction with Article 8

(*Continued overleaf*)

Date	Name	App. no.	Articles of the Convention invoked in complaint								Key issue	Significance	Decision/ Judgment
			2	3	8	10	11	12	14	Other			
02/06/05	*H.G. and G.B. v Austria*	11084/02 15306/02			X				X		Minimum age of sexual consent		Violation of Article 14 in conjunction with Article 8
13/12/05	*Love and Others v UK*	4103/04 5498/04 10617/04 14557/04 27313/04		X	X	X			X	13	Prohibition on homosexuality in armed forces		Inadmissible
19/01/06	*R.H. v Austria*	7336/03			X				X	6	Minimum age of sexual consent		Violation of Article 14 in conjunction with Article 8
01/02/05 02/11/06	*Kobenter and Standard Verlags GMBH v Austria*	60899/00				X					Freedom of expression		Violation of Article 10
07/11/06	*Ayegh v Sweden*	4701/05	X	X							Deportation of asylum seeker		Inadmissible
05/12/06 03/05/07	*Bączkowski and Others v Poland*	1543/06					X		X	13	Freedom of assembly	First successful Article 11 complaint	Violation of Article 11, Violation of Article 13 in conjunction with Article 11, Violation of Article 14 in conjunction with Article 11

Date	Name	App. no.	Articles of the Convention invoked in complaint								Key issue	Significance	Decision/ Judgment
			2	*3*	*8*	*10*	*11*	*12*	*14*	*Other*			
22/01/08	*E.B. v France*	43546/02			X				X		Discrimination in adoption of a child	First successful complaint against discrimination in adoption law	Violation of Article 14 in conjunction with Article 8
13/05/08	*N.N. and T.A. v Belgium*	65097/01			X						Respect for correspondence		No violation
04/11/08	*Courten v UK*	4479/06							X	1 of P1	Discrimination in taxation		Inadmissible
04/12/08	*Marangos v Cyprus*	12846/05		X						6	Right to a fair trial		No violation
02/06/09	*Small v UK*	7330/06			X				X		Minimum age of sexual consent		Struck off list
23/06/09	*M.W. v UK*	11313/02			X				X	1 of P1	Discrimination in social security benefit		Inadmissible
09/12/04 08/10/09	*Porubova v Russia*	8237/03				X				6	Freedom of expression		Violation of Article 10
02/03/10	*Kozak v Poland*	13102/02			X				X	6	Discrimination in housing provision		Violation of Article 14 in conjunction with Article 8

(*Continued overleaf*)

Date	*Name*	*App. no.*	*Articles of the Convention invoked in complaint*								*Key issue*	*Significance*	*Decision/ Judgment*
			2	*3*	*8*	*10*	*11*	*12*	*14*	*Other*			
24/06/10	*Schalk and Kopf v Austria*	30141/04			X			X	X	1 of P1	Discrimination in marriage	First Article 12 complaint deemed admissible	No violation
20/03/08 22/07/10	*P.B. and J.S. v Austria*	18984/02			X				X	1 of P1	Discrimination in insurance benefits		Violation of Article 14 in conjunction with Article 8
21/09/10	*Manenc v France*	66686/09			X				X		Discrimination in pension benefits		Inadmissible
21/09/10	*Santos Couto v Portugal*	31874/07			X				X	6	Minimum age of sexual consent		No violation
28/09/10	*J.M. v UK*	37060/06			X				X	1 of P1	Discrimination in payment of child maintenance		Violation of Article 14 in conjunction with Article 1 of Protocol 1

Date	Name	App. no.	Articles of the Convention invoked in complaint								Key issue	Significance	Decision/ Judgment
			2	3	8	10	11	12	14	Other			
21/10/10	*Alekseyev v Russia*	4916/07 25924/08 14599/09					X		X	13	Freedom of assembly		Violation of Article 11, Violation of Article 13, Violation of Article 14 in conjunction with Article 11
17/02/11	*Wasmuth v Germany*	12884/03			X				X	9	Compulsory payment of taxation to benefit churches opposed to homosexuality		No violation
31/05/11	*D.B.N. v the UK*	26550/10	X	X	X				X	13	Deportation of asylum seeker		Struck off list
20/10/11	*Stasi v France*	25001/07		X					X		Treatment in detention	First complaint from homosexual prisoner about sexual orientation discrimination to reach the Court	No violation

(*Continued overleaf*)

Date	Name	App. no.	Articles of the Convention invoked in complaint								Key issue	Significance	Decision/ Judgment
			2	3	8	10	11	12	14	Other			
17/01/12	*Zontul v Greece*	12294/07		X						6, 13	Treatment in detention	Successful use of Article 3 to complain about criminal justice response to rape of a (homosexual) male by a public official	Violation Article 3
09/02/12	*Vejdeland and Others v Sweden*	1813/07				X				7	Hate speech	First homophobic 'hate speech' case	No violation
31/08/10 15/03/12	*Gas and Dubois v France*	25951/07			X				X		Discrimination in second (step) parent adoption		No violation
12/06/12	*Genderdoc-M v Moldova*	9106/06				X	X		X	6, 13	Freedom of Assembly		Violation Article 11, Violation Article 13 in conjunction with Article 11, Violation Article 14 in conjunction with Article 11

Date	Name	App. no.	Articles of the Convention invoked in complaint								Key issue	Significance	Decision/ Judgment
			2	3	8	10	11	12	14	Other			
19/06/12	*K.N. v France*	47129/09	X	X						13	Deportation of asylum seeker		Struck off list
10/07/12	*A.S.B. v the Netherlands*	4854/12		X							Deportation of asylum seeker		Struck off list
09/10/12	*X. v Turkey*	24626/09		X	X				X	6,7,13	Treatment in detention	First successful use of Article 3 in respect of sexual orientation discrimination; First successful complaint about homophobic treatment in prison	Violation Article 3, Violation Article 14 in conjunction with Article 3
23/10/12	*Molnar v Romania*	16637/06				X	X			7, 9	Freedom of speech of anti-gay Christian		Inadmissible
13/11/12	*H. v Finland*	37359/09		X	X			X	X	2 of P4	Recognition of same-sex marriage following gender reassignment		No violation

(Continued overleaf)

Date	Name	App. no.	Articles of the Convention invoked in complaint								Key issue	Significance	Decision/ Judgment
			2	*3*	*8*	*10*	*11*	*12*	*14*	*Other*			
04/12/12	*Verlagsgruppe News GMBH and Bobi v Austria*	59631/09				X					Media disclosure of homosexual acts		No violation
04/12/12	*Rothe v Austria*	6490/07			X						Media disclosure of homosexual acts		No violation
04/12/12	*Küchl v Austria*	51151/06			X						Media disclosure of homosexual acts		No violation
15/01/13	*Eweida and Others v UK*	48420/10 59842/10 51671/10 36516/10							X	9	2 of the 4 applicants alleged violation of Article 9 rights when required by employment law to provide services to homosexuals	First case challenging equality law in respect of sexual orientation	No violation (in sexual orientation cases)
19/02/13	*X. and Others v Austria*	19010/07			X				X		Discrimination in second (step) parent adoption	First successful second parent adoption complaint	Violation Article 14 in conjunction with Article 8

Date	Name	App. no.	Articles of the Convention invoked in complaint								Key issue	Significance	Decision/ Judgment
			2	3	8	10	11	12	14	Other			
07/05/13	*Boeckel and Gessner-Boeckel v Germany*	8017/11			X				X		Discrimination in the registration of the birth of a child		Inadmissible
27/06/13	*M.K.N. v Sweden*	72413/10		X							Deportation of asylum seeker	The applicant did not assert a homosexual identity, but cited a previous homosexual relationship in his complaint	No violation
22/10/13	*Georgescu v Romania*	4867/03		X	X				X	5,6,13	Discriminatory treatment by police		Inadmissible
07/11/13	*E.B. and Others v Austria*	31913/07 38357/07 48098/07 48777/07 48779/07			X				X	13	Retention of criminal records relating to convictions for now repealed homosexual offences		Violation Article 14 in conjunction with Article 8, Violation Article 13
07/11/13	*Vallianatos and Others v Greece*	29381/09 32684/09			X				X		Discrimination in 'civil union' law	First successful complaint relating to exclusion from civil partnership law	Violation Article 14 in conjunction with Article 8

Index